Military Confidence-Building
and
India-China Relations
Fighting Distrust

Military Confidence-Building and India-China Relations

Fighting Distrust

Edited by

Dipankar Banerjee

and

Jabin T. Jacob

PENTAGON PRESS

Military Confidence-Building and India-China Relations: Fighting Distrust
Edited by: **Dipankar Banerjee & Jabin T. Jacob**

ISBN 978-81-8274-708-1

First Published in 2013

Published by

PENTAGON PRESS
206, Peacock Lane, Shahpur Jat,
New Delhi-110049
Phones: 011-64706243, 26491568
Telefax: 011-26490600
email: rajan@pentagonpress.in
website: www.pentagonpress.in

Printed at Aegean Offset Printers, Greater Noida

Contents

Preface

This volume by the Institute of Peace and Conflict Studies (IPCS) is part of a project under the Asian Security Initiative of the John D. and Catherine T. MacArthur Foundation. This three-year project from 2009 to 2012 was aimed at developing a framework for regional cooperation in Southern Asia—to sustain and strengthen the process by which India and China would cooperate on the key challenges affecting their bilateral relationship and to involve their smaller neighbors in their economic growth stories.

The IPCS identified three core areas—*strengthening military confidence-building measures on land and in maritime issues between India and China, expanding economic activity along the Sino-Indian border areas* and *developing infrastructure for connectivity between India and China.* This volume under the first of these issue areas puts together papers presented initially at a conference held in Beijing, China in March 2010 and subsequently revised, together with supplementary papers and documents.

The conference was notable for the presence of not just academic specialists and retired military personnel of wide-ranging professional experience but also for the contributions of serving military officers from both India and China. It was therefore, a unique and important dialogue and the editors have sought to preserve the distinct perspective each contributor brought to the proceedings. This book represents the first occasion where India and China have engaged each other at a senior level on such sensitive issues.

While some papers have been updated, most reflect the context and security environment of the time the conference was held. That said, subsequent events have shown that they remain relevant to the current Sino-Indian security context. The global economic crisis is far from fully resolved and Sino-Indian relations continue to be at a difficult stage with concerns on both sides about the other's military build-up in the border areas. Some of the ideas put forward in these papers for improving CBMs such as reviving anti-terrorism exercises and expanding anti-piracy cooperation are today finding greater acceptance.

In recent years, there have been some setbacks in the military relationship owing to China's visa policy involving India's Jammu and Kashmir and Arunachal Pradesh In addition, there has been a perception in India in recent years that the number of Chinese 'incursions' across the Line of Actual Control has been on the rise. Whatever the truth, these perceptions have played an important role in setting the agenda for Sino-Indian relations.

In September 2012, Chinese Defence Minister Gen. Liang Guanglie finally returned then Indian Defence Minister Pranab Mukherjee's visit to China in 2006. One interpretation for Gen. Liang's visit to India was that with a major leadership transition underway at home, increasing tensions with its East Asian neighbours over maritime territorial disputes in the East China and South China Seas and the United States' rebalancing towards Asia, China perhaps looked for a measure of calm and stability in its west. Nevertheless, it is also important to note the significance of this return visit following the signing of the *Agreement between the Government of the Republic of India and the Government of the People's Republic of China on the Establishment of a Working Mechanism for Consultation and Coordination on India-China Border Affairs* in January 2012. The possible resumption in the near future, of bilateral army exercises suspended since 2008, is a very significant result of this visit.

As will be evident from the papers, there are both subtle and sharp differences in the perspectives emanating from the participants of the two countries. Yet, there is also consensus that as two rising powers, India and China will increasingly have a lot to do together at the regional and global levels and that their cooperation needs to be strengthened and expanded. It is hoped that the debates engendered in this volume will be taken up further and contribute to just such a strengthening and expansion of Sino-Indian ties not just in the security domain but also in other fields.

The editors are sincerely grateful to the John D. and Catherine T. MacArthur Foundation for entrusting this study to the IPCS. We would also like to express our gratitude to the many Indian and Chinese participants at the Beijing conference and to the final contributors to this volume. The editors also specially thank Rukmani Gupta who was both a key organizer of the conference and a participant. For their help with editing and proofreading the text and various other inputs, thanks are also due to several researchers at the IPCS over the three-year period of the project. This volume would not have come to fruition without their efforts. The editors are also grateful to Rajan Arya and Beena Rehman at Pentagon Press for the speed and efficiency with which this volume has been produced.

New Delhi **Dipankar Banerjee & Jabin T. Jacob**
October 2012

List of Contributors

Cdr. Kamlesh Kumar Agnihotri, Research Fellow, National Maritime Foundation, New Delhi

Maj. Gen. (Retd) Dipankar Banerjee, Mentor, Institute of Peace and Conflict Studies, New Delhi

Maj. Gen. (Retd) Gong Xianfu, Deputy Chairman, China Institute for International Strategic Studies, Beijing

Dr. Jabin T. Jacob, Assistant Director and Fellow, Institute of Chinese Studies, Delhi

Prof. Srikanth Kondapalli, Centre for East Asian Studies, Jawaharlal Nehru University, New Delhi

Maj. Gen. (Retd) Pan Zhenqiang, Senior Adviser, China Reform Forum, Beijing

Brig. (Retd) Arun Sahgal, Consultant, Institute of Peace and Conflict Studies, New Delhi

Prof. Swaran Singh, Centre for International Politics, Organisation and Disarmament, Jawaharlal Nehru University, New Delhi

Prof. Wang Fan, Director, Institute of International Relations, China Foreign Affairs University, Beijing

Sr. Col. Wang Guifang, Chinese Academy of Military Sciences, Beijing

Prof. Xia Liping, Dean, School of Political Science and International Relations, Tongji University, Shanghai

Ms. Zhang Yidan, Research Associate, Institute of International Relations, China Foreign Affairs University, Beijing

1

Sino-Indian Military CBMs—Efficacy and Influences

Maj. Gen. (Retd) Dipankar Banerjee and Jabin T. Jacob

India and China have yet to resolve their long-standing boundary dispute. But in recent years they have built a carefully crafted architecture of Confidence-Building Measures (CBMs) to prevent possibilities of any adverse developments along the disputed border. The IPCS-MacArthur Project on Military CBMs and Sino-Indian Relations attempted to examine the state of CBMs as perceived by leading experts from India and China. How have these held up to the pressures of recent years? What are the specific nature and features that each would like to pursue? Where do national perceptions merge or contend? What additional measures might be needed to strengthen those already existing?

The 1996 Agreement between India and China on Confidence Building Measures in the Military Field along the Line of Actual Control (LAC) in the India-China Border Areas, that followed an earlier Agreement in 1993, pledged non-aggression, prior notification of large troop movements, a 10 km no-fly-zone for combat aircraft, and exchange of maps to resolve disagreements about the precise location of the LAC. The 2005 Agreement on the Political Parameters and Guiding Principles for the Settlement of the India-China Boundary Question, stepped up from treating the issue from a purely military viewpoint to a political question. Since 2003, India and China have appointed Special Representatives at the political level to address these issues. They have met roughly twice a year until 2010, but the underlying suspicion on both sides has not disappeared. Meanwhile border incidents continue to occur with these being played up particularly in the Indian media.

Against such a background, it is important to revisit CBMs between India and China to judge how they operate, what their limitations are and what influences them as also, to see what needs to be done to further strengthen them and make the possibility of serious military engagement along the border areas infeasible.

Sino-Indian Military CBMs[1]: Effect and Efficacy

Volker Rittberger, Manfred Efinger and Martin Mendler define CSBMs (Confidence- and Security-Building Measures) as:

> "Collective arrangements about the function and use of military power in peacetime. They are designed to confirm non-aggressive intentions of all states and therefore build stable expectations concerning their military activities. However, CSBMs do not substantially restrain the sovereignty of states to choose their own national defense policy. Therefore, they can be classified as a pragmatic contribution to peacefully managing the classical 'security dilemma' based on both the proscription of the threat or use of force and the right to military self-defense".[2]

James E. Goodby defines CSBMs as possessing the following characteristics:

"(1) they deal with the operations of military forces, not with their capabilities;

(2) at a minimum they provide a framework for exchanging information about the nature of military operations;

(3) they should encourage nations to act during normal times in a way that would serve to eliminate causes of tension and reduce the dangers of misunderstanding or miscalculations;

(4) they should promote habits of co-operation among adversaries;

(5) preferably, they should serve to reinforce stability or restore equilibrium during periods of intense international confrontation;

(6) agreement on such measures is based on the assumption that the nations involved desire to avoid conflict, but since this assumption could change it is important that such a co-operative security regime should contain measures of verification necessary to deter or detect deception".[3]

By Goodby's definition, Sino-Indian military CBMs have achieved their goals but it could well be asked if habits of cooperation have really developed between the two sides. Even though border meetings have now become a routine feature following a regular and predictable pattern; it needs to be asked if these are as yet a substantive exchange or dialogue. Indeed, it is open to question if well-articulated rules of adjustment and norms of behaviour have yet emerged between the Chinese and Indian militaries.[4] Military-to-military exchanges such as the visits of senior officials or joint exercises have been plagued by problems. Joint exercises were terminated after a pair of exercises in each other's countries while visits by senior officers have led to problems with the issuance of Chinese visas for Indian officers resulting in cancellation of some visits, which in turn has exacerbated difficulties in relations. Similarly, the assumption that the opposite side wishes to avoid conflict is not entirely borne out by the nature of both the interactions and suspicions that arise or linger on the two sides. In this context, perhaps, it is especially the Indian side that does not seem to trust Chinese intentions. Most of the suspicion seems to arise from an Indian focus on the rising capabilities of the Chinese military in addition to perceptions about the nature and intent of its activity in the form of the so-called border incursions across the LAC. Thus, the first characteristic of CSBMs is not necessarily fully applicable in the Sino-Indian case and nor therefore, can the sixth characteristic be achieved.

In Rittberger et al.'s study, the authors argue that the United States and the Soviet Union had a shared interest in managing their rivalry so as to control its costs and risks. This shared interest was backed also by a recognition that one, a cooperative, orderly, and stable bilateral relationship was desirable and two, that regional and global institutions and arrangements created additional order in the international system from which the two superpowers could also benefit even if indirectly.[5] Can we assume that India and China think similarly, especially when they are not quite at the top of the world order like the US and the USSR were, and when there are other complicated bilateral dynamics in the immediate neighbourhood? One only needs to consider Sino-Pak and Indo-Pak relations, for example, while the two countries' bilateral relationship with the US are no less important.

Further, as Rittberger et al. have argued, even as the United States and the Soviet Union subscribed to these longer range goals, they continued to have rather fungible and somewhat divergent conceptions of what the norms or rules and modalities of a more cooperative relationship and of a better-structured international system ought to be. And despite talk of Asian values and the Asian century, India and China are in a similar situation and perhaps even just as sharply divided over the norms that they espouse in the international system. One needs only to look at the fairly clear call India made for respecting international law in the case of the contretemps over the INS Airavat,[6] to see that India and China are some distance apart in their understanding of how international law and norms should operate.[7]

In the US-Soviet case, the norms and rules of the CSBM regime were complied within an almost routine manner, not only because of short-term calculations of prudent behaviour but out of a longer-term interest in creating uniform expectations about what constituted permissible military activities and what did not.[8] In the case of Sino-Indian relations, this level of convergence it would appear is yet to be achieved. A simple case in point is the fact that there is no unanimity even over an approximate length of the disputed boundary. The Chinese hold the length of the disputed boundary to be approximately 2,000 kms (see Wang Guifang in this volume)—which implies leaving out the section that is part of the Indian state of Jammu and Kashmir, ostensibly because it is disputed territory – while Indian sources put the length at about 3,500 kms (see Arun Sahgal in this volume).

Also in the US-Soviet case, the CSBM regime, while unable to address the possibility of war in case of a capabilities mismatch, appears to have reduced, even overcome, the perceived threat of a surprise attack and thus contributed to stabilization of security relations.[9] In the case of Sino-India relations there might be no overt threat of surprise attack—even if there is a perception that the capability gap is widening in China's favour—but the absence of such threat also possibly encourages low-level tensions to continue and given their history or at least perceptions of history on the Indian side, such low-level provocations also increase Indian hostility and mistrust of the Chinese. As David B. Dewitt argues, "the possibility of waging war increases because of the reduced probability of severe escalation. In this sense, war becomes a tactical instrument of politics, and CSBMs, coupled with other defensive measures, simultaneously may reduce the severity but increase the frequency of violent confrontation".[10]

Successful CBMs can eventually lead to questions about whether prevailing assumptions on both sides about the strategic intentions of the other side continue to be valid or need to be re-assessed.[11] However, even though Sino-Indian CBMs might be viewed as largely successful, they do not necessarily mean there is evolution towards greater understanding on both sides or a strategic reevaluation towards improving the chances for continued maintenance of peace. Rather, the perception or worry, at least on the Indian side, seems that any absence of war is merely a prelude to greater Chinese assertiveness. In this sense, CBMs between India and China have failed to serve their primary purpose and Chinese border 'incursions' seem to add weight to such a perception. This contributes to India's attention on Chinese military modernization and its own attempts at matching this modernization drive. Dewitt highlights this paradox when he states, "while contributing to peace, CSBMs may actually be part of a logic which supports the need for states to arm to the point of sufficiency for conventional deterrence".[12] It is in this context, that we would argue somewhat counter-intuitive to conventional thinking that military modernization and the achievement of unambiguous military parity at least in the likely theatre of conflict, is necessary before CBMs can really take effect.

It is perhaps an acknowledgement of this state of affairs which has led to the creation of a new border mechanism in 2011 between the two sides that involves a hotline between the Indian Joint Secretary in charge of East Asian affairs in the Ministry of External Affairs and his counterpart in the Chinese Ministry of Foreign Affairs to be used in case of incidents on the LAC. Institutionalization however, has still a long way to go and are often stymied by procedural factors.[13]

Critics of CSBMs have argued that their relevance to Western concerns about military security has been limited or non-existent and skeptical about whether CSBMs ever reduced measurably the danger of surprise attack.[14] This point is particularly relevant in the context of Indian suspicions of Chinese motives and of predictions such as those made by one Indian writer of an impending Chinese attack on India in 2012.[15] At the same time, notification, observation and inspection mechanisms help allay such fears. The question therefore needs to be asked if in the Sino-Indian context, such activities as the exchange of visits to each other's military facilities and extant verification mechanisms are sufficient or need to be upgraded. Worryingly, even the limited sets of exchanges are often waylaid by political incidents, for example, the contretemps in 2010, over the denial of a proper visa to a senior Indian military official who was supposed to lead a military delegation to China.[16]

Sino-Indian CBMs: Domestic and Geopolitical Influences

How do the domestic factors in each country and the international context affect adherence to and implementation of CBMs in the Sino-Indian context?

Without doubt, both domestic and international factors have had a deep impact on the weight accorded and uses found by each side to CBMs on the LAC. In other words, both India and China, have adopted a fungible view of the implementation of CBMs depending on both their domestic constraints and their perceptions of whether the prevailing international situation is in their national interests.

On the domestic front, several reasons might be put forward for both India and China. One, it is an inevitable consequence of economic growth that governments will have more money to invest in public goods such as road and telecom infrastructure, for example. And given, the under-development of Tibet, it should not be surprising that a lot of attention has been focused on infrastructure development along the LAC with India. Therefore, a case can be made that Chinese infrastructure development in this region is not so much targeted against India—even if it can be put to that use—but is an outcome of development priorities especially under its Western Development Strategy. Indeed, the same justification can be used for India's own rapidly developing infrastructure in its border areas.[17]

Two, given Chinese national and strategic sensitivities associated with Tibet, the outbreak of violence in Tibetan areas inside China since 2008 have added to Beijing's concerns and suspicions about India especially as the latter hosts the Tibetan government-in-exile. John Garver has in fact, argued that even as China seeks improvement of relations with India, keeping the territorial dispute with India ongoing—in the form of the insistence on the 'return' of Arunachal or its seeming intractability on Tawang—is part of a dual-track approach to making sure India refrains from "trouble-making" in Tibet.[18]

Moving on to wider geopolitics, it is inevitable that as simultaneously rising powers with growing international responsibilities Sino-Indian relations will increasingly be affected by issues of global import. In this context, as long as the boundary dispute remains unresolved, problems and confrontations along the LAC will not so much be the result only of differences in perceptions as to where the LAC runs but also be affected by externalities such as events in the wider region and in the world where the two countries might confront each other. The world and indeed, Sino-Indian relations, have changed substantially since the treaties of 1993 and 1996. This change has been reflected in the bilateral context by the move to towards Special Representative-level talks in 2003 and the 2005 Agreement on Guiding Principles and Political Parameters that appeared to indicate not only a move towards a political solution of the boundary dispute but also a reduction of emphasis on the military side of things along the LAC.

It must be noted that in 2005, the Sino-Indian Agreement on Political Parameters and Guiding Principles was actually overshadowed by the accord Indian Prime Minister Manmohan Singh reached with US President George W. Bush on a civilian nuclear deal just over two months later. The Chinese were perhaps surprised by this new US-India bonhomie and perhaps anticipated that wherever this was headed would be to the detriment of China. While they initially sought to play along by offering their own version of civilian nuclear cooperation with India,[19] nothing much came of this and they eventually sought to fire over the shoulders of a small group of nations that sought to oppose the deal at the NSG in September 2008.[20] Also unlike Japan, which was left feeling similarly surprised and aggrieved by the Shanghai Communiqué of 1972 by which the US established formal relations with Beijing, China is in a position to demonstrate its unhappiness, both with the US and India. In the case of India, this unhappiness has perhaps been expressed in the form of increased incidents along the LAC or perhaps even a go-slow in the boundary negotiations. Thus, dynamics of the Sino-US relationship could affect the Sino-Indian relationship as it might China's relations with a host of other countries.

Thus, the case can well be made that "confidence" is lacking on multiple fronts in the Sino-Indian relationship which in turn parlays into ineffectiveness or even a lack of priority accorded to military CBMs along their disputed boundary. This is a vicious and dangerous cycle, and one to which the political and military leaderships of both countries will have to pay greater attention.

Structure of the Book

The second and third chapters by Maj. Gen. (Retd) Dipankar Banerjee and Maj. Gen. (Retd) Pan Zhenqiang respectively are expositions of the strategic outlooks on Sino-Indian ties from New Delhi and Beijing respectively carried out with a view to outlining differences between the two sides as well as areas of possible congruence and the reasons thereof. In the fourth chapter, Brig. (Retd) Arun Sahgal provides a view albeit from the Indian side of the working of military CBMs and their shortcomings. The Chinese view outlined in the fifth chapter by Sr. Col. Wang Guifang notes that resolution of the boundary dispute while of vital importance in promoting bilateral relations has become increasingly affected by nationalist feelings on both sides abetted by strident media commentary.

Nuclear CBMs form the focus of the sixth chapter. Here, Prof. Srikanth Kondapalli conducts a detailed study of the perceptions of both sides insofar as strategic CBMs are concerned noting that while the two sides do not maintain their nuclear forces on full alert and both have a no-first use policy, a formal and binding agreement between the two sides is necessary to increase trust levels. Prof. Xia Liping in the seventh chapter and Cdr KK Agnihotri in the eighth, focus on what is likely to become an increasingly important domain in strategic developments between both sides, namely the high seas. With rising naval capacities on both sides, India and China will soon run into each other more often in the Indo-Pacific Oceans and begin to impinge on each other's strategic areas. Already, some indications are evident in developments in the South China Sea since 2010 that have involved standoffs between China and other claimants in the area, as also Indian concerns over Chinese scientific explorations in the Indian Ocean

Region. It is therefore, imperative that serious thinking should begin on CBMs in the maritime domain as well.

Chapters 9 and 10 are another dyad of studies of possible bilateral CBMs this time in the anti-terrorism domain. While both countries claim to suffer from the scourge of terrorism, that it means different things to each country is evident from the respective essays by Maj. Gen. (Retd) Gong Xianfu and Prof. Swaran Singh. That however, does not reduce the desirability, according to the two authors, of both nations cooperating in countering terrorism.

Chapter 11 by Prof. Wang Fan and Ms. Zhang Yidan focuses on the impact of the media and think-tanks on Sino-Indian relations. This is a particularly important dimension of policy studies given the increasing spread and influence of the media in both countries. In fact, Sino-Indian relations have certainly been affected negatively by the spin Indian news channels in particular, have given certain incidents. This chapter analyses the consequences and implications that think-tanks as well as the visual and broadcast media have had in both countries. The final chapter by Dr. Jabin T. Jacob contextualizes the major treaties signed between India and China since the end of the Cold War. It examines their content in terms of the CBMs outlined, and how these reflect the state of the bilateral relationship as well as possibly, internal developments in each country.

Conclusion

What of the way forward? How long will Sino-Indian CBMs be governed by the principle of minimum achievement? Will effective CBMs contribute to the solution of the boundary dispute? Can the two countries reach an agreement on arms control in their border areas? Can thresholds of notification for military exercises be lowered or the lead time extended? Can quantitative ceilings be established on both military deployments as well as personnel in the border areas? Can the definition of border areas itself be expanded? Can on-site inspections be increased in both scale and frequency? It is patently clear that there is a need to carefully examine these and other related questions at several levels. Initially perhaps, non-official forums—to be followed later by official mechanisms—can be used to examine and exchange views on such issues as military doctrine, implementation experience, and the constraining of the size, duration, frequency, and other characteristics of out-of-garrison activity.[21]

As Dewitt has pointed out, one of the reasons for the success of CSBMs in Europe was the fact that "in spite of occasional rhetoric to the contrary, the central authorities of all the major European states accord[ed] each other legitimacy of governance".[22] As India and China come into their own as global powers, and emerge as role models for other countries, their ideological differences—on the basis of domestic political systems—might well widen and cause each to question the legitimacy of the other's political system if not actively seek to undermine it. The tendency of the Chinese side to blame the Indian media and its reportage of alleged border incursions for the deterioration of Sino-Indian ties, points to a deeper malaise, namely one of Chinese unwillingness to accept or inability to understand the workings of the Indian political system. There could thus, be grounds for a breakdown of CBMs, despite functional relationships in trade and commerce.

More than ideological differences however, internal governance issues in each country can also hamper communication and agreement on military CBMs. As Dewitt has argued,

> "Where the exercise of force remains central to the maintenance or enhancement of state or communal authority, and where interstate conflict (and often intercommunal conflict) is a defining characteristic of the regional system, the introduction of CSBMs may well run counter to the interests of the leadership because such measures are meant to constrain their freedom of military action... in situations where military power is a necessary component of political authority and an integral part of the political culture, the very acceptance of CSBMs may be problematic".[23]

While Dewitt was referring to the authoritarian regimes of the Soviet bloc, here the reference is to China. The increasing role of the Chinese PLA in the country's foreign policymaking has already come to attention[24] and in a context where China's civilian leaders lack military experience but the Communist Party of China holds the PLA to be the Party's army, that army can be expected to make multiple demands, including political ones, of the civilian leadership. This in turn can complicate China's relations with key countries such as the US or India, which are or may be perceived as challengers to China's global dominance.

At the end of the day, as is well understood, lack of information about relative military capabilities forms an important cause of war. In the case of Sino-Indian relations, the problem extends to lack of mutual understanding of each other's societies, political systems and cultures. In such a context, the threat of conflict only increases. Since their boundary dispute is an active one, the chances of confrontation escalating along the LAC are all the greater. It is therefore imperative that the role of military CBMs between the two sides be properly understood and the CBMs themselves carefully drawn up and effectively implemented. Further, it must be understood that military CBMs along the LAC do not function in a vacuum and that domestic factors in each country and the international context also play roles in the legitimacy and efficacy of these CBMs. The chapters in this volume are efforts at understanding such complexity from the perspectives of both scholars and practitioners of the two states.

NOTES

1. In the case of NATO-Warsaw Pact relations, "before 1981 the term 'Confidence-Building Measures' (CBMs) was used to refer to the measures agreed to between the superpowers in the 1960s and in the Helsinki Final Act (1975). The term 'Confidence and Security-Building Measures' (CSBMs) was introduced into the CSCE process (especially by Yugoslavia) to describe the qualitative differences between the relevant provisions of the Helsinki Final Act and the measures proposed at the Madrid CSCE follow-up meeting (1980-83)". See fn.1, Volker Rittberger Manfred Efinger and Martin Mendler, "Toward an East-West Security Regime: The Case of Confidence- and Security-Building Measures", *Journal of Peace Research*, Vol. 27(1), February 1990, p.71.
2. Ibid., Rittberger et al., p. 70.
3. Quoted in ibid., pp. 58-59.
4. See David B. Dewitt, "Confidence- and Security-Building Measures in the Third World: Is There a Role?" *International Journal*, Vol. 42(3), Summer, 1987, p. 513.
5. Rittberger et al., op. cit., p. 55.
6. Ben Bland and Girija Shivakumar, "China confronts Indian navy vessel," *Financial Times*, 31 August 2011, http://www.ft.com/cms/s/0/883003ec-d3f6-11e0-b7eb-00144feab49a.html#ixzz1WguaKVu4. In late July 2011, the INS Airavat was leaving a Vietnamese port after a scheduled visit, when an unidentified Chinese warship demanded over the radio that the Indian ship identify itself and explain its presence in what it said were Chinese waters. The Airavat proceeded on its way without replying, completing the rest of its mission.
7. Rittberger et al., op. cit., p. 55
8. Ibid., p. 56.
9. Ibid., p. 56.
10. Dewitt, op.cit., p. 521.
11. Rittberger et al., op.cit., p. 56.
12. Dewitt, op.cit., p. 535.
13. A case in point is the report in October 2011 of the Indian Prime Minister's Office being unable to establish a hotline with China because India has been unable to come up with a suitable encryption technology and this, after the Chinese side had delivered its on decryption equipment several months ago. Samanta, Pranab Dhal, "Delhi's hotline to Beijing waits for room in PMO, tech upgrade to match the Chinese," *Indian Express*, 16 October 2011, http://www.indianexpress.com/news/delhis-hotline-to-beijing-waits-for-room-in-pmo-tech-upgrade-to-match-the-chinese/860460/0.
14. Rittberger et al., op. cit., pp. 65-66.
15. Bharat Verma, "Unmasking China", *Indian Defence Review*, Vol. 24(3), July-September 2009, www.indiandefencereview.com/2009/08/unmasking-china.html.
16. The exchanges were resumed in 2011. *Times of India*, "Indian military delegation arrives in China on goodwill visit," 19 June 2011, http://articles.timesofindia.indiatimes.com/2011-06-19/china/29676804_1_indian-military-delegation-goodwill-visit-military-exchanges.
17. For more on this aspect see, Jabin T. Jacob, "The Sino-Indian Boundary Dispute: Sub-National Units as Ice-Breakers", *Eurasia Border Review* (Hokkaido University, Japan), Vol. 2(1), Summer 2011, pp. 35-45.

18. John Garver, "The Unresolved Sino–Indian Border Dispute: An Interpretation", *China Report*, Vol. 47(2), May 2011, pp. 101-15.
19. See Jabin T. Jacob, "Indo-US Nuclear Deal: The China Factor," *Special Report*, No. 14, Institute of Peace and Conflict Studies, March 2006, http://www.ipcs.org/IPCS-Special-Report-14.pdf.
20. Jabin T. Jacob, "Behind the Stonewall," *Indian Express*, 11 September 2008, http://www.indianexpress.com/news/Behind-the-stonewall/359970/.
21. These questions have been raised in Volker, op.cit., pp. 68-69.
22. Dewitt, op.cit., p. 512.
23. Ibid., p. 534.
24. See for example, John Pomfret, "Dispute with Japan highlights China's foreign-policy power struggle", *Washington Post*, 24 September 2010, http://www.washingtonpost.com/wp-dyn/content/article/2010/09/23/AR2010092306861_pf.html ; Thomas J. Christensen, "The Advantages of an Assertive China: Responding to Beijing's Abrasive Diplomacy", *Foreign Affairs*, Vol. 90(2), March/April 2011, http://www.foreignaffairs.com/articles/67477/thomas-j-christensen/the-advantages-of-an-assertive-china; Daniel Blumenthal, "Riding a tiger: China's resurging foreign policy aggression", *Foreign Policy*, 15 April 2011, http://shadow.foreignpolicy.com/posts/2011/04/15/riding_a_tiger_chinas_resurging_foreign_policy_aggression.

2

India-China Relations in the 21st Century—Seeking Confidence and Convergence

Maj. Gen. (Retd) Dipankar Banerjee

Exordium

India and China, the two largest civilizational states in history, have had a long and checkered relationship. Experts have generally shared one of two views. Some have argued that due to the formidable barrier of the Himalayas, contact between the two countries was minimal and hence relations were neither close nor substantial. Yet, others have contended that in spite of the times and the nature of connectivity of that era, what contacts did exist were significant and positive. As we look ahead to the future, we will have to craft a mutual relationship based on this shared past but without yet an adequate understanding of each other's concerns and interests. This at a period when China is already once again among the world's leading powers and India is slowly and steadily moving ahead to reassume a significant global role. It will be a challenge for both countries.

What is not contested in our historical relationship however, is that bilateral relations were mutually beneficial. These were related to trade and commerce through the 'silk routes', exchange of religious teachers and treatises and intellectual exchanges between scholars, which took place both in China and at the famous Nalanda University in India.[1] The Silk Route had several branches in the west some entering northern India. In Southeast Asia, China's southern Silk Route met India's trade routes from Orissa and West Bengal (Kalinga and Bengal of the Maurya dynasty) though not always simultaneously. These resulted in the harmonious mingling of two civilizations best exemplified today in the composite cultures to be seen in Thailand and the Indo-Chinese countries. This harmonious co-existence of two major civilizations also ensured a peaceful Asia and till the 18th century the domination of the global economy by China and India.[2]

This history of amity and friendship later made possible Rabindranath Tagore's visit to Shanghai at the invitation of Chinese scholars in the 1920s and the subsequent opening of the Cheena Bhavan (China House) in Shantiniketan for Chinese studies.[3] At the invitation of Zhu De in 1937, Jawaharal Nehru as the President of the Indian National Congress sent a medical mission to Yennan with five doctors and medical equipment.[4] The Mission provided valuable medical support for a couple of years, but Dr Dwarkanath Kotnis remained in China till his death in 1942.[5]

This was the foundation on which India and China attempted to build a relationship of *Hindi-Chini bhai bhai* (Indians and Chinese are brothers) in the 1950s, when both became free after a long period under foreign domination.

The Border Issue

The clash on the border in 1962 was, in the span of history, a mere blip.[6] The casualties suffered by both sides were small especially when measured against China's casualties in the Korean War (1950-53) and even Vietnam War (1979) or India's in the Second World War. But, this conflict was perceived in both countries in very different ways. A small part of an entirely unprepared Indian Army with indifferent political strategic guidance was beaten and badly humiliated. India felt deeply betrayed, by China and also by its own leaders who had kept the people in the dark and allowed itself to be surprised.[7] For China this was a conflict in the periphery, taking place a decade after the Korean War. It was also when the 'Great Leap Forward' in China was taking a massive toll of lives in the countryside. As a consequence little is known in China even today of this 'skirmish' in its remote borderland.[8]

The tension lasted about two decades with diplomatic relations normalized and restored at the ambassadorial level in 1976. A process of active engagement to resolve this issue began in 1981 with the visit of China's foreign minister to India in 1981.[9] Efforts have continued ever since, with regular frequency and at different levels.

The asymmetric perception of the nature of the conflict has complicated finding an acceptable solution to the border problem. In India's perception, this remains a major obstacle to good relations. Hardliners in India will always point to this unresolved problem to attribute motives to China and hold back measures for cooperation. In China, however, this is a minor issue, which can be solved later. Deng Xiaoping had said in 1988 that, if the present set of leaders could not resolve the border question, then it should be left to the next generation to resolve. Meanwhile, there is no consensus, even on the length of the border.[10] For India the border question remains a litmus test of Beijing's friendship and good intentions towards India. Yet, neither side seems to be ready to make the necessary compromises that are essential to resolve this issue left behind by history.

Even though tensions on the border remain, it has been otherwise peaceful and stable. No serious exchange of fire or hostility has disturbed the Himalayan serenity in about three and a half decades. Regular meetings at the border help ensure peace and tranquility and are conducted with great goodwill and ceremony. The latest bilateral agreement signed in New Delhi on 17 January 2012, the India-China Agreement on the Establishment of a Working Mechanism for Consultation and Coordination on India-China Border Affairs, lays down a mechanism of consultation at an official level which will further help in dealing with local border problems.[11]

A month before the last Special Representative meeting in Delhi, in December 2011, Indian Prime Minister Manmohan Singh, had said that he was convinced that the Chinese leadership wanted a peaceful resolution of all problems between the two countries, including the long-running border dispute. Responding to this, the Chinese foreign ministry spokesperson had said a few days later that, China was "ready to work with India to enhance the China-India strategic partnership".[12] If this remains the official policy of the two governments then a reasonable and acceptable resolution of this problem can be found through further consultations.

It is in this backdrop that it is important to discuss enhancing confidence between India and China in the context of Asia and the world and building convergence over critical issues of international concern.

India's Perception of China's Rise

Recent decades have witnessed one of the most remarkable economic developments in the history of the world, the reemergence of China. Never before has such a large country grown its economy continuously at an average of over ten per cent a year for over three decades, as China has done since the early 1980s. India has viewed China's rise over the years with amazement and high appreciation. China's rise occurred at a time when there emerged the perception of a Western decline and Japan began its long stagnation in the 1990s.[13] In turn, it not only lifted a large number of China's people out of poverty, "but it lifted all boats in Asia" particularly in China's neighborhood. When the Asian economic downturn occurred in 1997, it was China that stood firm with its currency exchange rates and which, with its rising economy helped the rest of the region to recover, indicating clearly its changed geopolitical importance in Asia.

India's GDP too, has grown, since 1991, when it gave up its socialist economic policies, but at a significantly lower annual rate than China. It remains well behind China today in economic growth, but its trajectory is clearly on a major upward trend. Taken together this has led to a situation where for the first time in world history, two very large countries next to each other have grown simultaneously and are today among the leading nations in a world that is becoming smaller every year under the process of globalization.[14]

Both India and China have benefited from these developments. Implementing the policies of normalization in all spheres even as the border question was being negotiated, bilateral trade between India and China has multiplied. From a little under a billion US dollars less than 15 years ago, it has reached US$70 billion in 2011 and continues to rise sharply. Though concerns are expressed in New Delhi periodically over the asymmetric nature of this trade—India exports mainly raw materials and imports finished consumer goods also suffering a serious imbalance—it benefits too, from this process.

This normalization of bilateral relations has seen a number of very substantive positive outcomes. Bilaterally it has allowed major confidence-building measures to be established. Senior political and military leaders visit and interact with each other often. A bilateral strategic dialogue has taken place every year since 2009. Each of the three military services has undertaken joint exercises with the other. An 'observer status' is accorded to the other in the Shanghai Cooperation Organization (SCO) and the South Asian Association for Regional Cooperation (SAARC) respectively. There are sideline discussions between leaders in many international forums. Finally, regular bilateral dialogues at functional level address many issues for enhancing mutual cooperation.

India and China and the Asian and Global Orders

At the outset, it is important to stress the difference in the respective positions of India and China in the global order. China has already 'emerged' as a great power, second today, only to the United States in terms of comprehensive national power.[15] It is the largest trading nation and the 'factory' of the world, with over US$3 trillion in currency reserves and an annual GDP of about US$6 trillion. Its current annual GDP growth rate, though likely to slow in the current period of global recession, still comfortably leads the rest of the world. Compared to this, India is an 'emerging' power with decades to catch up on China. In terms of per capita and total annual GDP, India's is about a quarter to one-fifth that of China.[16]

This asymmetry shows in a number of critical areas even as it is recognized that India too matters and that its voice, which already has weight in Asia, will increasingly matter in the world as well, in future. India—often called the "back-office" of the world—is a strong information technology hub and emerging as a global innovation centre. But, its cumulative impact on the world still remains significantly less than China's. Finally, in addition to economic power China also has global political influence as a permanent member of the UN Security Council, the only country from Asia.

This comparison becomes sharper when seen in the context of hard military and space power or in the ability over the next decades to project this power abroad. China's defence spending growing at ten per cent annually over two decades has led to a formidable military capability. Its army is the largest in the world and rapidly modernizing. Major advanced weapon systems are presently manufactured indigenously. The more prominent modernization has been in its naval capabilities where it is beginning to project its influence far afield. It is expanding in the Pacific Ocean beyond the "first island chain" and in the Indian Ocean extending its reach to the East coast of Africa. Its aircraft carrier development program will in the near future provide it the type of naval expeditionary capability that it had only during the period of the famous Admiral Zheng He five centuries ago. China is today, a leading space power with advanced satellite systems that could be developed for military use and an effective anti-satellite missile capability. It has an advanced space exploratory program with manned missions, which is heading for rapid expansion.

India too, has a modest military modernization program, stymied somewhat by the absence of implementation and constant slippage in acquisition targets. Its total defence including modernization budget remains at a little over one-third that of China's. But, these limitations are overcome in some measure through building strategic partnerships with major countries in Asia and the world. This reduces its current military requirements for security far from home and reduces overall expenditure.

India's strategic partnership with the US, in particular, opens up many possibilities for cooperation, which might add to its aggregate strength and global influence. It is important to understand the nature of this Indo-US strategic partnership. It is neither an alliance nor a close coordination of defence planning with the aim of mounting joint military operations. It provides an arrangement for useful exchange of views, developing inter-operability and an ability to launch joint coordinated humanitarian operations. It envisages significant arms purchase and manufacturing possibilities and in the near future of joint weapons development and research. While, there are no agreements yet to include joint communications or the hosting of US troops in India, extensive joint exercises are carried out by India with the US military every year, more than what it does with any other country. Over the years, this has enabled the building of a genuine partnership between India and the US, which today includes many facets other than military cooperation.

While India does not have the same influence as China in global security issues it too, is deeply involved around the world as a member of several international bodies. Along with China, it engages other continents under the Brazil-Russia-India-China-South Africa (BRICS) partnership. Annual heads-of-government meetings and other meetings on the sidelines of various international conferences help understand and build relations across continents.

Developments in the Asia-Pacific Region

These developments are taking place in a larger Asia-Pacific region that is witnessing major changes. It is necessary to reflect briefly on the nature of these changes and how they impact on both India and China. The first change, is the centrality of Asia in global geo-strategy, both in terms of its rapid economic growth and also on issues related to security concerns and military development. Second, is America's recent rebalancing towards the region committing it to deploy some 60 per cent of its military resources in the Asia-Pacific. Third, is that many of the new issues and potential hotspots are located in the sea rather than on land.

The US presence in Asia-Pacific has been a reality since the end of the Second World War and most countries in the region have welcomed it. It has facilitated the economic growth of several countries in the region and is seen by them as a stabilizing factor. The American imperative of dealing with terrorism led to a greater focus in Iraq and Afghanistan leading to a temporary absence from the Asia-Pacific during the Bush presidency. With the winding down of those commitments, a return to the Asia-Pacific is a natural phenomenon and has been taking place for some years now. This presence has been a positive development. The humanitarian assistance provided by the US military during the 2004 tsunami devastation in Southern Asia sometimes in collaboration with regional militaries helped alleviate severe distress. The continuation of other potential conflict situations, is again leading to an attempt at renewing military relationships with the US, by some countries of the Association of Southeast Asian Nations (ASEAN).

In the second half of the last century, security concerns in Asia were focused on post-colonial territorial issues and resolving land boundaries often around China's borders. These resulted in Asia's major wars at the time. Today's concerns are focused more on the seas and on maritime boundaries, many of which remain disputed. This is being compounded by the possibility of energy resources under the seabed and the need to secure the sea lines of communication which are vital for regional trade and hence prosperity. This affects the entire Indo-Pacific oceanic space, which is merging and mingling to form one large geo-strategic zone. In this region, according to a former Indonesian defense minister, the interests and concerns of both India and China remain intertwined.[17]

Three principal issues in Asia and perhaps the world are of major concern in matters of security. First, is the Korean peninsula and the nature of the North Korean state and its nuclear capability. Next, are questions over island territories in the East and South China Seas. Third, is the potential for instability in the Afghanistan-Pakistan region post-NATO and International Security Assistance Force (ISAF) pullout in 2014. China is involved in all of them, while India is concerned with the last two and in addition with other potential developments specifically in the Indian Ocean.

Unlike other regions of the world, Asia does not have a security architecture or a continent-wide structure to address issues of peace and security and regional cooperation. It is true that under the ASEAN a regional order is in the process of being structured. It has gradually attempted to create some of the mechanisms that will help build these. As of now it remains essentially a dialogue mechanism with varying compositions and a mix of track-1 and track-1.5 arrangements, with ASEAN at its centre. Provided it is an inclusive grouping of all countries in Asia, including Australia and New Zealand it should be a welcome development and supported by larger outside powers. It must be recognized that it does not have a security responsibility. The ASEAN Regional Forum (ARF) is merely a discussion forum of a political nature and the more recently initiated ASEAN+8 defence ministers dialogue is merely a forum for them to meet annually. It may be in the interest both of India and China to help ASEAN build and strengthen these institutions.

With the end of the Soviet Union in 1990 Central Asian countries emerged as independent sovereign states. Initially both India and China developed good bilateral relations with all these newly independent countries. But Indian efforts were stymied by the absence of a common border and access and in spite of its desire was unable to build stronger ties.[18] On the other hand, China with the help of Russia founded the SCO in 1996, with the aim of enhancing regional stability and building cooperation.[19] At the end of the first decade of the 21st century, the SCO is a major bulwark against NATO expansion in Asia and provides today a mechanism through which China has extended its influence over this region and accesses the considerable natural resources of these countries, while also providing a degree of security and stability. Though this cooperation may be more tactical than strategic according to Robert Kaplan, and even though there may be an element of competition between Russia and China, it still remains an effective forum through which Beijing exercises its influence over the region.[20] The SCO conducts major annual military exercises ostensibly for counter-terrorism, which in practice has a considerably larger scope. India is an 'observer' in the SCO, as are some other neighbours, but effectively excluded from its decision-making processes.

In the south of the continent, is the South Asian Association for Regional Cooperation (SAARC), established in 1985 with seven members and now with Afghanistan as its eighth member. It has nine observer nations including China and the EU. The SAARC is essentially meant for regional economic cooperation patterned on the ASEAN and meant to facilitate trade and commerce, but today includes collective counter-terrorism cooperation as well. Though meant to be much more intimate and with a larger agenda, its potential is stymied by lack of cooperation between member countries. China has good bilateral relations with all SAARC countries and a particularly close one with Pakistan. Overall, this is a welcome development and Chinese companies particularly in infrastructure and communication are making very valuable contributions.

The time has come to examine how some of these regional organizations could in the future expand and cooperate in terms of memberships and functions. This might help build an inclusive architecture that will facilitate all-round cooperation in terms of trade and commerce, use and exploitation of resources and ensuring common security for all members. Should there be substantial improvement in India-China relations, this should not be an insurmountable problem.

The area that is rapidly becoming a theatre for trans-continental concern is the Indo-Pacific oceanic region. The areas of maximum interest lie in the northern Indian Ocean and the eastern Pacific. It is through the waters of these oceans that ply the densest sea-borne traffic in the world. China, Japan and South Korea are the states most affected, but Australia, the US and India are also just as significantly involved. It is the route through which the Persian Gulf oil and gas reach its most thirsty consumers and by which the world economy is powered. It is also the region where India-China cooperation and convergence must play the most important role. Yet, different perceptions prevail. For China, these waters are of vital concern as through them ply most of its commerce with Europe and from where it receives a bulk of its energy requirements. In this context, its desire to break out of the 'first island chain' in the Pacific is quite understandable. Its growing desire to secure the Indian Ocean routes from pirates as well as other challenges have led to a policy of greater presence around the Indian Ocean rim through strategic treaty arrangements and port construction activities. Recently, China has been involved in constructing a naval base at the Seychelles.[21] These are of course understandable, and from China's perspective, necessary. But, there has been a lack of transparency in China's efforts regarding its presence as well as force accretions, which taken together have created the impression of a "string of pearls" in the Indian Ocean aimed at restricting India's influence over this oceanic space, which accidentally also bears India's name, but does not allow it any proprietary rights.[22]

When analyzed in the context of China's rapid military modernization, which again is the consequence of its economic growth and ability to devote much greater resources to its defense, gives rise to a feeling in the region of sudden and alarming presence. In New Delhi, China's naval presence in the Indian Ocean and its maritime activities across the region is observed with some anxiety.

China-Pakistan Relations and India's Concerns

Any analysis of Sino-Indian relations has to take in to account China's close relations with Pakistan and its impact on India. At the outset, I would like to emphasize that there is no reason for India to object to Beijing's close and growing cooperation with Islamabad. Foreign policy is a sovereign right of independent nations to be formulated and pursued in the national interest. Yet, its impact and consequences need also to be considered as it may impinge on relations with other states and influence other interests. China can equally point towards growing India-US relations as a counter.[23]

It is acknowledged that having strong friendly relations with a South Asian country, which facilitates maintaining links with other Islamic countries further west are very significant objectives for Beijing. Besides, in the first two decades of the establishment of the PRC, breaching the Western powers' "ring" around China would have been an important objective as well. Therefore, the assurance in 1955 at Bandung from the Prime Minister of Pakistan, Mohammad Ali Bogra to Zhou Enlai, that his country's membership of SEATO was not targeted against China but intended at developing its own military capability against India, would have been very welcome to Beijing. Even though Islamabad continued to play a double game on this with the US, it was apparently acceptable to Washington, till at least 1965.

Two aspects of current China-Pakistan relations are of major concern for India. One, is the nuclear and strategic weapons cooperation with Pakistan and the other is PLA presence in Gilgit-Baltistan.[24] China's support to Pakistan's nuclear programme is said to have begun from the early 1980s and have continued ever since. There may be doubts as to how far Pakistan's nuclear and strategic weapons programme would have actually progressed without this support, but of greater concern is its continuance, including supply of nuclear reactors at Kahuta. Even though there have been several positive developments in India-China relations, this aspect still continues to be a major concern to India's strategic thinkers and affects India's position on strengthening bilateral confidence-building measures (CBMs).

One of these positive developments was perhaps Chinese President Jiang Zemin's advice to Pakistan's legislators in November 1996, when he emphasized,

> "Properly handling existing disputes in the spirit of seeking common ground while setting aside differences... We should look at the differences or disputes from a long perspective, seeking a just and reasonable settlement through consultations and negotiations while bearing in mind the larger picture. If certain issues cannot be resolved for the time being, they may be shelved temporarily so that they will not affect the normal state-to-state relations".[25]

This was a message to Islamabad to follow China's path in developing all-round relations with India even as the border question was to be left for the next generation to resolve.[26] A policy that Deng Xiaoping had suggested in 1988 and which has since been followed by India and China. However, there is no reason to believe that Pakistani leaders paid much heed to this advice. The most blatant violation of this principle was the Kargil operations launched by Gen. Pervez Musharraf in 1999, who was later the Pakistani head of state till 2007. Yet, Jiang Zemin's statement and perhaps a nuanced shift in policy then on Kashmir went largely unnoticed in India.

The other issue that may have more direct influence on Sino-Indian confidence-building is the reported presence of PLA soldiers in Gilgit-Baltistan. This was originally reported by Selig Harrison, a reputed US reporter in the *New York Times* in August 2010, where he said that between 7,000 and 11,000 PLA soldiers have been present in the region ostensibly for road construction.[27] This was countered by Pakistani authorities, but a rejoinder was given by Harrison the following month in the *International Herald Tribune*.[28] Indian assessments suggest that a minimum of 4,000 PLA soldiers are presently deployed there. Chinese authorities have countered this by stating that only a few civilians are present to support infrastructure and other constructions after the severe floods in Pakistan in 2010. Though it is accepted that the Karakoram Highway across the Khunjerab Pass linking the region with Xinjiang is being improved and a certain number of construction workers from China would be present, greater clarity on this from China would be welcome and may be achieved through transparency and related CBMs.

Tibet Question

A greater concern in China today appears to be over the Dalai Lama and Tibet. The Tibet issue should have been considered settled when India recognized in 2003 that "Tibet Autonomous Region is part of the territory of the People's Republic of China and reiterates that it does not allow Tibetans to engage in anti-China political activities in India".[29] But, the presence of over a hundred thousand Tibetans in India including the Dalai Lama, and their activities in India though peaceful, but often highlighting the absence of freedom in Tibet, is naturally anathema to China. The ultimate resolution of the Tibetan issue is indeed a purely domestic matter for the government in China, to be settled by it considering its own national security and in consultation with the people of Tibet. India can do little about it. Any suppression of peaceful demonstration within India by this diaspora is not in the purview of Indian national law and cannot be prevented.

The Dalai Lama personally does not undertake any activity in India that will compromise his spiritual standing. In 2011, he also relinquished all his temporal powers. Taken together, it is India's firm view that the Tibetan question should not come in the way either of stronger India-China relations or of the resolution of the border question.

Nuclear Issues

The most important issue for India and China to seek convergence and build confidence is the nuclear question. China became a nuclear weapon power on 16 October 1964. At great hardship to its people and with remarkable dedication of its scientists, it mastered the technology of nuclear explosion. Mao Zedong had assessed the external security situation to be grave enough to warrant developing this capability. He declared that ensuring security for a nation was the supreme responsibility of its leaders. He also declared at the outset that China would never be the first to use this weapon and would never do so against a country that did not possess this weapon. India's nuclear doctrine and policy is essentially the same and does not target any specific nation. It is a certain capability that the nation will keep as a deterrent and consider using only when attacked by another nuclear weapon power.

This bilateral nuclear weapon environment has been further complicated by Pakistan's acquisition of nuclear weapons. In Indian perception, influenced by western assessment and analyses, Islamabad's links with both China and North Korea in its nuclear and missile developments have made it much more complex. The management of this environment thus becomes an issue of the highest priority for confidence building in the region.

Over the last 15 years, both India and Pakistan have built an adequate number of nuclear bombs and a range of weapon systems to deliver the weapons. The time has now come to ensure that these weapons are neither used in conflict, nor their components allowed to fall into the hands of non-state actors who could cause untold devastation to millions. Yet, no collective dialogue has even started to address these questions. While an Indo-Pak dialogue process exists where a nuclear dialogue mechanism could be built, none exists in the case of India and China. It is necessary to overcome the obstacles to ensure that these weapons do not become part of the equation in any future relationship in Asia.[30]

It is true that a substantial nuclear weapons elimination process would require global engagement. But, a measure of adequate confidence-building through transparent measures of engagement and dialogue that will set up requisite cooperation arrangements can surely be addressed between India, Pakistan and China. Effective confidence along these lines between all three countries, ensuring "no-first use", transparency and effective safety and security of nuclear weapons, along with stable demarcated borders have the potential to dramatically alter the strategic relationship between these three countries.

Building Convergence and Confidence

The immediate and long-term objective for both India and China remains ensuring a reasonable standard of living for their large populations. There can be no other compelling purpose for either nation given the present state of development in both countries. Hence, a cooperative relationship between the two largest nations in Asia is an imperative. Some measures to this end are discussed in brief.

- Remove all irritants in bilateral relations related to the border question. Accepting an immediate solution on delineation may not be possible, strengthen further confidence-building. This may be done through implementing existing agreements, reducing troop levels and developing greater transparency across a range of areas. Accepting that each will have security concerns independent of the other, concede that there will be no equality or symmetry, but adequacy.

- Enhance the scale and quality of bilateral annual strategic dialogue to include discussions on Pakistan, terrorism and Af-Pak.
- Establish bilateral strategic nuclear dialogue to build confidence, strengthen "no-first use" doctrines and build consensus on nuclear weapons elimination globally.
- Facilitate the establishment of an Asia-wide security structure based on ASEAN that will help facilitate dialogue and discussion, provide early warning of conflicts, enable resolution mechanisms and promote conflict resolution.
- Consider sponsoring an Indo-Pacific Ocean security arrangement in partnership with littoral countries that will help promote and secure trade and reduce maritime competition.

Conclusion

Good relations between India and China have the potential to shape the future of Asia and the world. Together, they constitute nearly 40 per cent of the global population. Their economies have the potential to continue to grow significantly higher than other countries well into the future, in spite of global fluctuations. Both have great power aspirations, but both also face daunting challenges of resource scarcity, environmental pollution, climate change, and energy insecurity. And this, in a world where the global order is still set by Western powers, even though their capabilities are declining.

NOTES

1. Amartya Sen, *The Argumentative Indian: Writings on Indian History, Culture and Identity*, New Delhi: Penguin Books, 2005.
2. For example, in 1820 China's GDP was 32.9 per cent of the global GDP and India's was 18.8. Also, Angus Maddison "The World Economy Historical Statistics", OECD, 2003. Angus Maddison cited in *Macronomics*, "Long term Macro views—as per Angus Maddison," 1 May 2010, http://macronomy.blogspot.in/2010/05/long-term-macro-views-as-per-angus.html.
3. Shantiniketan or the 'abode of peace' was the University founded by Tagore in Paschimbanga (West Bengal) with his award money from the Nobel Prize for Literature in 1913.
4. Huang Hua, *Memoirs*, Beijing: Foreign Language Press, 2008, p. 398.
5. Dr Kotnis is a hero both in China and India. His story has been much written about in both countries and even a popular Indian film made in commemoration. See for example among many others *China Daily*, "Indian Doctor's Selfless Service Remembered," 10 September 2005, http://www.china.org.cn/english/culture/

141496.htm. His Chinese wife Guo Qinglan, passed away on 28 June 2012 in Dalian at age 96. Tributes were paid to her memory and to Dr Kotnis by the Chinese Government and the Indian Embassy, Beijing. See *Times of India*, "Dr Kotnis's wife passes away in China at 96," New Delhi, 29 June 2012, http://articles.timesofindia.indiatimes.com/2012-06-29/china/32471565_1_india-and-china-indian-embassy-chinese-foreign-ministry. The External Affairs Minister in India at Delhi on June 29 also sent condolences. Ministry of External Affairs, Government of India, "EAM condoles the passing away of Mme Guo Qinglan," *Press Releases*, 28 June 2012, http://www.mea.gov.in/mystart.php?id=530219682.

6. In June 1991, the author was one of two Indian Generals who visited China at the invitation of the PLA, resuming military to military contact between the two nations cut off for 34 years due to the War. During the few days of our stay we were often accosted by friendly officials, cadres, scholars and others who would spontaneously say words to the effect that; "we have been friends for 5,000 years but have had a difficult period for only 20 years—let us be friends again".
7. There is a long narrative of this in the Indian media, parliamentary proceedings and scholarly research. Books authored by Indian Army officers involved in this conflict during this period reflect this sentiment. Brig John Parshuram Dalvi, who was Commander of 7 Infantry Brigade, who fought in the Namka Chu Sector in the Kameng Division of Arunachal Pradesh in 1962 and was subsequently a prisoner of war in China, wrote the book, "Himalayan Blunder: The Curtain-raiser to the Sino-Indian War of 1962" (Dehradun: Natraj, 1997)). The book was initially banned in India but later allowed to be reprinted.
8. During this author's first visit to China in 1991, nobody seemed quite aware of the 1962 conflict. The situation is somewhat different now. With greater awareness and opening up of its recent history, a number of Chinese scholars today are writing about this war.
9. Hua, *op.cit.* p. 412.
10. Due to the nature of the dispute there is no agreement or clarity on the length of the border itself with both countries having a different view. India considers it to be 3,488kms long, while China claims it is about 2,000kms. See for example Krishnan Ananth, 'Officials dismiss China's Kashmir border claims,' *Hindu*, 20 December 2010, http://www.thehindu.com/news/national/article963655.ece.
11. Ministry of External Affairs, Government of India, "Agreement between the Government of the Republic of India and the Government of the People's Republic of China on the Establishment of a Working Mechanism for Consultation and Coordination on India-China Border Affairs," 17 January, 2012. See Appendix.
12. Krishnan Ananth, "China welcomes Manmohan statement on Border Issue", *Hindu*, 25 October 2011, http://www.thehindu.com/news/international/article2570427.ece.
13. Paul Kennedy, *The Rise and Fall of the Great Powers: Economic Change and Military Conflict from 1500 to 2000*, London: Fontana Press, 1989. It made a great impression in the Asia-Pacific including India in the 1990s and seemed to suggest a sudden decline of the US, which of course proved utterly premature.
14. See for example the paper authored by Wilson, Dominic and Roopa Purushothaman, "Dreaming with BRICs—the Path to 2050," Goldman Sachs, Global Economics Paper No 99, 1 October 2003, http://www.goldmansachs.com/korea/ideas/brics/99-dreaming.pdf. This study has predicted that by 2050 China, the US and India in that order will be by far the leading economies of the world.
15. For a comparison of the difference in years between the state of development in India and China in different categories of social indicators, please see, "Chasing

the Dragon," *Economist*, 3 October 2011, at http://www.economist.com/blogs/dailychart/2011/10/comparing-india-and-china.

16. One of the best recent comparative study of the economic performance of both countries is that of Mohan Guruswamy and Zorawar Daulet Singh, *Chasing the Dragon: Will India Catch Up with China?* Delhi: Pearson Longman, 2009.
17. Juwono Sudarsono, "Redefining ASEAN security in the region," *Jakarta Post*, 5 May 2011, http://www.thejakartapost.com/news/2011/05/05/redefining-asean-security-region.html.
18. India's annual two-way trade with Central Asia is in the order of US$500 million while China's is 60 times more at about US$30 billion as of 2011.
19. The SCO Website at http://www.sectsco.org/EN/. Originally known as the Shanghai Five when it was formed in 1996, it became the SCO after Uzbekistan joined in 2001.
20. "Robert D. "Kaplan on the Shanghai Cooperation Organization (Agenda)," *Stratfor*, (video), 8 June 2012, http://www.youtube.com/watch?v=7LJqziSRI6o.
21.
22. See for example an article in Maseeh Rahman, "Chinese plans in Seychelles revive Indian fears of encirclement," *Guardian* (UK), 22 March 2012, http://www.guardian.co.uk/world/2012/mar/22/china-seychelles-indian-fears-encirclement.
23. Though it would be correct to state that whatever the nature of India-US relations, it is not in the nature definitely of "deeper than the oceans and higher than the highest mountains" as Sino-Pakistani relations is often characterized. Indo-US relations are at best a partnership between equal but far away partners sharing a common vision of the future but following different paths. India is not even a "major non-NATO partner" of the US, which Pakistan is.
24. China has consistently denied the presence of any PLA personnel abroad including in Gilgit-Baltistan. Yet, western reports and internal analyses in India have cast doubts regarding this assertion.
25. Aparna Pande, "Pak-China; Changed Equations", *Indus-Asia Online Journal*, 26 August 2009, http://iaoj.wordpress.com/2009/08/27/pak-china-changed-equations/.
26. Ibid.
27. Selig Harrison, "China's Discreet Hold on Pakistan's Northern Borderlands", *New York Times*, 26 August 2010. http://www.nytimes.com/2010/08/27/opinion/27iht-edharrison.html, accessed on 20 July 12.
28. Mian Jahangir Iqbal and Selig S. Harrison (rejoinder), "China's Presence in Pakistan, *New York Times* (Letters to *the International Herald Tribune*), 8 September 2010, http://www.nytimes.com/2010/09/09/opinion/09iht-edletters.html. Mian Jahangir Iqbal was the Pakistani Press Counselor General to Pakistan's Permanent Mission to the United Nations in New York.
29. Ministry of External Affairs, Government of India, "Declaration on Principles for Relations and Comprehensive Cooperation between the Republic of India and the People's Republic of China," 23 June, 2003. See Appendix.
30. A number of limited utility nuclear CBMs exist between India and Pakistan and these have been observed by both sides. There is thus no reason to doubt that similar arrangements of a more substantial nature can also be built between all three countries.

3

The Rise of India and China-India Relations

Maj. Gen. (Retd) Pan Zhenqiang

One of the spectacular developments in Asia in the past two decades has been the rise of India. Together with the rise of China, the emergence of India as a potential world power promises to dramatically alter the regional as well as world economic and security architecture. At the same time, the rise of both India and China is bound to have a profound impact on the bilateral relations between the two Asian giants. How does China view the rapid development of India? Will the two countries become strategic partners, not only living peacefully side by side, but also working together to strive for a better world order? Or are they destined to fight for greater influence as rivals in the world, and in Asia, in particular? The present paper attempts to offer a Chinese view on these questions, and concludes by arguing that the two great nations need to join efforts to overcome obstacles that are in the way of forming a more constructive, cooperative partnership for the future.

Rising India

India's rapid economic development began later than China's. It was not until the early 1990s, that New Delhi began serious economic reforms. But since then, India has ensured its economic growth has stayed on the fast track for the past two decades. From 1980-2002, India's annual growth rate reached 6 per cent. The figure even climbed to a record 7.5 per cent during 2002-06. In the face of a global recession starting from 2008, India was one

The views expressed in the paper are the author's own, and do not necessarily reflect those of any other individual or institution.

of the least affected countries in the world thanks to its robust policy of generically expanding domestic demands and relaxed financial regulations. While many other major countries are grappling with the economic downturn, India succeeded in realizing economic recovery in the latter part of 2009, with a 6 per cent annual growth rate that year, and possibly over 7.5 per cent in 2010. By end 2011, India's GDP has reached US$1.5 trillion, ranking it as the 12th among old economic powers. Judged according to the PPP standard, India has become the fourth largest economy in the world (next only to the US, Japan, and China), with its GDP being as high as US$3.39 trillion. This economic miracle has helped India to substantially reduce its population below the poverty line and created a growing middle class.

What makes many Indians especially proud is that the country seems to have embarked on a road to development built on India's own strength. As one senior analyst noted:

> "China's strength has been its ability to mobilize capital and labor to develop its manufacturing sector, fueled by massive injections of foreign direct investment (FDI) and enormous government infrastructure spending, India, on the other hand, has had to rely more on its large pool of highly educated knowledge workers and the sheer savvy of its private sector managers. As a result, China dwarfs India as a manufacturing powerhouse, while India shines in its software and business outsourcing services. It is a case of brawn versus brains".[1]

Building on this technologically innovative edge, India has produced a number of national business giants like Infosys and Wipro, which have demonstrated powerful technological leverage in the international market. The technological advantage leads many pundits in the research community, in India in particular, to be extremely confident that although less visible, India may have greater potential than China for development in the future. One of these optimistic predictions, for example, suggested that in the coming 50 years, India would see an annual economic growth rate of 5.8 per cent, China 4.9 per cent, the US 1.8 per cent, and Japan 1.4 per cent. India would surpass Italy in terms of GDP in 2015, France in 2020, Germany in 2025, being next only to the US, Japan and China. The prediction went on to claim that while three nations—Brazil, Russia, and China—among the BRICs may start to see a decline in their economic performance by 2050, India alone would continue to progress with an annual growth rate of 5 per cent, with the prospect that India could become the largest economy in the world by that time.[2]

Whether all these predictions could come true is worth further debate, considering that India, like any other major developing country, may also experience many constraints both domestically and internationally in its future economic development. However, India's booming economy today with its huge potential in the future has already set a stage for the change of its political environment at home as well as reorientation of India's foreign and security policy based on the shift of the balance of forces in the Asian context.

Fast-paced economic development on the domestic front had helped the ruling Congress (I) Party to greatly consolidate its power base. Elections to the Lower House of India's Parliament from 16 April to 13 May 2009, saw the overwhelming victory of the coalition led by the Congress (I), and the defeat of the opposition both from the right and the left. In particular, it has dramatically reduced the power of the main opposition—the Hindu nationalist Bharatiya Janata Party (BJP), leading to the erosion of the traditional pattern in India's domestic politics, characterized with the contention of two major parties. The Congress (I) is more or less free to pursue its policy objectives, and ensure domestic political stability.

The economic rise of India has far-reaching impact on both India's foreign and security policy. India has long cherished an ambition to become a world power, playing a leading role in shaping Asian unity free of manipulation from the Western or any other major power. In line with this vision, India had tried to create a third block in the form of a non-aligned movement outside the competition between the two world superpowers during the Cold War. However, owing chiefly to its lack of strength, India was hardly able to play that role. Instead, New Delhi soon found itself to be virtually marginalized when it came to international affairs, and was even forced to be allied with the Soviet Union to augment its position in its contention with Pakistan and China. India's influence continued to be largely confined to the subcontinent and it was only when New Delhi's economy began to take off that the opportunity for change in its political circumstances emerged. With the steady progress of its economic performance, India's dream of being a world power seems within reach; its foreign and security policies are becoming increasingly proactive.

The first indication of such a change in India's policy was its clear interest in engaging in cooperation to manage economic, political, and security affairs in the Asia-Pacific. In 1992, India launched the Look East Policy, which was primarily aimed at improving relations with ASEAN as well as other nations of the region such as China, Japan and Korea to facilitate more regional cooperation. Since the beginning of this century, India has succeeded in becoming a summit level partner of ASEAN in 2002 and getting involved in some regional initiatives such as the BIMSTEC and the Mekong Ganga Cooperation Initiative and becoming a member of the East Asia Summit (EAS) in December 2005. Economically, for the fist time India's trade volume with the Asia-Pacifica countries (excluding the US) surpassed the total of its trade volume with Europe and the US put together, in 2004. That year also saw the value of the total import and export of India in the Asia-Pacific reach US$56 billion, with the export being US$29.4 billion, and import US$26.6 billion, accounting for 46 per cent and 35 per cent in India's foreign trade respectively.[3]

Second, building on its growing status as a more influential international player, India did not lose the opportunity to reorient its traditional policy of balancing various major powers to promote its own interests. Although the collapse of the Soviet Union has fundamentally changed the nature of India's allied relations with Russia, New Delhi nevertheless has continued to attach importance to maintaining close cooperation with Moscow. But the new focus evidently has been on rebuilding partnership with the Western powers, the US in particular. The readjustment could not have happened at a more optimum time as all the major powers outside the region are now vying for closer cooperation with India. This growing interest has been fuelled apparently by the potential of India's huge economic strength, but is also motivated by strategic calculations.

Claiming that it was the US policy "to help make India a major world power in the 21st century," Washington has been anxious to enhance its efforts to upgrade its relations with New Delhi particularly after the 9/11 terrorist attacks. The aim is to intensify collaboration with India across a range of issues on the global agenda. For the first time, India no longer refused the role of the US in South Asia, as it used to. Instead, New Delhi has welcomed the proactive American involvement in the security affairs of the subcontinent. What was of special significance was the Indo-US nuclear agreement signed in July 2005. According to the agreement, India agreed to separate its civilian and military nuclear facilities and place all its civilian nuclear facilities under International Atomic Energy Agency (IAEA) safeguards. In exchange, the US agreed to work towards full civilian nuclear cooperation with India. The importance of this accord lies in the fact that it represents the American acceptance and acknowledgement of India's status as a nuclear weapons state. and also India's rising capabilities and ambitions of being a great power in Asia.

India also succeeded in the fast improvement of its relations with other major players in the world. New Delhi, for example, has been significantly upgrading energy and security cooperation with Japan, clearly to ensure its own energy security and due to shared apprehensions about China. Today, India has become the biggest recipient of Japan's Overseas

Development Assistance (ODA) program. India-Japan trade has seen an annual increase of over 20 per cent. In 2007, then Japanese Prime Minister Shinzo Abe visited India, expressing Tokyo's wish that the two countries would work together "to transform the notion of a broader Asia into reality at an early date". In Japan's perspective, the idea of a "broader Asia" covers the whole Pacific Ocean, the US, and Australia.

Interestingly, while India's new focus on strengthening relations with the Western powers has a clear calculation to compete with China for influence in South Asia as well as in the world, New Delhi has also demonstrated a strong interest in building up more cooperative relations with Beijing. This omni-directional, diplomatic offensive on the part of India features one important characteristic of its strategic thinking in the new international context, namely, of ensuring maximum strategic leverage by balancing one major power against the other while carefully stressing its own independent orientation, and indicating that it will be nobody's ally or subordinate. This orientation today, however, still gravitates more strongly toward the West, the US in particular, than ever before.

Last but not least, India's rising ambition for the status of world power finds unique expression in its unusual enthusiasm for strengthening and upgrading its military capability. As one specialist on Indian affairs described:

> "Economic growth underpins India's ability to provide adequately for the nation's growing defense needs. India has emerged as one of the largest arms buyers in the global market in the last few years... India, the world's fourth-largest military power, has embarked on an ambitious plan to modernize its largely Soviet-era arms since the late 1990s as it started asserting its political and military profile in South Asia and the Indian Ocean region. India's armed forces have become increasingly ambitious, talking of their own revolution in military affairs. In line with India's broadening strategic horizons, its military acquisitions are shifting from conventional land-based systems to means of power projection such as airborne refueling systems and long-range missiles. India is setting up bases abroad, patrolling the Indian Ocean to counter piracy, protecting the crucial sea-lanes of communication, and demonstrating a military assertiveness hitherto unknown. A continuation of this trend is premised on India's ability to sustain its present economic growth trajectory".[4]

India's military ambition of being one of the world's foremost military powers, finally led to its decision to become an open nuclear-armed state in 1998. The nuclear option was the logical result of New Delhi's belief that nuclear weapons are the most effective short-cut to world power status. The comment by the former Indian Army Chief of Staff General K. Sundarji made on the US invasion of Iraq in 1991 brought home this conviction. He said: "[Coalition members] could go in because the US had nuclear weapons and Iraq didn't... The Gulf War emphasized once again that nuclear weapons are the ultimate coin of power".[5] Thus one may well argue that India's nuclearization was more politically than militarily motivated. From a purely military point of view, in fact, India's acquisition of nuclear weapon capability added little to its security, as the Indian nuclear status inevitably triggered Pakistan—its long-term rival in the subcontinent into also going overtly nuclear and developing a nuclear doctrine. The fact that the emergence of two nuclear weapon states in South Asia generated not only a risk of an uncontrolled nuclear arms race in the region, but also neutralized India's conventional superiority over Pakistan, complicated, if not reduced security for India in South Asia.

In the meantime, India has been most proactive in seeking defense and military cooperation with the Western powers in an attempt to further consolidate its position of strength. Again, the US has become the new target for India. The lifting in 2001 by the US of all its sanctions against New Delhi imposed in response to the call by the UN Security Council after India's nuclear tests, removed all obstacles to military and defense collaboration between the two countries. In 2005, the US and India signed a bilateral Defense Framework, which was regarded as an event of great significance, to boost the US-Indian defense cooperation. The Framework envisaged a series of cooperative measures, unimaginable in previous times, including expansion of joint military exercises and exchanges, defense trade, and the establishment of a bilateral defense procurement and production group from both countries. More prosaically, it also identified issues for building the bilateral defense collaboration and achieving greater inter-operability of their forces across the spectrum. Specifically, this agreement looks to promote cooperation in multinational operations, counter-terrorism, the promotion of regional peace and security, fighting the proliferation of weapons of mass destruction and calls for expanded cooperation on missile defense, disaster response, combined operations, peacekeeping operations, and increased intelligence exchanges. Both countries agreed in their discussions on the inclusion of a review of all the outstanding security issues on South, Central Asia, Southeast Asia, China, the Gulf, and so on. Similarly, in response to both, the deal with Washington and the latter's sale of up to 36 F-16C/Ds to Pakistan, the Indian Air Force is calling for an acceleration of its own upgrades, especially as the legislative "wheels are in motion" for the US to formally approve the initial delivery of 18 Block 52 Pratt & Whitney PW 100-229 powered F-16/C/Ds with an option for 18 more.

India's interest extended even further to strengthening its military capability to have secure control of the sea lines of communication in the South China Sea and the Indian Ocean. To that end, New Delhi has invested heavily in upgrading its naval forces. For example, India has stepped up efforts to build its first made-by-India aircraft carrier, which has reportedly over 40,000 ton displacement, with a maximum cruise speed of 28 miles per hour, and maximum range of 8,000 miles. The carrier was expected to be launched by the end of 2010, and commissioned in 2014, enabling India to greatly expand the scope of its naval activities.[6] Though there has been a delay, the direction of developments seems clear. India also attached importance to shore up both bilateral and multilateral maritime cooperation with Australia, Japan and members of the ASEAN countries in addition to the US, all of which India has been successful in concluding agreements with regarding maritime defense cooperation. Of particular notice were India's efforts to enhance defense cooperation with those ASEAN countries of geographical significance. These countries include Vietnam, for example, who can offer India the use of its port of Cam Ranh Bay; and Singapore, which holds the Malacca Strait, the strategic route between South China Sea and Indian Ocean. Although deliberately keeping it low profile so as not to anger China, India has nevertheless shown interest in the idea of coalition, based on the so-called shared value of democracy for the maritime cooperation with the US, Japan, Australia in the Asia-Pacific as well as in the Indian Ocean. New Delhi participated in the first ministerial meeting among these four powers in Manila in May 2007, a large scale joint military exercise in the Bay of Bengal among these countries, as well as in Singapore in September the same year.

Chinese View of India's Rise

China welcomes the rise of India, and does not view the rise of India as a threat. In China's view, the two countries have the same bitter, humiliating experience of Western colonialism in modern history, and share almost completely the same historical task for domestic development each in a vast, pluralist and complex environment at home. In order to accomplish this daunting task, both are desperately in need of a peaceful and stable international environment, including a more just and fair international structure and order. The two countries share common views on many vital international issues like pushing for the development of global multipolarity, opposing the dominance of world affairs by any major power or group of powers, calling for a greater role of the United Nations in maintenance of world peace and security and promotion of development, and safeguarding the interests of the developing countries in the face of the often bullying actions of developed countries, to name a few.

China and India have a solid foundation for cooperation. As two great and ancient civilizations, they enjoy long-standing good relations and friendly exchanges for more than 2,000 years, learning from each other and being inspired by each other. Today, as two emerging world economies, they are in a good position to complement each other to achieve common development and a world better suited for their sustained security. It is against this backdrop that successive Chinese leaderships have consistently attached great importance to, and striven for the better bilateral relations between the two countries.

In the early years of the Cold War, the two countries enjoyed a honeymoon period, working together against the Western colonialist hegemony. Mao Zedong, at that time, stressed that "Despite our differences in ideology and social system, we have a large common ground, that is, we both need to deal with imperialism".[7] Leaders from both countries joined hands in producing the famous five principles of peaceful co-existence, which reflected the strong voice of the newly independent nations for peace and security and respect for norms in international relations. Even after the tragic military conflict in the border areas of the two countries, Beijing had cherished a wish that grievances over the border dispute from both sides would be transient, and that the two nations would eventually revert to their normal, friendly relations. As Mao Zedong once put it at a time still poisonous with the aftermath of deep mistrust following the border clashes, "India is a great nation, and the Indian people are a great people. After all, peoples of the two countries want to be friends. We cannot keep on quarrelling like this for ever. Please convey my best regards to your president and prime minister".[8] To Mao's message came the immediate positive response from the Indian side, assuring that "we are prepared to start the dialogue in the hope of reducing and eliminating the tension and hostility that have enveloped our two neighboring countries".[9]

When the world entered into the post-Cold War era, leaders of both China and India became more aware that the two countries needed to re-embark on a road of reconciliation and chart a way toward greater cooperation. Then Indian Prime Minister Rajiv Gandhi first broke the ice by a visit to China in 1988, paving the way for thawing of the diplomatic impasse that had lasted over two decades. It was during that visit that Deng Xiaoping, the chief architect of China's reform and opening-up program, said to Prime Minister Gandhi,

> "Under the present favorable and peaceful international circumstances, China and India have a common responsibility to mankind—to develop. ... If China and India are developed, we can say we have made our contributions to mankind".[10]

Based on this belief, China holds that,

> "China and India are the two biggest developing countries in the world. We have a combined population of 2.5 billion, 40 per cent of the world's total. A China-India relationship featuring peace, friendship, win-win cooperation and common development not only serves the fundamental interests of our two countries and peoples, but also contributes to global peace and development. It will make a profound impact on Asia and the whole world. That is why we say that China-India relations have moved beyond the bilateral context and assumed global and strategic significance".[11]

The Chinese view has been echoed by the Indian side in almost the same language on many occasions. When meeting his Chinese counterpart Wen Jiabao in Thailand on 24 October 2009, Indian Prime Minister Manmohan Singh emphasized that:

> "India won't deem China a threat and hopes to develop strategic cooperative partnership that is harmonious, stable and strong with China. It is in the fundamental interest of both countries and is also conducive to the region and the world at large".[12]

On a more recent occasion, the Indian Prime Minister also stressed that "the Indian government devotes itself to advancing India-China comprehensive strategic partnership and is glad to see the progress made in bilateral ties. As long as the two countries speak in one voice, the world will listen".[13] Such are the perspectives of the leaders of both countries, bringing home the mainstream views and sentiments of the two great nations. Thanks to their joint efforts, China-India relations have enjoyed sound momentum of all-round growth since Rajiv Gandhi's visit. Efforts were first made, at this time, to explore a way to settle the border dispute—a point of friction in the relations between the two countries. Although the efforts in this respect have not seen major breakthroughs, the two countries succeeded in concluding agreements on measures to strengthen peace and stabilization along their borderline in 1996 and 1998 respectively. These military confidence measures have been contributing significantly to the maintenance of relative peace ever since.

Since the turn of the century, China-India relations have enjoyed even greater dynamism in their all-dimensional cooperation. Chinese Premier Wen Jiabao visited India in 2005; and the two sides announced the establishment of a strategic and cooperative partnership for peace and prosperity. In 2006, Chinese President Hu Jintao paid a successful visit to India, during which the two sides issued a Joint Declaration and adopted a ten-pronged strategy to deepen this partnership. When Prime Minister

Manmohan Singh visited China in May 2009, the two sides signed 'A Shared Vision for the 21st century', taking the relationship to a new level.

As a result, friendly exchanges and cooperation between the two countries have been expanding in many important fields such as economy, trade, culture, tourism, defence and people-to-people contact. In 2008, the two-way trade volume of the two countries reached US$38.6 billion. In the first seven months of 2009, it amounted to US$33.5 billion, up by 63.8 per cent from the corresponding period of 2008. Interactions between the two countries through both official and unofficial channels have becoming increasingly busier. Beijing and New Delhi successfully organized the "China-India Friendship Year" and the "China-India Year of Friendship through Tourism" in 2006 and 2007 respectively. Youth delegations composed of about 100 people each have exchanged visits several times. There are now over 40 direct flights between the two countries each week. The two militaries also conducted their first defence dialogue and first joint counter-terrorism army exercise in 2008.

Of course, despite all these impressive achievements, prospects for Sino-Indian relations still seem clouded with uncertainty. Old differences and disputes that persist have meant that the two countries have added challenges, stemming from the fast changing international environment and the reorientation of India's foreign and security policy.

In the field of bilateral relations, the unresolved border dispute remains the most serious issue that divides the two countries. From China's perspective, the China-India boundary has never been formally delimited. As the issue involves sovereignty and territorial integrity, it has often stirred the most sensitive national feelings in both countries. Neither side has much room to manoeuver. Under the circumstances, the only feasible way out is an agreement that the two countries should follow the spirit of peace, friendship, consultation on an equal footing, mutual respect and mutual accommodation, and resolve the boundary question through negotiations in a patient manner. Pending an ultimate solution, they should work together to maintain peace and tranquility in the border areas. Fortunately, the past few years have seen impressive progress in the negotiations between the two special representatives assigned by each government on the boundary question in line with this spirit. The two sides have agreed on the political parameters and guiding principles and encouraged discussion on a framework for eventual settlement. The challenge, therefore, is how to translate them into more concrete results, a task that requires not only the political wisdom and courage of the state leaders in their decision-making, but also continued efforts aimed at winning the support of domestic public opinion in both countries.

Tibet is another issue that the two countries need to further address in order to strengthen mutual confidence in future cooperation. That Tibet is an inalienable part of China has been universally accepted by the international community. The claim of India that it has a special interest in Tibet has been a source of mistrust and tension between the two nations, often leading many Chinese to question New Delhi's motivation, including its role in instigating the fleeing of Dalai Lama and allowing his 'government-in-exile' on its territory. Although India's recent reaffirmation of its position recognizing Tibet as part of China's territory was a great help in strengthening mutual confidence and trust, continuing to allow activities of separatist orientation on Indian soil remains a cause for great concern for China with respect to New Delhi's strategic intentions.

In the international field, fast growing international interactions among major players around South Asia have dramatically changed the security landscape in the region and beyond, and will thus have a profound impact on China-India relations in the future. Looking ahead, three evolving sets of trilateral relations may have a most important implication, for better or for worse:

> The first set of the tripartite relations are the interactions among China, the US and India. This is going to be the most significant, but also most complex tripartite relationship in the future. In the changing South Asian context, each of the three countries seem to strive to strengthen its relations with the other two, while avoiding being isolated by preventing them from getting too close. On India's part, New Delhi seems to hope that its power of diplomacy might induce both China and the US to court India, exacting greater concessions from both of them for its maximum benefits. At the same time, it harbours the fear about a so-called prospect of G2—meaning a world under a China-US condominium at the expense of India's core security interests. Washington evidently wants to use India as a strong constraint against China, but not without the fear that the two Asian giants may get too close together at the expense of American interests. On the part of China, the apparent inclination of India towards closer cooperation with the US has also magnified its concerns, if not alarm, over being encircled by a hostile coalition. Clearly, each side seems still to look at tripartite relations as a zero-sum game. And as long as they do so, it will be difficult for them to refrain from manipulating bilateral interactions for narrowly defined national interests. Both China and India in particular need to take care of each other's security concerns and core interests, and avoid miscalculation while pursing cooperation with the US.

The second set of trilateral relations is of China, India and Pakistan. Beijing's policy is clear and explicit. China will continue to maintain good and cooperative relations with Pakistan but not at the expense of India's interests. Nor would its effort to improve its relations with India be at the expense of Pakistan's core interests. The dilemma, however, is that both India and Pakistan, as two major rivals in the subcontinent, continue to look at the tripartite relations as a zero-sum game. Any enhanced cooperative measures by China with either of the two would invariably be regarded by the other as a provocation and even threat to the other. The only way to break out of this vicious circle seems to lie in the prospect of substantial improvement in relations between India and Pakistan themselves. When these two countries succeed in ameliorating their suspicions and hostility towards each other, China would be in a better position to push for a healthy development of the tripartite relations. The past years have seen some progress in the bilateral relations between India and Pakistan, each being aware that their differences and disputes can only be solved through a peaceful and diplomatic channel, and that cooperation rather than confrontation is in their best interests. On the other hand, the picture is still murky, given rising international terrorism and Islamic extremism in South Asia, the growing instability in Pakistan, and the impulse of India to resort to a tougher line towards its disputes with Pakistan. All these could become factors that could quickly throw India-Pakistan relations onto a confrontational track, which will not only fuel tensions in South Asia, but also complicate China's relations with India.

The third set of trilateral relations among China, India and Russia could also, in the long run, have a significant impact on the situation in South Asia, and China-India relations as well. Although still emerging as major economies, the three countries, which together stretch over 20 per cent of the total global landmass and represent 39 per cent of the global population, have huge potential in their role in world affairs. More important, all the three countries share the same basic world outlook with a common desire of seeing progress of democratization of the international relations, development of a multi-polar world order, and strengthening the diversity of world cultures and civilizations. They naturally have the same wish to strengthen cooperation for their best interests. On 2 June 2005, the foreign ministers of the three countries held an "informal meeting" in Vladivostok for the first time, signifying that trilateral relations have been lifted to the official level, and attracting worldwide attention. Since then, nine rounds of such meetings have been held, adding greater dynamism to their cooperation, particularly in the field of non-traditional security. The ministerial meetings have also served as a platform for the exchange of views and the exploration of ways to enhance cooperation among the three countries on many vital security issues. Undoubtedly, this set of tripartite relations would work towards a more balanced power structure in the subcontinent, and thus offer greater incentives for closer ties between China and India. On the other hand, both China and India may also face new challenges to their bilateral relations in a more complex context, in which balancing relations with various major powers could become the central focus.

Another equally important international factor that will affect China-India relations is the evolving global efforts to fight international terrorism. Since President Barack Obama took office in 2009, he has clearly shifted the US focus on terror from Iraq to Afghanistan and the Northwest area of Pakistan with the consequent dogged resistance by international terrorists and violent insurgents in South Asia. Despite the increasing efforts of the military mop-up campaigns, the US will still face a long-term uphill struggle to destroy Al Qaeda and the remnants of the Taliban in the region, and achieve substantial progress towards stabilization of Afghanistan and Pakistan. China shares the US objective of removing the threat of terrorism as well as sustained peace and stability in South Asia. However, Beijing often finds it difficult to agree with the US strategy that so heavily relies on the large scale use of military force. This difference of approach has been further aggravated by the US double standard in defining international terrorism based on its selfish national interests and rather obscure motivations. Under the circumstances, international anti-terror efforts in South Asia continue to be characterized by a great deal of complexity and uncertainty, a factor that will have implications on China-India relations. Coordination of their anti-terror policy in the region, therefore, would be increasingly essential in order to substantiate their strategic and cooperative partnership between the two nations.

Lastly, China and India have also to work together with other members of the international community to address nuclear proliferation in South Asia. The regional security arrangement and China-India relations in particular, have witnessed a nuclear element since the nuclear explosions by both India and Pakistan in 1998. To China, this not only means a potential nuclear arms race between the two rivals in South Asia, but also complicates its threat perception vis-à-vis India. India's use of China as a pretext for going nuclear has further strengthened mistrust between the two countries. Beijing has consistently hoped both India and Pakistan would halt their nuclear programs, contributing to the strengthening of non-proliferation. On the other hand, it is also obvious that there is simply no way to turn the two de-facto nuclear armed states back into non-nuclear weapon states. But that should not mean that nuclear proliferation is an irresolvable issue in South Asia. From China's perspective, many steps could be conceivable for India and Pakistan to be engaged in the disarmament and nonproliferation efforts under the condition that they do not formally receive the legitimacy of the recognized nuclear-weapon states. For instance, New Delhi and Islamabad should be encouraged to continue their bilateral talks on nuclear confidence measures to strengthen nuclear stability so as to minimize the danger of misjudgment and overreaction. Both countries should also make efforts to secure their nuclear facilities and material and maintain controls on nuclear-related exports to prevent terrorists from using them. More important, the two countries should ratify the Comprehensive Test Ban Treaty (CTBT), and decide on a moratorium on the production of fissile materials, at an early date, pending negotiation of a fissile material production cut off treaty (FMCT). These measures, if realized, could help define an effective approach to nuclear cooperation with countries that have not signed the NPT; they are also conducive to enhancing confidence building and strategic stability between China and India.

Conclusion

With the fast development of the two countries, China and India seem to both have an impulse to seek greater voice in international affairs, to join the international community as equal partners, and to contribute more to the peace and security of the world. This is understandable, given their historical background and the huge potential as world powers. However, excessive eagerness to change and upgrade their world status in a short period of time could run the risk of developing a sort of rashness that harbours unrealistic expectations, and action beyond affordability or achievability. After all, both will remain developing countries for a long time to come, constrained by their huge domestic problems. Internationally, the Western powers, who have long been the chief beneficiary of the existing world order, will never be happy to see the rise of both China and India, and will do everything possible to slow down their development. In addition, both countries face similar, if not the same, task of building a lasting friendly, peaceful and stable neighborhood. All these are important reminders for the leaders of the two countries to remain sober-minded regarding their current status, and the common challenges both countries will be confronted with in the future. Both need to go a long way before they can expect to become true world powers. And in this long and arduous process, China and India need to support each other. Only in this context can the two nations see the real fundamental interests that bind them together, and the significance of building better, long-term ties of cooperation.

To build a better strategic and cooperative partnership, the two countries need a new vision, which truly avoids the Cold War mentality. Despite profuse expressions of goodwill towards each other by state leaders of both countries, one can still perceive a trust deficit between the two countries—an element of lingering mistrust and thinly-veiled calculations against each other in their policies. This is particularly so on the part of India as New Delhi, on many occasions, does not even care to hide its intention to contain China's rise by its military buildup and closer collaboration with the US. There is even a suggestion that India should be allied with the Western powers to cope with China—supposedly the greatest threat India is going to face in the future. That is, indeed, a dangerous point of view as it, if put in practice, will not only dramatically jeopardize peace and stability in South Asia, but will also force China to take steps to respond, putting China-India relations back on the confrontational track. This is hardly in the best interests of India. At this crucial time of change, both China and India should take special care to guard against Western powers, including the US, sowing seeds of discord among them for their own benefits.

The two countries also need to more effectively address the role of their domestic public opinion for a better, friendly relationship. With rising comprehensive strength, both countries seem to have seen the rise of nationalism at home with higher expectations, demanding greater respect from the world. These sentiments often turn the public emotional and irrational when dealing with disputes abroad, if misinformed or misguided. In the case of China-India relations, China's rise, the border dispute, Tibet, nuclear weapons, and even a small border incident, could suddenly be turned into big issues, invariably labeling China as a threat to India. In this respect, the media and non-governmental organizations (NGOs) could play a particularly crucial role as they are dominant in shaping the views of the public, as well as various government agencies. If history is any guide, this bilateral relationship has been often the victim of these distorted national emotions, since the border clashes in 1962. The problem still persists today. The media and NGOs in both countries, thus, have a special responsibility to guide the leadership to work towards creating a more propitious domestic atmosphere for sustained strategic and cooperative partnership between the two great nations.

Notes

1. David Plott, "The Language of Awe: the Rise of China and India", *Global Asia*, 2 (2), Fall 2007, p. 104.
2. Dominic Wilson and Roopa Purushothaman, "Dreaming with BRICs—the Path to 2050", Goldman Sachs, Global Economics Paper No 99, 1 October 2003, http://www.goldmansachs.com/korea/ideas/brics/99-dreaming.pdf
3. Anand G. Iridharadasl, "Rising India Remains Torn Between East and West", *International Herald Tribune*, 15 August 2005.
4. Harsh V. Pant, "Indian Foreign and Security Policy: Beyond Nuclear Weapons",

Brown Journal of World Affairs, XV (II), Spring/Summer 2009, p. 225.

5. Keith B. Payne, "Deterrence in the Second Nuclear Age", Leington: University Press of Kentucky, 1996, p. 28.
6. Nie Yun, "India's First Carrier Is to Be Launched by the End of This Year", *Xinhua*, 10 January 2010. Quoted from *Jiefang Ribao*, Shanghai, 11 January 2010.
7. Dai Chaowu, "Cold War and India's Foreign Policy and Its Relations with Major Powers" (in Chinese), 26 June 2009, http://history.news.163.com/09/0626/16/5COF89NQ00013FLN.html.
8. Mao made this comment at a reception on 1 May 1970, to the Indian Charge d' Affairs, Brajesh Mishra, who was later National Security Advisor under Prime Minister Atal Behari Vajpayee.
9. See Zhu Hua, "Zhou Enlai and the 30 Years of Sino-Indian Relations" (in Chinese), 13 August 2009, http://club.china.com/data/thread/5688138/2704/06/49/1_1.html. The quotes are translated by the author.
10. Yang Jiechi, "For Peace and Friendship, Win-Win Cooperation and Common Development", 8 September 2008, http://www.fmprc.gov.cn/eng/wjb/zzjg/yzs/gjlb/2711/2713/t511825.htm.
11. Ibid.
12. Ministry of Foreign Affairs, People's Republic of China, "Wen Jiabao Holds Talks with Indian Counterpart Singh", 24 October 2009, http://www.fmprc.gov.cn/eng/wjb/zzjg/yzs/gjlb/2711/2713/t623101.htm.
13. Ministry of Foreign Affairs, People's Republic of China, "Hu Jintao Meets with Indian Prime Minster Singh", 15 April 2010, http://www.fmprc.gov.cn/eng/zxxx/t682899.html.

4

Sino-Indian Military CBMs—Reducing Tensions, Building Confidence

Brig. (Retd.) Arun Sahgal

China and India, the world's two most populous and largest neighbours in Asia share nearly 3,500kms of land border.[1] As fast-growing economies both countries are likely to evolve as major global players in the next few decades. A partnership between these two countries is virtually an imperative for peace and prosperity not only for the two billion plus peoples of China and India but for Asia and indeed the whole world. This is an objective reality that governments of both the countries must consciously work to achieve. But, how far it is feasible, what should be done to make it happen and how to build up mutual trust and cooperation for the benefit of the people of the two countries, as well as of Asia and the world? The basic issue is how to reduce competition and increase cooperation.

At the very outset, it is important to reflect on what have been China's and India's approaches to each other, their perceptions, value systems, worldviews and strategic objectives. The answers provide an invaluable backdrop for a review of Sino-Indian relations and interactions over the past 60 years in their bilateral, regional and global dimensions. This would enable the drawing of an objective picture of the realities of the relationship and contrast those realities with the rhetoric which continues to enclose it. An objective assessment of these inputs would reveal whether a 'partnership' existed in the past and if it exists today and if it does not what steps should be taken to achieve it in the future. The issue also becomes important and relevant in the context of solving bilateral disputes, most importantly the "boundary issue".

India-China Relations: The Objective Reality

For the past 2,200 years, China has maintained itself as a political and unitary entity without interruption. This has been possible because of the strong central and authoritarian rule domestically and domination of the periphery by Chinese rulers. This, in a sense, constitutes the essence of China's political legacy and the pivotal centrality of the Chinese state both in the domestic and external contexts. Hierarchy is a very important concept in the Chinese worldview. Both historically and in the modern era, Chinese rulers have used power through violence to continue their legacy. All of this has become an integral part of Chinese tradition. Shorn of ideological shrouds, policies of the new People's Republic of China have been motivated to an extent by these legacies and traditions and moulded by cold calculations of national interest under a pragmatic, realist and unsentimental leadership. China's objective has been the reassertion of its traditional and historical centrality in its immediate neighbourhood, in the tradition of the long-established system of institutionalized inequality in relations between the Middle Kingdom and the peripheral tributary states, with a China-centric and China-dominated Asia as the long-term goal.

India's China policy on the other hand has been marked by friendship, sentimentalism, diffidence, brinksmanship, wishful thinking and engagement. Despite positive political overtures there has been growing negativism in their relations. The negative elements include slow progress in the boundary talks marked by the Chinese claim on Tawang, and indeed, over the whole of Arunachal Pradesh, China's continuing military modernization together with incremental buttressing of its military posture in Tibet in terms of rapid force deployment and sustainment capability, and forward development of logistics and communications infrastructure, together with growing border incursions including, even in settled areas like Sikkim. Despite several confidence-building measures in place there have been tensions between the two countries right through 2009. India perceives Chinese coercive tactics aimed at keeping tensions alive.

Adding to incremental tensions has been the growing stridency of the anti-India rhetoric within the Chinese think-tank community particularly those associated with the Peoples' Liberation Army (PLA). The chorus has been joined by the influential state-controlled media and bloggers and there is a sense of nationalistic jingoism permeating among the people vis-à-vis India. However, developments in 2010 coinciding with the celebration of 60 years of diplomatic relationship could portend better ties between the neighbours, even as both charter their trajectories towards being important players in the multipolar system.

Security Dilemma

Security dilemma is a concept in international relations theory according to which one state's drive to increase its security measures, could have an unintended negative impact on the security of another state, which, in turn, is forced to respond by enhancing its own security leading to a cycle of competitive moves that could result in an expensive and potentially destabilising arms race and in the worst case, to conflict. Thus, the dilemma faced by states is whether or not to develop countervailing capacities and capabilities to enhance their security, as it could paradoxically have an opposite effect.

The context of the security dilemma for China and India lies in the growing asymmetry between their military capabilities. India's security threat is China's sustained military modernization, development of strong defence industrial complex and forays into new types of warfare like space and cyber warfare, exacerbated by the unresolved boundary dispute between the two countries. It is true that China's military modernization may be driven by factors that have very little to do with India, but given the existence of the territorial dispute, and the perception that China is a revisionist state with respect to that dispute, India cannot ignore the possibility that China's capabilities could be redirected against it at some point in the future, however remote this may appear to be. The situation is complicated by the fact that, India's military modernization on the other hand, does not appear to exert the same effect on China, partly because it is more measured and modest than Chinese efforts. The perception that India is the status quo state may also be the reason that China is less wary about India's military capabilities, although off late there is an attempt to overplay India's modest attempts at military modernization.[2]

Seen from the above perspective, the lack of Chinese political will for settling the boundary dispute can be seen as a deliberate act of coercion. The positions of India and China on the territorial dispute have evolved over the years, but there remain glaring gaps which despite upgradation of the dialogue to political level have not produced a historic breakthrough. It is in this context, the issue of the strategic value each side places on the territory possessed by the other also becomes relevant.

From the Indian perspective, the important issue is the fact of growing Chinese military capabilities. There is, of course, the question of whether these are India-specific or reflect China's own growing security dilemma underscored by its attempts to be an important global and predominant Asian player. Here the issue gets complicated for India, particularly even if the argument of Chinese military modernization taking place in a broader strategic context was to be accepted. How does one explain Chinese infrastructural and logistical developments coming right up to the LAC? Added to these are regular border intrusions and encroachments and bellicosity in the Chinese media all through 2008-09.

It is in the backdrop of these developments that India has to reflect upon its own security needs and answer the question whether its capabilities are sufficient to ensure a relative status quo or defence advantage. India must also assess if it trusts in China's intentions at least in the short to medium term, examine the capability gap and whether it was widening to undermine the existing strategic balance between the two countries. Answers to the above questions together with the objective reality of the possibility of an early and equitable boundary settlement will force Indian planners to upgrade their military posture from dissuasion to deterrence, thus possibly unleashing a cycle of costly military capability infrastructural development. Thus, the settlement of the existing boundary dispute and maintenance of peace and tranquillity on the borders become imperative.

It is heartening to note that despite wariness over each other's strategic intentions and continued tensions, relations between India and China continue to be managed in a friendly and cooperative manner without any major flare-up. Both countries have by and large maintained peace and stability along the disputed borders. Two instances of clashes along the Sino-Indian boundary took place in 1967 at Nathu La along the Sikkim-Tibet border and in 1987 at Sumdurong Chu in Arunachal Pradesh, which were swiftly managed without undue escalation. The two militaries have largely maintained a non-confrontational posture along the Line of Actual Control (LAC), despite recent tensions, displaying a degree of maturity and self-confidence.

Boundary Issue: Rapprochement and CBMs

Former Indian Prime Minister Rajiv Gandhi's visit to China in December 1988 could be credited as an initiative of rapprochement in bilateral relations. It was after this visit, that the first major step in military diplomacy and Confidence-Building Measures (CBMs) was taken in the path-breaking September 1993 Agreement on the Maintenance of Peace and Tranquillity along the LAC which was a virtual no-war pact. This was followed by the 1996 Agreement on Confidence-Building Measures (CBMs) in the Military Field along the LAC. These two agreements led to the next step of "Adopting the Political Guidance Principles for the Settlement of Boundary Question" signed during Chinese Premier Wen Jiabao's visit to New Delhi in April 2005. This was pursued as a strategic objective with the purpose that would advance the basic interests of both the countries. The central theme was commitment to maintain peace and tranquillity on the border. The 2005 Agreement which called for the early clarification and confirmation of the LAC and to respect and observe the LAC, adopted additional CBMs to the 1996 Agreement, the most significant among which were the establishment of border meeting points at Kibithu-Damai in the Eastern Sector and Lipu Lekh Pass in Uttaranchal in the Central Sector; exchanges between commanders of the relevant military regions of China and the army commands of India, exchanges between training institutions, and sports and cultural exchanges between the two armed forces.[3]

With this agreement, the "three step" strategy for the resolution of the boundary dispute was put in place. The first step was putting in place political guiding principles for settling the boundary dispute, the second was creating the framework agreement for the implementation of guiding principles and the final step was to delimit the boundary.

It needs to be underscored that these agreements not only laid the groundwork for settlement of the long-standing boundary dispute but also for improving bilateral engagement between the two armed forces and enhancing military-to-military cooperation. As a result, the navies of the two countries participated in joint exercises off the Shanghai coast in China in 2003 and met again in 2005 in the Arabian Sea off the Malabar Coast and in 2007 off the cost of Qingdao.[4] The Chinese were also invited as observers during the Indian Army's war game exercises in the Western Sector in 2005. India meanwhile, sent observers to the China-Russia joint exercises in August 2005 at the invitation of the Chinese Ministry of National Defence.[5]

A comprehensive push on promoting bilateral military relations remained on track following the visit of the then Indian Defence Minister Pranab Mukherjee, to China in May 2006. The visit led to the signing of a Memorandum of Understanding (MoU) that called for the institutionalization of frequent exchanges between the officials of the Ministries and the armed forces through an Annual Defence Dialogue, in addition to developing an annual calendar for joint exercises and training programmes.[6]

As a consequence of these measures there has been regular interaction between the two sides which includes visits by senior military officials including those of service chiefs and corresponding visits by PLA Chiefs of General Staff and other high-ranking functionaries. To further enhance mutual cooperation and promote understanding between the two armed forces, the two sides have also conducted low-level military exercises in Kunming in 2007 and in Belgaum in 2008. Follow-up exercises in 2009 in China were not held owing to simmering tensions between the two sides although the official explanation was that these were not planned. Notwithstanding this, a third round of Sino-Indian army exercises are likely to be scheduled in the near future. In addition, as per the remarks of the Indian Air Force Chief, the first ever joint air exercise with China are also being planned sometime in 2012.[7]

Impact of Military CBMs

Sidhu and Yuan have divided Sino-Indian CBMs into three broad categories—declarative principles, information exchange and constraining measures. They contend that most of the current CBMs fall in the first two categories where the emphasis has been to institutionalize measures to keep tensions as low as possible by preventing accidents and maintaining tranquillity along the LAC as also to agree upon guiding political principles for an eventual settlement.[8]

There can be no doubt that military CBMs have resulted in graduated and reciprocated reduction of tensions along the LAC with practically no incidents of cross-border firing in recent times. This has resulted in lowering of tensions despite periodic reports of intrusions and patrols straying across the Line of Actual Control.[9] These in a sense are the major gains when seen in comparison to the situation obtaining along the Line of Control with Pakistan where despite similar agreements cross-border infiltration and firing continue. It needs to be acknowledged that relative peace along the LAC in a military sense has allowed India to reinforce its counter-insurgency efforts along the northern and western borders with Pakistan by allowing redeployment of some of the formations from the east. Some of these formations have since moved back to their original locations in the east, giving a false impression of build up in the eastern theatre.

Thus, from the Indian perspective, peace and stability along the LAC have been particularly helpful in containing cross-border terrorism from Pakistan. Additionally, over the last few years at least, Chinese and Indian forces have engaged each other near the LAC in a series of interactive activities such as mountaineering expeditions, celebration of national days, cultural and sporting activities and exercises bringing about greater degree of transparency, confidence and understanding of respective military capabilities. Another and perhaps an important payoff of the relative peace along the LAC has been the breathing space and confidence that the Special Representatives have for a negotiated settlement of the boundary issue, even if there appears to be little forward movement.

Analysis of Sino-Indian CBMs

Notwithstanding the fact that existing CBMs have managed to maintain peace and stability along the LAC, it has however, not helped in changing fundamental threat perceptions or the security outlook, from hostile and suspicious, to cooperative understanding. The effective implementation and verification of specific force reduction measures have yet to occur, partly because of the difference in perception regarding the LAC itself, which is yet to be clearly defined. This has led to loss of security consensus and the consequent flaring of tensions and border violations. While these have not resulted in escalation to hostilities, in 2008-2009, the situation deteriorated to the extent that there was a real fear of things spinning out of control.

A security deficit is evident between the two countries. This has been causing periodic tensions along the border despite the several CBMs and improvements in political and economic relations.[10] There are several factors contributing to this apparent security deficit.

Despite large numbers of CBMs, joint exercises and visits by senior military and defence officials, tensions continue to prevail along the LAC with a number of ground and aerial intrusions in Ladakh, Central Sector, Sikkim and Arunachal Pradesh. Further vitiating the bilateral atmosphere are frequent, belligerent Chinese statements questioning India's territoriality by asserting claims to Arunachal Pradesh, and objecting to the Indian Prime Minister's visit to the state. Further, there have been cartographic excesses in terms of excluding Jammu and Kashmir as part of India and including Arunachal Pradesh in Chinese maps. These are 'excesses' because China has been shifting its position. From acknowledging territory to be disputed to now acknowledging POK as Pakistani territory by laying no restrictions on issue of visas to citizens of POK but giving citizens of Indian J&K stapled visas. They have also started massive investments in POK in the infrastructure and development sectors.

The situation has been exacerbated to the extent that the two Prime Ministers had to meet on the sidelines of various multilateral summits to restore relative normalcy. The reason for these tensions is primarily because of non-resolution of the LAC alignment or the broader resolution of the boundary dispute despite 13 rounds of dialogue between the Special Representatives, clearly indicating a lack of political resolve on the part of Chinese interlocutors, in accepting actual LAC alignment in Eastern and Western Sectors (so far, maps of only the Central Sector have been exchanged), leading to misinterpretation and misunderstanding of the LAC alignment.

A second factor causing misunderstanding is the rapid pace of Chinese military modernization, and infrastructural build-up in Tibet including improved communications, forward logistic infrastructure and new airfields. What is worrisome is that storage and infrastructure building in the Tibet Autonomous Region (TAR) are much beyond the needs of local populace or even the forces deployed there. There is no doubt that on the Indian side too there are communications and other developments but these are first, extremely limited and nowhere near as extensive as those in TAR and second, purely defensive in nature mostly in terms of strengthening the existing posture in reaction to developments in Tibet.

The issue gets exacerbated by proactive Chinese doctrinal thinking including such concepts "active defence" and "local wars under conditions of informationalization".[11] Backed by a build-up of capabilities this new thinking in China does raise legitimate concerns in India. It is just as true that Chinese may have concerns about the Indian military modernization, and developments in the Northeast; however these are nowhere near the scale of those in TAR.

The basic issue is that China has gone in for massive upgradation of infrastructure, building up of airfields and now rail inks which come right up to the border. According to Indian assessments, China which maintains some eight border guard divisions can build up close to 20 divisions in Tibet in one campaigning season. The Indian response to this challenge includes raising two additional mountain divisions and associated equipment to meet this challenge.[12]

The third issue relates to deployment of tactical and strategic missiles in the TAR[13] and the danger posed by these in terms of an asymmetric warfare doctrine. Both short- and medium-range ballistic missiles with conventional or nuclear warheads are perceived as coercive tools, which could result in escalation of even local tensions.

Strengthening Existing CBMs and Improving Implementation

Given the aforementioned backdrop let us now address the issue of how existing CBMs can be improved or enhanced to prevent future escalation and to build cooperation and confidence. To further improve the existing CBMs, the following measures are proposed.

The first and foremost requirement is to speed up delineation of the LAC in the Western and Eastern Sectors including the exchange of maps. This is important to prevent inadvertent crossings and intrusions that can lead to standoffs between the two armies and can be done without prejudice to the formal positions of either side. Such a step will go a long way in reducing tensions.

Second, and in the same vein, there is a need to increase the number of designated places for border meetings to be held. Presently, there are three sites identified for flag meetings namely Spanggur Tso, in Ladakh, Nathu La in Sikkim and Bum La along the India-China-Bhutan border in Arunachal Pradesh. In addition, successful flag meetings have been also been held at Kibithu on the trijunction of India, China and Myanmar which merits formalisation. However, there is no meeting point in the Central Sector; the proposal to include Lipu Lekh is under discussion and needs to be expedited. Once these places are formalized then at least in sectoral terms there will be a formalised mechanism in place to deal with local issues arising along the LAC to include intrusions, inadvertent crossings, exchange of information on a number of issues like disease, natural disasters and so on.

Third, and even more important, there is a need for specific and periodic sector-level meetings to discuss disputed segments of the LAC as provisioned in the Agreement on Peace and Tranquillity along the LAC. If there is no mutual agreement, a joint survey to determine respective claims should be embarked upon.

Other issues relate to dealing with increasing air intrusions and proximity flying by Unmanned Aerial Vehicles (UAV). While an agreement exists for maintaining a safe distance of one kilometre from the border, there have nonetheless been apprehensions about increased aerial activity along the LAC. To diffuse tensions, a separate meeting or representation of air force commanders at the border meetings of sectoral and regional commanders should also be considered to discuss all problems relating to air intrusions and delineation of flying zones.

Another area requiring institutionalisation is the method, scale and content of effective verification measures and of the supervision required for the reduction of military forces and the maintenance of peace and tranquillity. This issue needs to be addressed at the various sectoral and regional commander meetings suggested earlier.

Joint adventure activities, study tours and visits by middle- or functional-level officers to build up better understanding and confidence between the two deployed forces could also be undertaken.

CBMs at Higher Echelons

As mentioned earlier, during the Indian Defence minister's visit to China in May 2006, a memorandum of understanding (MoU) was signed for holding regular Defence Dialogue between the two countries. Under the MoU there would be frequent exchanges between the leaders and high-level functionaries of the Defence Ministries and the armed forces of India and China, including an Annual Defence Dialogue to review progress in defence exchanges and make suggestions. The two sides would endeavour to hold joint military exercises or training programmes in areas of mutual interests, with each side inviting senior military officers to witness military exercises. The MoU also established a mechanism for study tours for senior- and middle-level service officers and relevant civil officials, as well as a mechanism for studies in each other's military academies and exchanges in agreed fields.

Although there have been three rounds of defence cooperation dialogue and a number of issues of mutual concern have been discussed, these deliberations are not adequately or suitably structured. A more structured framework for defence cooperation is required for bringing all stakeholders together. Consultations should preferably be broken up into various working groups comprising military, civilian and technical experts to discuss mutually-agreed issues and recommend specific measures to be discussed in the exchanges pertaining to issues concerning regional security, national defence policies, military exchanges and cooperation. In fact, these deliberations should lay down a calendar of exchanges, visits and exercises between the two sides.

Another important means to help diffuse tensions would be the establishment of a hotline between the respective regional and military command headquarters. This will help immediate resolution of tensions without getting embroiled in laborious diplomatic procedures. The Indian experience with Pakistan shows that this is a very effective means of diffusing tensions between professionals.

Other Means of Enhancing Mutual Cooperation

An important but sensitive issue for joint consideration is enhancing mutual cooperation on the intelligence exchange front, particularly on terrorism, drug trafficking and small arms infiltration. This gains salience in the backdrop of a rising tide of radicalism and fundamentalism. Developments in the Afghanistan-Pakistan region clearly point to the fact that the Taliban and other radical groups, far from being marginalised, are resurgent and giving US-led coalition forces a hard time. Both China and India have large stakes in stability and containment of radical forces in the region and India has additional concerns regarding the activities of Indian insurgent groups operating from neighbouring countries. Exchange of information and regular dialogue between senior intelligence functionaries including heads of intelligence will go a long way in improving understanding of the activities of radical groups and build momentum towards greater intelligence cooperation.

Mutual technical cooperation in the defence field can also be considered. China has developed an elaborate, extensive and indigenous defence industrial base; India too is similarly attempting to indigenise defence production in key areas. Thus, the scope exists for initiating technical defence cooperation dialogue particularly in the exchange of information and expertise in mutually-decided areas and in undertaking joint development projects. Such endeavours will not only be cost effective but go a long way in allaying mutual suspicions.

Another area of higher echelon CBMs is pre-notification of missile testing with the aim of preventing misunderstandings or misinterpretation and promoting a stable environment of peace and security between the two countries. The idea would be to inform each other of a time window and likely impact area, preferably outside of a pre-specified exclusion zone. This agreement can also include a decision not to deploy tactical or other missiles, including cruise missiles, within a mutually-agreed specified area. This issue assumes significance in the backdrop of reports of increasing deployment of missiles in the TAR and misperceptions on the Chinese side about Indian deployments.

Conclusion

One of the major factors contributing to a security deficit is the non-resolution of the long-standing boundary dispute. Whereas it is fully recognized that there are many complications and misperceptions affecting its resolution, both sides need to show political courage to resolve the dispute. The boundary dispute distracts both countries from building a strong cooperative and mutually beneficial relationship. This is particularly important when China has resolved such disputes with all its neighbours barring India and Bhutan.

Next, pending a final boundary settlement, there is an urgent need to have an agreed boundary alignment through the exchange of marked maps. So far only maps of the Central Sector have been exchanged and despite a number of meetings, those of the Western and Eastern sectors have still not been exchanged. In the backdrop of increasing border tensions in the form of intrusions and so on the issue assumes greater urgency.

It will also be in the interest of both sides to restrain their media and internet blogs to the extent possible, from hyping tensions and engaging in provocative writing. It is important in this context for the government on both sides to issue periodic statements, giving factual positions and preventing speculation. An important method of diffusing tensions could be increased exchanges between the strategic communities of the two sides and writings which attempt to put such issues in perspective rather than indulging in unnecessarily provocative analysis. As developing countries, both need to address a multitude of social and economic challenges internally, and unwarranted tensions only distract them from the difficult and onerous tasks at home.

NOTES

1. The figure is quoted from the official website of the Indo Tibetan Border Police Force, http://itbp.gov.in/.
2. Sankhya Krishnan, "India's Security Dilemma vis-a-vis China: A Case of Optimum or Sub Optimum Restraint?" *RCSS Policy Study* (47), 2009, pp 8-9.
3. See the text, Ministry of External Affairs, Government of India, "Protocol between the Government of the Republic of India and the Government of the People's Republic of China on Modalities for the Implementation of Confidence Building Measures in the Military Field Along the Line of Actual Control in the India–China Border Areas", 11 April 2005, See Appendix.
4. Bhartendu Kumar Singh, "Military Diplomacy and Sino-Indian Relations", IPCS, *Article*, No. 2309, 5 June 2007, http://www.ipcs.org/.../india.../military-diplomacy-and-sino-indian-relations-2309.html.
5. Bhartendu Kumar Singh, "Military Diplomacy: The Future of Sino-Indian Military Relations?" *China Brief*, (23), 8 December 2008, http://www.jamestown.org/single/?no_cache=1&tx_ttnews[tt_news]=34236.
6. Ibid.
7. *Sify News*, "India, China to undertake joint air exercise in 2012: IAF chief", 23 February 2010; http://sify.com/news/india-china-to-undertake-joint-air-exercise-in-2012-iaf-chief-news-general-kcxlEdgbcff.html.
8. W. P. S. Sidhu and Jing-dong Yuan, *China and India: Cooperation or Conflict?* Boulder, CO: Lynne Rienner Publishers, 2003, p. 127.
9. An intrusion is defined here as a wilful act more in the form of symbolism aimed at staking claim to a piece of territory, while straying on the other hand, is an inadvertent act.
10. This latter is apparent in the strides in Sino-India trade and close collaboration on contentious global issues like climate change and the Doha Round among others.
11. For more on this aspect, see Gordon Housworth, "Informationalization in Chinese military doctrine affects foreign commercial and military assets", *Intellectual Capital Group*, 31 May 2007, http://spaces.icgpartners.com/index2.asp?NGuid=E2605D41B8DC46A58813E69E976EC8A1.
12. *Times of India*, "Army plans to raise Arunachal and Sikkim Scouts for China border", 18 May 2010, http://timesofindia.indiatimes.com/india/Army-plans-to-raise-Arunachal-and-Sikkim-Scouts-for-China-border/articleshow/5941569.cms; *DNA*, "Indian Army raising two divisions close to China border", 15 February 2010, http://www.dnaindia.com/india/report_indian-army-raising-two-divisions-close-to-china-border_1348336, and Bharat Verma, "Unmasking China", *Indian Defence Review*, Vol. 24, No. 3, Jul-Sep 2009, 13 June 2011, http://www.indiandefencereview.com/2009/08/unmasking-china.html.
13. *Pioneer*, "China deploys CCS-5 missiles on India border", 17 August 2010, http://www.dailypioneer.com/276667/China-deploys-CCS-5-missiles-on-India-border.html.

5

Viewpoints on Enhancing Military CBMs along the China-India Border

Sr. Col. Wang Guifang

In recent years, the China-India border issue has become a focus in bilateral relations and an important topic in the internal and external affairs of the two countries, receiving wide domestic and international media coverage. Prime Minister Manmohan Singh of India once said that the disagreements between China and India would not disappear by themselves, and deserve careful study and research. The nature of China-India border issue and its status in the security strategy of both countries have been listed as a priority topic on the agenda of both governments as well of many pundits in both countries. To resolve the issue, therefore is of vital importance to evaluate and promote bilateral relations.

The Nature of the China-India Border Issue

China and India share a border line of more than 2,000 kilometres, with a disputed area of about 125,000 square kilometres, divided into the western, middle and eastern sections along the long border line. The central bone of contention is not in the middle section, but in the eastern and western sections. The eastern section is actually controlled by India, while the western section by China. Both countries claim sovereignty over the disputed areas in both sections. The two countries have been frequently quarrelling with each other in the media, running into deadlock in diplomacy, and making little progress in seeking resolution. In short, passed down as a historical relic and also compounded by geostrategic conflict, the border issue between the two countries is extremely complicated.

First, the border issue is a leftover from history. It had originated from the British colonial policies. India insists on the validity of Simla Agreement of the British Indian government and the McMahon Line, refusing to make concessions in the eastern and middle sections that it controls, and even demands sovereignty over Aksai Chin in the western section. China, meanwhile holds that as a product of colonialism, the McMahon Line is of no legal effect, and that colonial treaties should not constitute the legal basis for the eventual resolution of the border issue.

Second, the border issue concerns national feelings. Recent years have witnessed continuous economic growth in both China and India. Despite the grave financial crisis across the world since 2008, both China and India have maintained a high growth rate. Against the backdrop, there are evidently growing national sentiments in both countries which called for the governments to take tougher line with the other side. In India, there are people, who criticize China's policies and wonder why China has solved almost all border issues with its neighbouring countries but not with India. There are people in China, who are not happy either. In their view, after the border war ended in 1962, the Chinese army immediately withdrew to the original positions. The Indians, instead of responding in a positive way, seemed to take advantage of China's reconciliatory stance, and demanded more compromises from China. Many people in China felt that the Chinese people were subjected to unfair treatment by history, and had to swallow the ill effects of colonialist policies. They demanded that China should not allow this to happen again. With such a confrontational psychology from both sides, it is natural that the border issue has become an outlet of nationalist feelings and a symbol of safeguarding national dignity.

Third, the border issue has been turned into a political issue. One of the recently disputed issues in the eastern section is Tawang. As part of South Tibet of China in history, it is the birthplace of the sixth Dalai Lama, boasts the second-largest monastery after Lhasa, and is regarded as a holy land of substantial significance by the Tibetans. Therefore, the border issue is not simply a question of the territorial gain or loss. It is often combined with complicated national and religious feelings, involving the government's ethnic and religious policies as well as political stability in society. On India's side, both the visits by Prime Minister Singh to Arunachal Pradesh and the permission for the Dalai Lama to visit Tawang seemed to highlight the assertion of India's sovereignty over Tawang. They are also meant to be a signal to the people at home and abroad that India would not give in to China's alleged hard-line policy. Used as a political bargaining chip, the border issue seems a crucial and sensitive political factor in the domestic affairs of India.

Fourth, the border issue is amplified by the media. In this respect, what is noteworthy is that the mainstream Western media has often played up China-India contradictions on the border issue with ulterior motives. An attempt to play one side against the other served the interests of the Western countries by ensuring their dominance in the world order. Unfortunately, there are voices from both countries that seemed to take delight in echoing the Western media's view by exaggerating the differences between the two sides, and have fanned the hostile feelings against each other among the two peoples. Bharat Verma, editor of *Indian Defence Review* predicted in an essay in *The Times of India* that a nervous China would attack India sometime before 2012. This kind of instigation has enormous negative media impact, and severely impedes a political solution to the border issue. To a great extent, the extremist, irrational and non-objective report exacerbates the political environment on the border issue.

The Status of the Border Issue in the Security Strategy of China and India

No doubt the border issue has been on the top of the agenda of both capitals as the central issue in their bilateral regulations. As long as the issue persists, the development of a sustained, effective partnership would be greatly restrained. In line with this perception, the two countries have been making great efforts to seek a peaceful solution on a fair, just and reasonable basis. High-level dialogue has been going on; a series of agreements have been reached to strengthen confidence; and a working mechanism, including setting up of the negotiation platforms and process, has been established. As a result, the two countries have succeeded in reaching consensus on the guiding principles as well a roadmap for the eventual resolution of the border issue. All these achievements have provided a good basis for progress in the future.

Looking ahead, China and India may find even greater incentives to seek resolution of the border issue against a broad backdrop of the global transformations and readjustment. The two countries face a similar external security environment. Both of them need to concentrate on economic development at home, and to foster friendly relations with their neighbouring countries. In short, a peaceful solution of the border issue is in their best strategic interests for the promotion of peace and prosperity as well as for the realization of their strategic goals.

On the other hand, the border issue involves sovereignty, territorial integrity, and the national feelings of the people of the two countries. Neither side should act in a rash manner. A great deal of spadework needs to be done, which includes, for example, upholding the negotiation on an institutional basis, and developing a more propitious environment as far as public opinion is concerned. In this respect, promoting a better appreciation of the issues involved and the backing of the of the people of the two countries is perhaps of particular significance, in order to ease the way for the two governments to seek eventual resolution of the border issue in the spirit of mutual respect, benefit and compromise.

Enhancing Military CBMs

Indian Prime Minister Singh said that the border issue was complicated, and required sound and sober minds of both sides to work on a final solution. Pending the solution, China and India should set as priority maintaining security and stability along the borderlines, and avoiding military confrontation between the two powers. In addition to strengthening political relations and economic cooperation, exploring ways to enhance military CBMs in the border areas and strengthening military cooperation between the two countries are of particular significance. In this respect, four suggestions might be in order:

First, establish strategic consensus between high-level military officials of both countries. Both China and India suffer from a trust deficit. To ensure security along the border areas, the military leaders of both countries should make full use of the current strategic dialogue mechanism, maintain institutional exchange channels, share relevant information on military security, and consult and discuss with each other in the spirit of equality, mutual respect and mutual benefit. Meanwhile, the military leaders of both countries should also work together to explore effective approaches to the implementation of military inspection along the borderlines, enhancing nuclear security (non-targeting and no-first-use principles), and promoting border crisis management, and so on, so as to provide an authoritative military and political platform for the future solution of the border dispute, and a mechanism for diminishing mistrust, removing psychological conflicts, and promoting mutual trust and confidence within the two militaries.

The second suggestion would be to improve military management along the borders. Working on the front line of defence, military officers in the border areas usually react in the most spontaneous and direct way. In recent years, affected by domestic and international media, military tension along the border has tended to grow. Both countries should improve military management and avoid unintended accidents in the border regions. When they do occur, both sides should refrain from politicizing them and escalating tensions.

Third, both sides should attempt to foster a friendly atmosphere along the border. Proportionate to new military developments along the border, efforts should be made to continuously reduce and control build-ups of army, air force, frontier services and paramilitary as well as of state-of-the-art arms and equipment. Both countries should inform each other of important military actions in advance such as conducting military exercises and upgrading major infrastructure, invite the other side as observers, so as to remove unnecessary suspicion between the two countries and create a peaceful atmosphere for mutual trust in the border areas.

Fourth, expand the scope of military cooperation. Joint military exercises at the tactical level of the army mark a good start, and should develop in the future. Meanwhile, we need to explore and expand to enrich the content of military cooperation, and push forward overall military relations between the two countries. For practical topics such as countering terrorist attacks and piracy and for humanitarian rescue, the two countries should carry out joint naval exercises, improve naval security cooperation and prevent military adventures. The two countries should exchange information on terrorist activities, transnational crimes and other aspects, enrich the content and upgrade the level of cooperation, assume an active role in stabilizing the border areas, creating more favourable conditions and lay more solid foundations for a final solution.

Conclusion

The solution of the China-India border dispute is of vital importance to the future development of both countries. It is also significant to the security of Asia and the rest of the world. To this end, both countries should adopt a new perspective, a new vision and a series of new measures to encourage new trends in China-India relations. By adopting new perspectives, both countries should aim at long-term security and development in line with the complicated changes in the international strategic architecture, and each other's security concerns. They should attach greater importance to their strategic common ground and mutual interdependence. They should also avoid repeating previous mistakes, and try to solve the border issue with patience, confidence and in good faith. By adopting a new vision, both countries should develop a new mindset in which neither side looks at the bilateral relationship as a zero-sum game. Only with this win-win principle can the two giants seek mutually acceptable measures on the basis of mutual understanding and compromise over the border dispute. By adopting new measures, both countries should be able to solve border disagreements and conflicts bilaterally and without outside interference, and particularly avoid being manipulated by external powers. The new perspective, mentality and measures will encourage a new trend in China-India relations, namely, a political solution through peaceful consultation on the border issue. Once we solve the border issue, one could imagine that a new era of bilateral relations between China and India will emerge. Thanks to the settlement of its last land dispute, China can get effective insurance as well as overall improvement of its security in the neighbourhood. On India's part, in addition to having a lasting insurance on its land borders in the north, the peaceful solution of the border issue may also provide good basis for resolving the Kashmir dispute with Pakistan. When meeting with George Fernandes, the then Indian Defence Minister, in April, 2003, Premier Wen Jiabao said that in the over 2,000 years since China and India began contact with each other, they had been friendly with each other for 99.99 per cent of time, and those conflicts that happened occasionally accounted only for 0.01 per cent in the long history of the interaction between the two great nations. To Wen's remarks, Fernandes also responded by expressing his wish that the two countries should make concerted efforts to bury the short period of misunderstanding, and embark on the road of mutual friendship with ever growing dynamism. He was right and it is high time for both China and India to act accordingly.

6

Sino-Indian Nuclear CBMs: Prospects for Cooperation

Srikanth Kondapalli

As two credible nuclear powers in Asia, adjacent neighbours, populous and rising countries in the 21st century, India and China have expressed their desire to seek a peaceful and stable global and regional order. Unlike all other nuclear powers in the world today, India and China also distinguish themselves in declaring a 'no first use' (NFU) position and also advocate global nuclear disarmament. Both support the several initiatives taken for nuclear weapons free zones, for instance, the Bangkok Treaty which legalizes the idea of such a zone for Southeast Asia. Both countries also share the view that nuclear weapons are last-resort defensive political weapons and that these can be used only for counter-nuclear retaliation efforts. Both have not placed their respective strategic forces on launch on warning and their missiles possibly un-fuelled and hence exhibit strategic restraint.[1] However, despite these commonalities, significant differences in status, approach, ideas and programmes exist between the two countries on nuclear issues.

China had started its nuclear programme in the 1950s with an explicit military dimension.[2] The United States and the then Soviet Union were cited as China's national security concerns during the Cold War period.[3] In India's case, the nuclear programme remained predominantly civilian from the 1940s.[4] However, the Indian programme acquired military dimensions by the 1980s and by 1998 explicitly cited China's proliferation of nuclear and ballistic missiles/technologies to Pakistan as the reason for such capability acquisition.[5] While China declared itself nuclear in 1964 and joined some international arms control and disarmament treaties such as the Nuclear Non-Proliferation Treaty (NPT) and Comprehensive Test Ban Treaty (CTBT), India has not been a party to any of these treaties, holding that the terms are discriminatory and privileges the "haves" over the "have-nots"—a discourse the Chinese elites are familiar with due to their opposition to the Partial Test Ban Treaty (PTBT) in the 1960s. However, in recent times, with constant reports about China's alleged continuing assistance to Pakistan in the strategic field and to deal with a two-theatre war, there have been voices in the Indian establishment calling for a departure from the NFU commitment.[6] Likewise, it has been argued in China that the Chinese NFU commitment is not applicable to its claims on territories or if the adversary attacks China's ICBM silos/strategic hubs.[7] There have also been reports about changes in the operational doctrines of the two countries.[8] Hence, if the above revisions in Indian and Chinese unconditional NFU are considered as true, it can be argued that these two Asian countries could hypothetically resort to nuclear war and therefore nuclear CBMs between the two become a necessity.[9]

Second, China does not recognize the *de jure* nature of the Indian nuclear programme, evident in China's support to the 1998 United Nations Security Council Resolution 1172, although as a *de facto* measure, from military operational perspective, China's Second Artillery Forces were reportedly targeting Indian cities and strategic hubs from early 1980s. If the Chinese plan to utilize conventional warheads, instead of nuclear warheads to mitigate the weaknesses in their air force's conventional capabilities,[10] then accidental nuclear retaliation also becomes a possibility as it would be difficult to know the exact payload (conventional/nuclear) of an incoming missile. This factor thus, points to the necessity for both countries to initiate comprehensive arrangements about missile CBMs.

Third, both countries have been increasingly spending enormous amount of resources—human financial and technological—to enhance their strategic weapons programmes. At China's 60th National Day parade in Beijing on 1 October 2009, for instance, new series of missiles were displayed. In the case of India too, the Agni-II and Agni-III missiles have been successfully tested and are being deployed and operationalized. Besides, both nations are also preparing for ballistic missile defence systems, which are aimed at neutralizing each other's strategic capability. Despite denials, both are possibly also acquiring tactical nuclear weapons, which provide for a greater role to the local commanders and hence increase the possibility of escalated tensions in the bilateral context.[11] Again, both countries are actively modernizing their nuclear arsenal towards miniaturization, and upgrading their ballistic missiles propellants with solid fuel technologies and MIRV capability.[12] They have also been reported to be acquiring permissive action links[13] necessary for automation of command and control systems in the rocket forces.[14]

Fourth, while both countries have NFU positions, in the light of the tensions growing between the two countries in the last couple of years,[15] it must be noted that no single effective mechanism exists between them to address nuclear accidents, strategic misperceptions and unintentional events. While conventional CBMs have existed between the two from 1996, there has been no agreement so far between India and China on de-targeting/non-targeting, or other de-escalation and risk-reduction methods. Even though both sides had initiated a strategic dialogue mechanism and announced the setting up of a hotline in June 2009 and agreed to cooperate on a civilian nuclear programme in November 2006, chances for accidental nuclear launches have not been addressed institutionally so far. These remain points of concern and highlight the nuclear- and ballistic missile-related risks between these two countries and the need for CBMs in the strategic field.

This paper traces mutual perceptions and explores the CBMs approach in general and, in the light of the arrangements made during the Cold War between several countries; it also offers some suggestions for CBMs between the two countries in the nuclear field. At the outset a few caveats need to be highlighted. Cold War-era active and overt confrontation no longer exists in an age of globalization, and interdependence between countries, including India and China, is inevitable. Yet, misperceptions can lead to deterioration of relations between the two countries.

Chinese Perceptions

While there has been a trend towards cooperation, nuclear issues have been a point of contention in Sino-Indian bilateral relations. A dominant perception in China is reflected in the following observation by a Chinese military newspaper,

> "Since the 80s India started pursuing a policy of 'regional deterrence' and a military strategy aimed at seeking a strong military strength and consolidating on the gains, containing China and deterring Pakistan, controlling weak and small neighbours and intercepting big power penetration outside the region and thereby clearing hurdles in its path towards becoming a world power".[16]

Also, in the aftermath of the Indian nuclear tests in 1998, China had been highly critical of such tests and argued that India should give up its nuclear option—but without providing an answer to Indian security concerns.[17] In 1998, the United Nations Security Council passed Resolution 1172 proposed by the United States and supported by China, calling on India and Pakistan to "cap, roll-back and eliminate" their nuclear programmes. Till this date, China has insisted that India should abide by this Resolution and give up its nuclear capability, while India maintains that it has neither signed any international arms control and disarmament treaties, and nor is the regional situation conducive to its security interests, which have been partly aggravated by the Chinese transfers of strategic weapons/ technologies to Pakistan. Another assessment, in the authoritative *World Military Yearbook of 2001* published by Chinese military constituents, argued that India had

- "minimum credible nuclear deterrence" to contend with China and deter Pakistan, and intended to extend second-strike capability in the Indian Ocean so as to check American influence.
- maintained defence strategy as "regional deterrence" (*diqu weishe*),
- formulated a strategic policy of waging limited war of hi-tech under nuclear deterrence conditions while preparing for changes from one theatre to multiple theatres.[18]

Subsequently, in the 2005 yearbook, it was argued that in its drive to become a "great power", India was following a policy of enhancing its nuclear arsenal and strengthening minimum credible deterrence and the triad.[19] Chinese military publications have also noted new developments in ballistic missiles in India, although most of these are less than 2,000 km in combat radius and would not be able to provide any effective deterrence against Beijing. Nevertheless, following the Indian success in launching Agni-III and plans for Surya ICBMs there has been a relative shrillness in Beijing's responses.[20]

Apart from opposition to the Indian nuclear tests, even Indian moves towards lifting sanctions and enhancing civilian nuclear commerce have been viewed with caution by China. These were reflected in the India-United States talks in the 1990s and more recently in the background of the United States-India 123 agreement. For instance, in the light of Strobe Talbott-Jaswant Singh talks in 1998-99, China had expressed its displeasure and argued that these violate international arms control and disarmament treaties. Sha Zukang, Director-General of the Department of Arms Control and Disarmament in China's Ministry of Foreign Affairs even went to the extent of questioning the legitimacy of such parleys between Washington and Delhi. He argued that the United States should not discuss with India on nuclear deterrence capability or support an Indian bid for UN Security Council permanent membership.[21] Sha further stated that China would insist on India signing CTBT unconditionally.[22]

China has cautiously watched the 123 civilian nuclear cooperation agreements in July 2005 and March 2006 between US and India, expressing reservations about the United States-India negotiations and their impact on international arms control treaties. However, in Article 8 Point 27 of the joint declaration of 21 November 2006 signed between Indian Prime Minister Manmohan Singh and visiting President Hu Jintao, China agreed "to promote cooperation in the field of nuclear energy with India". It also called for enhancing "exchanges in the related academic fields". There was a suggestion that China could benefit in the opening up of the Indian civilian nuclear market. However, since India is looking forward to setting up advanced 1,000 MW projects, it is likely that, given the Chinese lack of expertise in this field, China may not be a major beneficiary. Nevertheless, China could still benefit in the ancillary fields of raw materials supply and other areas. After the release of the text of the United States-India agreement on 1 August 2007, intense lobbying ensued between India and China on this issue as consent was needed from the 45-member NSG. However, Article 5 Section 6(b)(iv) of the United States-India agreement states that if disruptions to nuclear supplies take place, then the United States and India "would jointly convene a group of friendly countries such as Russia, France and the United Kingdom to pursue such measures as would restore fuel supply to India". This provision was put in to possibly minimize any Chinese pressure.

China portrays itself as a concerned actor by virtue of being a member of the Nuclear Supplies Group (NSG) which it joined in 2004 but China itself was admitted to the NSG with assurances of receiving advanced civilian nuclear technologies *on the condition* of abiding by non-proliferation regimes. Hence, although China still resisted a consensus in the NSG by citing the United Nations Security Council Resolution 1172 or with the help of other countries within the NSG, the extent of such opposition appeared in the final analysis, to be limited. The then Indian National Security Advisor however, did express his "disappointment" at the Chinese role at the IAEA and NSG meetings China's Foreign Minister Yang Jiechi for his part denied such a Chinese position.[23] Nevertheless, implicit adopting of such a non-cooperative posture by China would have stalled the flowering of "strategic partnership and cooperation" between India and China as envisioned under the Agreement of April 2005. For this reason, China has followed a careful approach on the issue utilising a lot of backdoor diplomacy. Overall, it can be argued that since the 1998 tests, India and China relations have exhibited turbulence and that this indicates that China has not really come to grips with the Indian nuclear reality.

Indian Perceptions

In contrast to the Chinese perceptions, Indian concerns are mainly focused on its national security needs. Major points emphasised in the Indian defence and security establishments are related to unstable conditions in South Asia. These issues pose a "security dilemma" for New Delhi as a result of Chinese missile deployments, ballistic missile defence, strategic submarine project and anti-satellite test. For instance, the Indian Ministry of Defence in its annual report of 1988-99 soon after conducting nuclear tests stated that "...the nuclear tests conducted by India...have helped forge a relatively stable national security environment for India.... (China's WMD transfers to Pakistan are a concern), India does not regard China as an adversary...".

The annual report for 2000-01 however, stated that "Every major Indian city is within reach of Chinese missiles.... The asymmetry...is strongly in favour of China...". The next annual report in 2001-02 stated: "...there are continuing reports of transfer of missile parts and components technology to Pakistan (from China)". The 2002-03 report reiterated:

> "... every major Indian city is within reach of Chinese missiles and this capability is being further augmented to include Submarine Launched Ballistic Missiles (SLBMs). The asymmetry in terms of nuclear forces is pronouncedly in favour of China and is likely to get further accentuated as China responds to counter the US missile defence programme. China's close defence relationship with Pakistan takes a particular edge in view of the latter's known belligerence and hostility to India and its acquisition of nuclear assets".

In the 2006-07 report, the Ministry stated:

> "The Chinese assistance to Pakistan's nuclear and missile programme has been a matter of concern as it has adversely impacted on India's national security environment. We have also taken note of the recent destruction by China of one of its own satellites in polar orbit through direct ascent anti-satellite test".[24]

In addition, Indian Ministry of External Affairs annual reports refer to "reliable and widespread" information about China's transfer of weapons of mass destruction to Pakistan.[25] Another major decision-maker, the 12th Lok Sabha Standing Committee on Defence argued:

> "...the Government should go ahead full steam in a time-bound manner to develop full range of missiles in addition to the variants of "AGNI" currently under development as a deterrent to potential enemies from using their ballistic missile capabilities against any of our assets".[26]

The above statements indicate that India is concerned with Chinese missile deployments in Delinga, Da Qaidam and Xiao Qaidam in "greater" Tibet (included in the Tibetan traditional places such as U-Tsang, Amdo and Kham) and Kunming military districts and the possibility of the more than 1,500 short-range ballistic missiles being shifted from Fujian and Zhejiang provinces to western areas in the event of a resolution of the Taiwan issue. According to Vijai K Nair, citing US Air Force National Intelligence Centre's declassified documents and Russian reports, China has been upgrading its nuclear and ballistic missiles to target India. Not only are the numbers of CSS-2 missiles at the 53rd Army at Jianshui (south of Kunming in Yunnan Province), with a range of 3,100km, not changed, but the training programme of the crew at Kunming training area is being enhanced, in addition to the probable replacement of CSS-2 by CSS-5 Mod1.[27] Large-scale training activities were reported from Datong field garrison, Haiyan training facility of the 56th Army (with missile bases at Da Qaidam, Delingha and Xiao Qaidam—all in "greater Tibet"). The communications infrastructure between missile bases in Jianshui-Kunming-Yunan-Chengdu-Lhasa-Haiyan-Datong (in southwestern and central China) are being upgraded for faster mobility.[28] Reports also indicate preparations by China for launching newer and longer-range missiles, and even anti-ballistic missile system in the Tibetan Plateau.[29] In January 2010, *Xinhua* reported that China had tested successfully "ground based midcourse missile interception technology".—indicating that this technology could be used for ballistic missile defence purposes of shooting down any incoming missiles (say, hypothetically, from India).[30]

Two other major developments have also triggered Indian concerns on China, namely, the planned deployment of a new strategic nuclear submarine in Sanya (Yulin) and the 2007 anti-satellite (ASAT) test. Recent reports indicate to the shifting of Type 094 Jin-class SSBN (with 8,000 km range Jl-2 SLBM) and construction of several berths to accommodate warships and tunnels that could lodge nearly 20 submarines at the Sanya (Yulin) base in Hainan.

On 11 January 2007, China officially acknowledged conducting ASAT operation when one of its missiles destroyed the ageing 750 kg Fengyun 1C weather-forecasting satellite launched in 1999. Reportedly this intermediate range ballistic missile (IRBM) with a kinetic interceptor was launched from Xichang range in Shanxi Province, and it destroyed the satellite at about 850kms above the earth's surface. Other ASAT programmes include lasers, micro-satellites, piggy-back satellites and electromagnetic weapon systems.

To mitigate its security concerns, India adopted a strategy of "deterring Pakistan and dissuading China" which now appears to be graduating from the above-mentioned position to that of "deterring Pakistan and deterring China".[31] This implies not only enhancing the nuclear stockpile and developing and deploying Agni-III missiles of 3,000 km and above range, but also configuring long-range aircraft for nuclear missions and efforts to build second-strike nuclear capability. In October 2007, India succeeded in testing Agni-III while in December 2007, it tested an interceptor missile as a part of its ballistic missile defence system. India had also expressed interest in possible import of Patriot Advanced Combat Systems-II from the US and Arrow missile systems from Israel in order to counter ballistic missile launches from Pakistan.

For India, the Chinese ASAT test is not a direct threat in the short term; however, it indicates that China can destroy the one and only military satellite that India possesses at the moment, thus putting at risk Indian military networks. The DRDO chief said that the test was a "matter of concern" but India is unlikely to test its own ASAT for the moment. An arms race in space is likely between the two countries in the longer run. The announcement by the Indian Air Force chief on establishing an Aerospace Command can be seen as a move in this direction.[32] Also, speaking on 5 November 2008 at the National Defence College, then Indian Foreign Minister Pranab Mukherjee said: "There are also new set of challenges which China poses such as the strategic challenge as China develops its capabilities in outer space...".[33]

India has indicated plans to respond to the naval base at Sanya with a similar base at Rambilli in Andhra Pradesh. The news about the Sanya base has gained wide coverage in India which prompted the Indian naval chief to argue in favour of discussing this issue at the Cabinet Committee on Security. As a result, eventually in July 2009, India launched the INS Arihant project for sea trials. The 6,000-tonne SSBN is to be equipped with SLBMs of a range of 700 km. Also, in February 2010, it was reported that India had unveiled a project to develop the submarine-launched Shaurya missile which can carry a one-tonne nuclear warhead over 750 km with a circular error probability (CEP) of 20-30 meters.[34]

CBMs in General

Strategic-level misperceptions and miscalculations can cost the two sides dear, especially if they are nuclear armed. The logical answer to prevent conflicts or even graduate to mutual trust is to implement CBMs. The concept of CBMs is linked to evolving a secure environment by a set of states or regions. They are intended to prevent conflict or reducing the risk of conflict between countries and to enhance mutual trust and confidence. The meaning and content of CBMs has undergone a change from the Cold

War period, though several different kinds of CBMs have existed before. During the Cold War, the CBMs had a military and strategic connotation, as seen in the European experience.

CBMs included measures towards transparency as reflected in advance notice of military exercises, inspections, or mechanisms for risk reduction efforts such as in the agreements of Helsinki in 1975, Madrid in 1983, Stockholm in 1986, Vienna in 1990, 1992 and 1994, and have been relatively successful in preventing conflict between the then NATO and Warsaw Pact blocs during the Cold War period. The 1962 Cuban missile crisis and establishment of "hotlines" between USSR and the United States is another example in avoiding misperceptions and accidental nuclear fallout. The 1974 West Asian initiatives for demilitarised zones between the Arabs and Israel and the Camp David accords of 1978 are other instances in which several CBMs came into being in the conventional field.

These CBMs intended to bring about transparency in the military field, concentrated on the following aspects: periodic publication of "white papers" on defence issues like concerns, doctrines, budgetary allocations, levels of force structures, equipment acquisitions, capabilities, training and military exercises, no use of force or threat to use force, agreements/MoUs, treaties, and high-level political, diplomatic and defence personnel visits. Miscalculations by the leaderships of the sides involved are reduced further through a regular flow of information, intelligence exchanges, the posting of observers at military exercises, inspections, exchange of defence personnel at defence colleges, and the use of diplomatic and multilateral approaches in solving or addressing national/regional/international problems.[35]

However, with the end of the Cold War between the United States and USSR and also due to several global changes, the nature of the CBMs also underwent a change from military orientation alone to non-military aspects as well. Alternate security paradigms have also been propounded to include issues related to common security, non-offensive defence, nuclear disarmament, military CBMs, détente from below, and so on. While the objective of security policies during the Cold War was based on threat assessments and measures to overcome such threats, in the post-Cold War period, risk management has emerged as the main objective.

To ensure transparency in the defence policies, both India and China have been publishing official papers on the subject. In the case of India, the annual reports of the Ministry of External Affairs and Ministry of Defence from the 1950s till the present elaborate on the policies, security environment, organizations, budgetary allocations, and equipment profiles, among other things. China is a recent entrant in the field with its release of six white papers related to security aspects from the mid-1990s.[36] India has initiated several CBMs with its neighbouring countries, as with others, though the CBMs with Pakistan have been relatively less successful, even if in the nuclear field, the two countries have achieved a mutual non-targeting of nuclear establishments as a major breakthrough in their bilateral relations. In the case of China, the CBMs initiated involve territorial aspects,[37] and the arms control and disarmament spheres, especially the 1964 nuclear no-first use, and de-targeting and non-targeting agreements with Russia and the United States in 1994 and 1998 respectively.

Indo-Pak Strategic CBMs

Compared to CBMs between India and China, such efforts between India and Pakistan are relatively extensive, although conflict prevention or trust at the strategic levels is still missing between New Delhi and Islamabad. Both countries had signed an agreement even before they became explicit nuclear states in December 1988 as a part of which they had commenced exchanging lists of nuclear installations in their respective countries from January 1992, after the agreement came into force in 1991. The agreement prohibits any attack on the nuclear installations of the other. On the first day of every year subsequently they have exchanged information regarding the nuclear installations, even in times when both countries appeared to be on the verge of conflict such as during the Kargil events or in the aftermath of the terror attacks on the Indian Parliament. In February 1999, the foreign secretaries of India and Pakistan also signed a MoU at Lahore to begin bilateral consultations on security concepts and nuclear doctrines, with a view of to developing measures for confidence building in the nuclear and conventional fields, aimed at the avoidance of conflict. The two sides undertook to provide each other with advance notification in respect of ballistic missile flight-tests, and to conclude a bilateral agreement in this regard; undertake national measures to reduce the risks of accidental and unauthorized use of nuclear weapons under their respective control; notify each other immediately in the event of any accidental, unauthorized or unexplained incident that could create the risk of a fallout with adverse consequences for both sides, or an outbreak of a nuclear war between the two countries; to adopt measures aimed at diminishing the possibility of such actions or such incidents being misinterpreted by the other; to identify/establish appropriate mechanism for this purpose; and to continue to abide by their respective unilateral moratorium on conducting further nuclear test explosions unless either side, in exercise of national sovereignty, decided that extraordinary events have jeopardized its supreme interests.[38]

The MoU also mentioned periodic reviews and improvement of links between the Directors-General of Military Operations of the two militaries. Subsequently, to further enhance CBMs, both countries decided in June 2004 to establish a hotline at the foreign secretaries' level and reduce risks and misunderstandings on nuclear issues. During the visit of then Indian Foreign Minister Natwar Singh to Islamabad in February 2005, it was also decided to establish a formal system of advance notification of missile tests.

Sino-Indian Strategic CBMs

CBMs in the strategic field hardly exist between India and China. Although there has been a slight revision in the Chinese position on the nuclear issue vis-à-vis India, one of the major hurdles for CBMs in the nuclear field between the two countries is the intransigence of Beijing in recognizing India's strategic weapons status, despite preparing to counter this in the operational sense. As suggested at the beginning, despite NFU pledges by both countries, several scenarios could pose serious problems between the two, such as bilateral political tensions, an unbridled arms race,[39] accidental nuclear fallout, lack of escalation control procedures, misunderstanding about the incoming conventional warhead in the event of limited border skirmishes, and so on.

Nevertheless, both countries have indicated that they are interested in talking about the issues at hand. Indian Foreign Minister Jaswant Singh's visit to Beijing in June 1999 after the Indian nuclear tests is one effort in this direction. China's efforts in this direction have been relatively tepid and it reportedly refused to entertain an Indian request for a bilateral NFU commitment.[40] Later, the first-ever security dialogue between the two countries was held by the Indian Joint Secretary (Disarmament) Rakesh Sood and the Director-General of the Asian Department of the Chinese Ministry of Foreign Affairs, Zhang Jiuhuan on 6-7 March 2000 at Beijing, where China told India to abide by the Chinese-backed UN Security Council Resolution 1172 of rolling back its nuclear programme.[41] The meeting came two weeks before US President Bill Clinton's visit to India. Later, in January 2001, Li Peng, head of the Standing Committee of the National People's Congress in a meeting with his Indian counterpart G.M.C. Balayogi, Speaker of the Indian Lok Sabha suggested that the two countries were not a threat to each other, while the latter suggested that both countries should work for universal nuclear disarmament.[42] The 2nd security dialogue was held in February 2001 and discussed the desirability of a genuine polycentric and equitable world and the prevention of an arms race in outer space, among other things.[43] At the 3rd Security Dialogue in September 2002, issues related to terrorism, regional and international security were discussed.[44] However, on the whole, there appears to be no progress on an understanding towards de-targeting between the two countries.[45]

In 2005, a new mechanism started between the two countries, namely, strategic dialogues, with the first such dialogue conducted at Delhi in January 2005, the second at Beijing in January the following year, the third at New Delhi in 2007 and the fourth in November 2010. Discussions included border issues, cooperation and coordination in regional and international affairs[46] but no major progress was achieved on nuclear/missile CBMs during these rounds of discussions as well.

However, despite tensions in bilateral relations, specifically on strategic weapons, there have been some cooperative efforts between India and China on nuclear issues in the recent past. It was reported that in the late 1980s, the Indian DRDO had purchased heavy water from China, although this has been mentioned as a "black market" transaction. In December 2003, Indian Atomic Energy Commission chief Anil Kakodkar had indicated that India was negotiating with China on export to the latter of about 30 tonnes of heavy water.[47] Further, Indian Foreign Minister Natwar Singh, in an effort to de-escalate tensions between the three Asian nuclear countries, had proposed in June 2004 that India, China and Pakistan should adopt a "common nuclear doctrine". While China did not make any comment, Pakistan had evinced interest, although there has been no major headway on this proposal so far.[48] These initiatives laid down the foundation for future efforts in the same direction. As mentioned previously, during President Hu Jintao's visit to New Delhi in November 2006, the joint statement with India referred to cooperation between the two countries in the civilian nuclear sector. In June 2009 again, both agreed to set up a hotline. There are also two MoUs that exist between the two countries on space cooperation, although they have not been really effective.

Conclusion

In the final analysis, it can be observed that there is a severe difference in perceptions between China and India on nuclear doctrines (despite NFU pledges), strategic weapons, ballistic missile defence, space development and deployment issues. While such deployment patterns do not indicate any current dangers—in a high-level or even a medium-level threat scenario—for long term stability in Asia and beyond, these two rising countries have to come to terms with each other's strategic weapons capabilities. It is argued further that escalating political tensions between these countries do create mutual suspicion which leads them to pursue a further enhancement of their respective strategic weapons programmes. As a result, unintentional and accidental use of nuclear weapons becomes a possibility. Strategic arms race, although denied by both, could logically result in mutual depletion of resources—if not immediate destruction. Conventional CBMs have provided a mode for expanding exchanges, peace and tranquility and de-escalation, while in the strategic sphere no major progress has been achieved so far. Hence, it is necessary for both sides to coordinate at the United Nations and adopt universal, comprehensive and non-discriminatory nuclear disarmament proposals. Although theoretically both are known to have kept their respective nuclear forces in de-alert conditions, it is imperative to negotiate a formal and binding agreement in this regard. Both should also have an agreement on de-targeting and risk reduction measures on the lines of those existing between India and Pakistan.

NOTES

1. For instance see Jeffrey Lewis, *The Minimum Means of Reprisal: China's Search for Security in the Nuclear Age*, Cambridge, MA: The MIT Press, 2007, pp. 15-16 and 18 and Bharat Karnad, *Nuclear Weapons and Indian Security: The Realist Foundations of Strategy*, Delhi: Macmillan, 2002.
2. See John Wilson Lewis and Xue Litai, *China Builds the Bomb*, Stanford, CA: Stanford University Press, 1988; Lewis and Xue, *China's Strategic Seapower: The Politics of Force Modernization in the Nuclear Age*, Stanford, CA: Stanford University Press, 1988; Mark A. Ryan, *Chinese Attitudes toward Nuclear Weapons: China and the United States during the Korean War*, New York: ME Sharpe, 1989; and Lin Chong-pin, *China's Nuclear Strategy: Tradition within Evolution*, Lexington, MA: Lexington Books, 1988.
3. The US reportedly planned to strike China with nuclear weapons on several occasions—in the 1940s, during the Korean War and on the Taiwan issue in the late 1950s. In addition, the USSR had also contemplated nuclear strikes against China after both fell out in the 1960s. See He Jinheng and Kang Shihua, "*He zhanzheng*" (Nuclear warfare), in *Zhongguo Dabaike Quanshu: Junshi* (*Chinese Encyclopaedia: Military Affairs*) 2 vols. Beijing: Chinese Encyclopaedia Publications, 1989, vol. 1, p. 365 and Xiong Guangkai, "The characteristics and impact of China's defense policy" in *International Strategy and Revolution in Military Affairs*, Beijing: Qinghua University Press, 2003. Declassified documents in UK indicated that to defend Hong Kong in 1961, the then British Foreign Secretary Sir Alec Douglas-Home wrote a letter to both Defence Minister Harold Watkinson and Prime Minister Harold Macmillan arguing for nuclear strikes against China. See *Daily Mail*, "Secret documents reveal Britain considered bombing China", 30 June 2006, http://www.dailymail.co.uk/news/article-393269/Secret-documents-reveal-Britain-considered-bombing-China.html.
4. On the Indian programme, see Karnad, op.cit.; Ashley Tellis, *India's Emerging Nuclear Posture: Between recessed Deterrent and a Ready Arsenal*, Santa Monica: RAND Corp., 2001; and Raju G. C. Thomas and Amit Gupta (eds), *India's Nuclear Security*, New Delhi: Sage Publications, 2000.
5. Indian Prime Minister Vajpayee said in a letter to the then US President Clinton that the "deteriorating security environment" in the neighbourhood drove India to test nuclear weapons. Further,
   "We have an overt nuclear weapon state on our borders, a state which committed

armed aggression against India in 1962. Although our relations with that country have improved in the last decade or so, an atmosphere of distrust persists mainly due to the unresolved border problem. To add to the distrust that country has materially helped another neighbour of ours to become a covert nuclear weapons state".
See *New York Times*, "Nuclear Anxiety; Indian's Letter to Clinton on the Nuclear Testing", 13 May 1998, http://www.nytimes.com/1998/05/13/world/nuclear-anxiety-indian-s-letter-to-clintonon-the-nuclear-testing.html?pagewanted=1?pagewanted=1.

6. For instance, in January 2003, the Indian government outlined an eight-point nuclear doctrine to include NFU, non-use of nuclear weapons against non-nuclear weapon states, global nuclear disarmament, establishment of a National Command Authority under civilian control, credible nuclear deterrence, right to use nuclear weapons in retaliation to chemical and biological attacks, strict export controls, participation in FMCT and unilateral moratorium on nuclear tests. See *Xinhua*, "India Outlines 8-Point Nuclear Doctrine", 5 January 2003, http://www.nti.org/e_research/profiles/india/nuclear/chronology_2003.html.
7. Given the current military technological advances in lasers, precision-guided weapons, information warfare, and so on, China's NFU position needs to be revised. According to Shen Dingli, Chinese strategists need "to analyze the new threat situation and reassess the logic of sitting idle after absorbing a first attack by non-nuclear unconventional attack, either by a state actor or a non-state actor". See Shen Dingli, "Nuclear Deterrence in the 21st Century", *China Security* (1), Autumn 2005, http://www.irchina.org/en/news/view.asp?id=402. See also Sun Xiangli, "Analysis of China's Nuclear Strategy", *China Security* (1), Autumn 2005, http://www.irchina.org/en/news/view.asp?id=401. However, according to Gen. Pan Zhenqiang, "China has consistently stressed that the first step should be the conclusion of a treaty by all nuclear weapon states not to be the first to use nuclear weapons. Such an agreement would be a significant confidence-building measure among these states to put their subsequent actions on the right track". See Pan Zhenqiang, "China Insistence on No-First-Use of Nuclear Weapons", *China Security* (1), Autumn 2005, http://irchina.org/en/news/view.asp?id=403.
8. China's operational doctrine at the conventional levels appeared to have graduated from a defensive to a pre-emptive strike (*xianfa zhiren*), while in the strategic spheres it has remained at counter-retaliation (*houfa zhiren*). However, some have argued that China is currently moving towards greater operational doctrinal flexibility, see Alistair Iain Johnston, "Chinese Nuclear Force Modernization: Implications for Arms Control", *Journal of Northeast Asian Studies* 2 (2), June 1983, pp. 13-28. See also Wang Wenmo (ed.), *Zhanlue Xue* (*Science of Strategy*), Beijing: National Defense University, 1999, pp. 347-70 and Wang Houqing, et.al (eds.), *Zhanyi Xue* (*Science of Campaigns*), Beijing: National Defense University, 2001 pp. 367-82. In January 2001, the then Indian Army Chief suggested that the Indian Army would be changing its tactics and methods of nuclear warfare. See Rahul Bedi, "General Sunderajan Padmanabhan India's Chief of Army Staff", *Jane's Defence Weekly*, 17 January 2001, http://www.nti.org/e_research/profiles/India/Nuclear/chronology_2001.html.
9. However, commenting on Gen. Zhu Chenghu's remarks in 2005 that China could possibly use nuclear weapons against the US to overcome China's conventional capability, Pan Zhenqiang argued that China's NFU pledge is a "theoretical pillar" of the country's nuclear policy and that Gen. Zhu's comments on possible use of nuclear weapons against the US to overcome China's lack of conventional superiority is "dead wrong" and that his "loose talk on the subject is very misleading

and sure to do serious damage". See Pan Zhenqiang, "China Insistence on No-First-Use of Nuclear Weapons", *China Security* (1), Autumn 2005, http://irchina.org/en/news/view.asp?id=403.

10. See Mark A. Stokes, *China's Strategic Modernization: Implications for the United States*, Carlisle Barracks, PA: Strategic Studies Institute, 1999, http://www.fas.org/nuke/guide/china/doctrine/chinamod.pdf.
11. For instance, in 1982 it was reported that a Chinese defense official told a French delegation that China had no tactical weapon deployed at "ground division or below" implying that tactical nuclear weapons might be held at a higher echelon. See Lewis, op.cit., p. 142. However, Charles Ferguson, Evan Medeiros and Phillip C. Saunders argue that China does not possess tactical nuclear weapons. See "Chinese Tactical Nuclear Weapons", in Brian Alexander and Alistair Millar (eds.), *Tactical Nuclear Weapons: Emergent Threats in an Evolving Security Environment*, New York, NJ: Brasseys, 2003, pp. 110-128. The Indian side has also emphasized the *strategic* nature of its nuclear programme. For instance, the then foreign minister Jaswant Singh argued, "...we do not see nuclear weapons as weapons of war fighting. In fact, India sees them only as strategic weapons, whose role is to deter use by an adversary. (Further,)...we have rejected notions of 'launch on warning postures' that lead to maintaining hair trigger alerts, thus increasing the risks of an unauthorized launch". See *Hindu*, "India Not to Engage in a N-Arms Race: Jaswant", 29 November 1999 http://www.indianembassy.org/inews/indianews_dec_99.pdf.
12. Various estimates suggest an increase in the quality production of nuclear fuels by China from the late 1970s. Thus by the early 1990s, it was estimated that the six nuclear fuel plants in China could produce about 25 tonnes of enriched uranium that could be sufficient for producing 1,500 nuclear weapons. Besides, it is estimated that China has a storage capacity of about 3.5 tonnes of plutonium that could produce nearly 2,000 nuclear weapons. See Robert S. Norris, Andrew S. Burrows and Richard W. Fieldhouse (eds), *British, French and Chinese Nuclear Weapons*, Boulder, CO: Westview, 1994, Chapter 6, pp. 324-356; John C. Hopkins and Weixing Hu (eds.), *Strategic Views from the Second Tier: The Nuclear Weapons Policies of France, Britain and China*, New Brunswick: Transaction Publishers, 1995; and Alastair I. Johnston, "China's new "old thinking": The Chinese concept of limited deterrence", *International Security*, 20(3), Winter 1995/96; and Stokes, op.cit.
13. This is a device for the security and safety of nuclear weapons and may consist of locks, encryption, and so on.
14. See Lewis, op.cit., p. 38.
15. The *Global Times* had published an article reminding India of the 1962 war, while a "Chinese strategist" recommended dividing India into 20-30 parts. See *Global Times*, "India's unwise military moves", 11 June 2009, http://english.people.com.cn/90001/90777/90851/6676088.html and *SiliconIndia News*, "China should break up India into 20-30 states: Chinese strategist, 10 August 2009, http://www.siliconindia.com/shownews/China_should_break_up_India_into_2030_states_Chinese_strategist-nid-60223.html. On the Indian side, besides the Navy and Air Force chiefs' comments on challenges from China, the Indian Army chief Gen. Deepak Kapoor said on 7 October 2009 that the army is preparing for a two-theatre war with Pakistan and China under nuclear conditions. See *OneIndia*, "Indian Army can counter Chinese threat: Army Chief", 7 October 2009, http://news.oneindia.in/2009/10/07/indian-army-can-counter-chinese-threat-army-chief.-html. Indian Defence Minister A K Antony told the first Consultative Committee meeting of the new Members of Parliament attached to the Defence

Ministry on 16 November 2009 that India should "build asymmetric capabilities against superior forces" and called for enhancing the strategic reach of the air force. See *Indian Express*, "India should build asymmetric warfare capabilities: Antony", 16 November 2009, http://www.indianexpress.com/news/india-should-build-asymmetric-warfare-capabi/542221/.

16. See Li Yanan, "India Dreaming to be a Military Super Power", *Liberation Army Daily*, 12 June 1999.
17. On the Chinese responses to the Indian nuclear tests and the background, see Wang Wenmo (ed.), *Zhanlue Xue* (Science of Strategy), Beijing: National Defense University, 1999, pp. 369- 370; Zhao Weiwen, *Yinzhong guanxi fengyunlu 1949-1999* (Record of stormy India-China Relations, 1949-1999), Beijing: Shishi Chubanshe, 2000, pp. 365-67. For the overall context, see John W. Garver, *Protracted Contest: Sino-Indian Rivalry in the Twentieth Century*, New Delhi: Oxford University Press, 2001; and Srikanth Kondapalli, "Chinese Military Eyes Southern Asia", in Andrew Scobell and Larry M. Wortzel (eds), Shaping China's Security Environment: The Role of the People's Liberation Army, October 2006 (Carlisle, PA: Strategic Studies Institute) pp. 197-282, http://www.strategicstudiesinstitute.army.mil/pdffiles/PUB709.pdf.
18. See the entry on "*Yindu*" (India) in *Shijie Junshi Nianjian 2001* (*World Military Yearbook 2001*), http://mil.qianlong.com/5051/2002-5-26/145@240422.htm
19. See the entry on "*Yindu*" (India) in *Shijie Junshi Nianjian 2005* (*World Military Yearbook 2005*), Beijing: Academy of Military Science, 2005, pp. 171 and 432.
20. On the Chinese reaction to the Agni-III's successful launch in April 2007 and plans for ICBM projects in India see D.S. Rajan, "India's Agni-III Missile in the Eyes of Chinese Strategic Experts", South Asia Analysis Group, Paper No. 2280, 2 July 2007, http://www.saag.org/common/uploaded_files/paper2280.html and Pratap Mohanty, "India Successfully Tests Missile Able To Hit China", *AFP*, 12 April 2007, http://www.spacewar.com/reports/India_Successfully_Tests_Missile_Able_To_Hit_China_999.html.
21. Sha was cited by C. Raja Mohan, "China Slams India's Nuclear Talks", *Hindu*, 18 January 1999, http://www.nti.org/e_research/profiles/India/Nuclear/chronology_1999.html.
22. *Hindu*, "China concerned over US Move on Indian N-Tests", 4 February 1999, http://www.nti.org/e_research/profiles/India/Nuclear/chronology_1999.html.
23. *Times of India*, See "NSG waiver: India issues demarche to China", 7 September 2008, http://articles.timesofindia.indiatimes.com/2008-09-07/india/27919229_1_nsg-waiver-nuclear-suppliers-group-unilateral-moratorium. See also, K. Subrahmanyam, "Don't Get Fooled by China", *Times of India*, 28 August 2007, http://articles.timesofindia.indiatimes.com/2007-08-28/edit-page/27953502_1_ring-magnets-proliferation-nuclear-suppliers-group.
24. Ministry of Defence, Government of India, *Annual Reports* (various years) (New Delhi).
25. See Ministry of External Affairs, Government of India, *Annual Report 1997-1998* (New Delhi) p. 3.
26. Lok Sabha Secretariat, "Action Taken on the Recommendations...", Standing Committee on Defence (1998-1999) Twelfth Lok Sabha, First Report New Delhi, July 1998, p. 3
27. For the bases, ranges of the missiles etc see Nuclear Threat Initiative, "Missile Overview", http://www.nti.org/e_research/profiles/China/Missile/index.html.
28. Vijai K. Nair, "The Chinese Threat: An Indian Perspective", *China Brief*, Vol. 1, No. 9, 8 November 2001, http://www.jamestown.org/programs/chinabrief/single/

?tx_ttnews%5Btt_news%5D=3763&tx_ttnews%5BbackPid%5D=191&no_cache=1,

29. See *Sing Tao Jih Pao* "China reportedly develops own missile defence system" 2 November 1999, p. A13 in *SWB FE/3682 G/17*, 3 November, 1999 and *Zhongguo Tongxun She*, "Army reportedly developing own Theatre Missile Defence system" 16 November 1999 in *SWB FE/3695 G/6*, 18 November 1999.
30. *Time*, "Missile defence system test successful", 11 January 2010.
31. Ninan Koshy had argued that India's nuclear doctrine shifted from "regional limited deterrent" to that of "regional overall deterrent". See Ninan Koshy, "Looking from India at the Spy Plane", Foreign Policy in Focus, 1 May 2001, http://www.fpif.org/articles/looking_from_india_at_the_spy_plane.
32. While attending the South Western Air Command's station commanders' conference, the Indian Air Force Chief Air Chief Marshal SP Tyagi said in January 2007 that an aerospace command needs to be established to exploit the outer space. See *Times of India*, "India to set up aerospace command: Air Chief", 28 January 2007, http://articles.timesofindia.indiatimes.com/2007-01-28/india/27880584_1_aerospace-command-aerospace-power-space-assets.
33. See Indrani Bagchi, "Finally, Pranab calls China a challenge", *Times of India*, 5 November 2008, http://articles.timesofindia.indiatimes.com/2008-11-05/india/27900493_1_india-and-china-india-china-chinese-president-hu-jintao.
34. Ajai Shukla, "Shaurya surfaces as India's underwater nuclear missile", *Business Standard*, 17 February 2010, http://www.business-standard.com/india/news/shaurya-surfaces-as-indias-underwater-nuclear-missile/385952/.
35. For the CBMs approach see Michael Krepon, et.al. (eds.), *Handbook of Confidence-building Measures*, Washington, DC: The Henry L. Stimson Centre, 1998 and relevant papers at http://www.stimson.org; Masahiko Asada, "CBMs in East Asia: A Japanese Perspective", *Asian Survey* vol. 28 (5), May 1988, pp. 489-508; Owen Greene, "Confidence-building in North-East Asia", *Bradford Arms Register Studies* (7), Boulder: Westview Press, 1996; and Malcolm Chalmers, "Confidence-building measures", in *Confidence-Building in South-East Asia*, Chapter 8, *Bradford Arms Register Studies* (6), Bradford: Westview Press, 1996, pp. 221-42. For the limitations of the CBMs approach see Marie-France Desjardins, "Rethinking Confidence-Building Measures", *Adelphi Papers* (307), Oxford: International Institute for Strategic Studies, 1997.
36. These six include "Arms Control and Disarmament" released in November 1995, and "China's National Defense" in July 1998, October 2000, December 2002, 2004, 2006, 2008 (released in January 2009).
37. On this connection between CBMs and border issues see Liu Huaqiu and Zheng Hua, "Confidence-building measures in Asia" in Michael Krepon (ed.), *Chinese Perspectives on Confidence-building Measures*, Report No. 23, May 1997, Washington, DC, The Henry L. Stimson Centre, 1997, pp. 1-14. They stress the specificities of Asian CBMs including their diversity, stress on general principles and guidelines, and incremental approach. For the evolution of Chinese views on CBMs see Xia Liping, "The Evolution of Chinese Views Toward CBMs" in the same book (pp. 15-37).
38. This MoU was signed by K. Raghunath and Shamshad Ahmed. See Ministry of External Affairs, Government of India, "Memorandum of Understanding", 21 February 1999.
39. Although both countries had played down the arms race factor, defence budgets of both countries are rising as are their strategic and conventional capabilities. However, in early February 2000, the then Indian NSA Brajesh Mishra argued that India did not intend to enter into a nuclear arms race with China. *Times of India*,

"We're Not Trying to Catch up with China", 7 February 2000.

40. Jaswant Singh replied to a question in the Lok Sabha on 1 December 1999 that India had "indicated (its) readiness to negotiate binding agreements on no-first use, bilaterally or multilaterally".
41. *Hindustan Times*, "India Rejects China's Call for Rollback", 9 March 2000.
42. *Hindu*, "Li Peng in India", *Frontline*, Vol. 18, No. 3, 03-16 February 2001, http://www.hinduonnet.com/fline/fl1803/18031260.htm.
43. For the official reply in the Indian parliament, http://www.meadev.nic.in/govt/parl-qa/loksabha/questn508.htm and http://www.meadev.nic.in/govt/parl-qa/rajyasabha/mar1-760.htm.
44. See http://www.meadev.nic.in/govt/parl-qa/loksabha/December 11-3333.htm. See also Jing-dong Yuan, "Sino-Indian relations: A new beginning", *Asia Times Online*, 19 January 2002, http://www.atimes.com/china/DA19Ad01.html.
45. Damon Bristow, "Indian and China hold first ever security talks to strengthen relations", *Jane's Intelligence Review*, April 2000, p. 3.
46. *Foreign Broadcast Information Service*, "China-India strategic dialogue manifests partnership", *People's Daily*, 12 January 2006, World News Connection File Number 985 Accession Number 219700118.
47. For these views see Nuclear Weapons Archive, "India's Nuclear Weapons Program: The Long Pause: 1974-1989" 30 March 2001, http://nuclearweaponarchive.org/India/IndiaPause.html and Gary Milhollin, "Dateline New Delhi: India's Nuclear Cover-Up", *Foreign Policy* (64), Autumn 1986, pp. 161-175.
48. *Space War*, "India Sets Dovish Tone with Pakistan, China in Call for Nuclear Coordination", 2 June 2004, http://www.spacewar.com/s2004/040602090246.lml 74psb.html.

7

Sino-Indian Maritime Cooperation: Strategic Environment

Xia Liping

Traditionally China and India have been continental powers. However, the two countries are now evolving as both continental and maritime powers (although China shows more interest in the Pacific Ocean and India exhibits more interest in the Indian Ocean). At the same time, the Indian Ocean is one of China's important sea lanes of communication (SLOCs) and India has increasing interests in the Pacific Ocean. Due to globalization, no country can possibly protect its SLOCs by itself.

New Rationale of China's Current Foreign Strategy and Security Policy

In recent years, China has developed a new rationale for its foreign strategy and security policy. First of all, it recognizes that the trend of economic globalization is one of the two major international trends in the world which is making countries interdependent and increasing common interests between them. Next, it calls for mutual respect for sovereignty, equality and mutual benefit, and peaceful coexistence between developed countries and developing countries. Finally, China insists also that developed countries should not regard developing countries as their stooges and should not use force against developing countries without authorization from the United Nations.

Giving up its initial reluctance, China has gradually accepted the key elements of international regimes, including the need for transparency, responsibility, consensus and refraining from the use of force.

(1) Transparency—participation in more international regimes and more exchanges with the international community has helped it make progress in achieving greater transparency of national security and economic fields.
(2) Responsibility—in recent years, China has taken up ever more international responsibilities. For example, China played a very positive role in organizing the three-party talks and the six-party talks on North Korean nuclear issue in Beijing in April and August 2003 respectively.
(3) Consensus—most multilateral international regimes need a consensus when they make major decisions on critical issues. China has paid increasing attention to consultation and dialogue with other countries on critical regional and international issues through different international mechanisms.
(4) Non-use of force—China put forward the New Security Concept with the aim of resolving disputes through dialogue and improving security through cooperation at its core.

All along, China has played a very important role in multilateral international forums. For example, China played a very positive and active role in initiating and developing the Shanghai Cooperation Organization (SCO), which has become an important sub-regional security and economic cooperation mechanism in Central Asia and one of the key regimes for Sino-Russian strategic partnership. Originally five countries—China, Russia, Kazakhstan, Kyrgyzstan and Turkmenistan—got together in the early 1990s to form the Shanghai Five for negotiations on resolving their border disputes, to establish CBMs and to realize disarmament along their border areas. Now the SCO is focused on cooperation in the fields of anti-terrorism, countering religious extremism and ethnic separatism as well as economic cooperation. With the establishment of the SCO, the Shanghai Six have developed what they call "Shanghai Spirit", which has been the guideline of this organization espousing mutual trust, mutual benefit, equality and consultation, respecting multi-civilization and seeking common development. In fact, the SCO is a new type of regional regime, which is not a military alliance and is not to be used as a tool against any other country, and is open to other countries.

The geo-economic theory on regional economic integration was put forward by Edward N. Luttwak and some other Western scholars in the early 1990s. They believe that countries have been competing under a new pattern called geo-economics since the end of the Cold War. Current examples for which are the European Union, which has made great progress in economic integration and political cooperation in Europe, and the North

American Free Trade Area (NAFTA) which has played an important role in economic integration of North America. Meanwhile, even though East Asian countries have been developing their economies very dynamically, they have lagged behind in economic integration as compared to the European Union and NAFTA.

Given these circumstances, China has been attaching more and more importance to regional economic cooperation for integration with its surrounding areas. For example, in November 2002, China reached an agreement with the Association of Southeast Asian Nations (ASEAN) to establish a Free Trade Area by 2010. In September 2003, Chinese Premier Wen Jiabao put forward the proposal to establish a Free Trade Area within the SCO. Some features of China's New Geo-economic Theory are:

(1) To put great emphasis on economic cooperation with its neighbouring countries including both developing countries and developed countries;
(2) To regard the establishment of free trade areas as one of the very crucial types of economic integration with other countries; and
(3) To let free trade areas be open to other countries.

In the 1980s, some American scholars, such as Robert Keohane and Kenneth Oye, put forward the cooperation theory, the main arguments of which establish that in international relations, interests of players do not always lead to confrontation with each other, and players can have mutual benefits from cooperation. The theory argues that international regimes should be strengthened so as to resolve disputes and conflicts through consultations, and to make cooperation a guiding principle in international relations. The concept of reciprocity should be amplified and be developed in international mechanisms, which can inspire cooperation, monitor actions of cooperation, reward those cooperating, ensure effective contact, and improve multi-level exchanges.

China has come to realize the benefits it can achieve by engaging in economic and security cooperation with other countries. At the same time, China has tried to incorporate certain features which derive from its own geopolitical limitations in cooperation theory, namely,

(1) To stress win-win results with other countries through cooperation;
(2) To establish multi-type and multi-level mechanisms of cooperation with other countries; and
(3) To go ahead with economic and anti-terrorist cooperation with developed countries despite unresolved disputes on human rights with such countries.

Contemporary deliberations have witnessed an increase in debates over what kind of power China should become. Some Chinese scholars hold that China should participate not only in existing international economic mechanisms, but also in existing international political mechanisms. It should let the United States maintain its leadership in these forums as it will be beneficial for China which can then operate in a peaceful environment and be able to gradually change the existing unreasonable rules of these mechanisms in favour of the interests of people of all countries. According to this theory, they support improvement of relations between China and the United States. However, some other Chinese scholars argue that the United States tries to contain China from rising as a great power and thus, hinders it from playing an important role in the international arena; in other words, the United States actually intends to weaken China. This debate is reflected in the decision-making processes and leaves imprints on China's foreign policy.

The debate also revolves around the issue of whether China should judge itself and get involved in international mechanisms on the basis of Euro-centric assumptions or establish theories of international relations with Chinese characteristics. Scholars have used several western theories of international relations, Marxian dialectical materialism and Deng Xiaoping's Thought to analyze China's contemporary international relations and based on these analyses have tried to put forward some new concepts. For example, Prof. He Fang holds that the world is now in the era of peace and development and China should adhere to peaceful means thereby, criticizing the viewpoint raised by a few Chinese scholars that China should indulge in an arms race with the United States in the aftermath of the NATO bombing of Chinese Embassy in Belgrade.[1] Also, Prof. Yang Jiemian puts forward the concept of "beyond geo-politics" to analyze relations between the major powers after 9/11.[2] The views of such Chinese experts influence both theoretical and policy changes.

China's Policy towards Neighbouring Countries

The first two decades of the 21st century are a period of important strategic opportunity for China. During this period China will focus its attention on building a well-off society in an all-out way. The objectives of China's modernization are to quadruple the GDP recorded in 2000 by 2020, and to become a mid-level developed country by 2050. In order to achieve these objectives, China needs a long-term peaceful and stable international environment, which can bolster China's economic development.

For the 21st century there are the three major tasks of historic significance for China: to propel the modernization drive; to achieve national reunification; and to safeguard world peace and promote common development.[3] In order to accomplish these three tasks of historic significance, China has developed some new concepts for its foreign strategy:

(1) Follow the historical tide and safeguard common interests of all mankind: China is ready to work with the international community to boost multi-polarization, promote the harmonious coexistence of diverse forces, and maintain stability in the international community. China will continue to improve and develop relations with the developed countries. Proceeding from the fundamental interests of all countries concerned, China will broaden the converging points of common interests and properly settle differences on the basis of the Five Principles of Peaceful Co-existence, notwithstanding the differences in social systems and ideologies. China will increasingly cooperate with the United State and other countries in setting up anti-terror mechanisms and dealing with regional security problems, such as the North Korean nuclear issue.

(2) Stress new concepts of security featuring mutual trust, mutual benefit, equality and coordination: Since the end of the Cold War, China has changed its security concepts according to the evolving international situation and interests of Chinese people as well as the necessity for world peace and development. China believes that to obtain lasting peace, it is imperative to abandon the Cold War mentality, cultivate a new concept of security and seek new ways to safeguard peace. It has to be kept in mind that the new concepts of security are in keeping with the trend of the era and have greater vitality.

China holds that the core of the New Security Concept should be mutual trust, mutual benefit, equality and coordination.[4] The new security concept should also be the guideline to resolve disputes in international security.[5]

On 7 October 2003, Chinese Premier Wen Jiabao stressed, "It is China's existing guideline to advance the vigorous development, peace and stability in Asia. It is an important part of China's development strategy to maintain good relationships with neighbours, make them secure and help them become rich".

"To maintain good relationships with neighbours" means that China will adhere to its philosophy of "making close and friendly relations with neighbours", so that they can cooperatively establish stable and harmonious relationships under the principle of living in harmony with surrounding countries.

"To make neighbours secure" means that China will vigorously maintain regional peace and stability, persist in improving mutual trust through dialogue and cooperation and in resolving disputes though peaceful negotiations. "To help neighbours become rich" means that China will strengthen cooperation for mutual benefit with its neighbours, and deepen regional and sub-regional cooperation in order to realize common development with other Asian countries.

Scope of the Sino-Indian Security Relationship and Strengthening the Strategic Cooperative Partnership

At present, China has put its relationships with major powers as the first priority of its foreign strategy, followed by its relationship with neighbouring countries as a critical leg of its foreign strategy, and finally, its relationships with developing countries as the foundation of its foreign strategy. India is a rising major power in Asia, a neighbouring country with China, and one of the biggest developing countries. India is the only country to fit in with all three standards. So China has paid special importance to its relationship with India.

The Sino-Indian relationship has recovered from the tensions between the two sides caused by India's nuclear tests in May 1998. Since Indian Prime Minister Atal Behari Vajpayee's visit to China in June 2003, both countries have made huge progress in their political and economic relations. Both China and India are large developing countries with one-third of the world's population. Therefore, it is necessary that the two countries accomplish economic and socially sustainable development to maintain peace, stability and prosperity in Asia as well as in the world. At the same time, both countries are rising powers in the international arena as well as influential neighbours so they should view their relations from a strategic perspective and make their best efforts in order to establish a long-term constructive and cooperative relationship. Both China and India have been long standing civilizations and take pride in their own unique histories. The two countries are peace-loving and their friendly exchanges go back to ancient times. Furthermore, both countries are initiators of the Five Principles of Peaceful Co-existence and have the same major objectives of realizing economic and social modernization. Hence, they should try to overcome the difficulties and obstacles in their relationship and revive these old linkages.

The significance of China's current foreign strategy and security policy is that it includes the concept of a period of important strategic opportunity and the will to safeguard the common interests of all mankind. These tenets of foreign strategy and security policy pursued by the Chinese leadership can be analyzed through a set of international relations theories, like interdependence theory, international regime theory, geo-economic theory, and 'cooperation for win-win' theory. In fact, China has given these theories a new rationale due to internal and external factors affecting China's global position and role. With the integration of China into the international economic and political order, it has pledged to continue its role as a major responsible power in international domain in the coming twenty years.

Relations between China and India can be studied at four levels: bilateral, sub-regional, regional, and global. Both countries share many common interests in these cross-sections of relations. On the sub-regional level, both China and India would like to see prosperity, stability and peace in South Asia and Central Asia and combat anti-terrorism and anti-piracy in the region. On the regional level, both countries would like to see economic integrity, prosperity, stability and peace in Asia and on the global level, both share many common goals, such as prosperity, stability and peace in the world and nuclear-non-proliferation. They would like to cooperate regarding financial crisis, climate change, and so on.

The Sino-Indian security relationship has gone through three major phases: of friendship (from 1949 to the end of 1950s), of opposition (from the early 1960s to late 1990s) and the strategic partnership from 2005 on. Although the relations between China and India improved till 1988, there were tensions again between the two sides following India's nuclear tests in May 1998. Relations however, improved with Chinese Premier Zhu Rongji's visit to India in January 2002 and then Indian Prime Minister Vajpayee's visit to China in June 2003. During these visits both countries agreed to strengthen their "long-term constructive partnership", as the fruition of the object put forward by the leaders of the two countries during Chinese President Jiang Zemin's visit to India in 1996. Since then, both countries have made substantial progress in their political, economic and security relations. After going through a long and winding road, China-India relations have entered a new stage of maturity.

In April 2005, during Chinese Premier Wen Jaibao's visit to India, both countries agreed to convert their cooperative partnership into a strategic cooperative partnership. They agreed that the development of trade and diplomatic links between the two nations was in their common interest as also contributing to regional and world peace and stability. During Wen's visit, the two governments inked an agreement on political guiding principles for solving the border issue. This was the first political document signed by the two countries since 1981 when the two countries started negotiations on settling border disputes. The agreement provides that "the differences on the boundary question should not be allowed to affect the overall development of bilateral relations... The two sides will resolve the boundary question through peaceful and friendly consultations. Neither side shall use or threaten to use force against the other by any means". It also declared that India and China would "make meaningful and mutually acceptable adjustments to their respective positions on the boundary question, so as to arrive at a package settlement to the boundary question... The boundary settlement must be final, covering all sectors of the China-India boundary". Further, "Bilateral strategic and reasonable interests, and the principle of mutual and equal security" would be kept in mind while arriving at a final settlement. The Sino-Indian border has been tranquil with no confrontation since 1993.

The two countries should look at their relations from a strategic and long-term perspective. They should continue to use the Five Principles of Peaceful Co-existence as guidelines in future agreements to strengthen Sino-Indian relations. The two countries should resolve their border disputes in the spirit of mutual benefit as well as mutual understanding and accommodation through negotiations. Such Sino-Indian agreements or policy guidelines for solving the border issue will help the Special Representatives of the two governments in negotiating territorial claims besides helping the experts who delineate the boundary on a map and on the ground.

The two countries should further strengthen the dialogue on strategic and security issues and should further enhance defence exchanges and CBMs between the two militaries so as to enhance mutual trust. China and India should also increase economic and trade cooperation to provide a strong material basis for strategic cooperation. They should recognize that they share similar long-term fundamental interests.

Rise of Non-Traditional Threats in the Pacific and Indian Theatres

After the end of the Cold War, and especially since the 9/11 incident, the system of international relations has been witnessing a transformation from one of balance of power in international anarchy to a new one mainly characterized by mutual interdependence between countries. But this transformation is likely to continue over a long period. In the contemporary world, with rising transnational challenges, major threats come more from non-state actors such as terrorists and pirates.

The transition period will be full of complicated struggles and the road will be tortuous as it will witness an increase in such incidents. During the transition, terrorism will pose a severe threat to the international community. Alongside, the threat of piracy is also set to increase in the Indian and Pacific Oceans. The impact of other non-traditional security threats on international relations is also rapidly rising.

Non-traditional security threats are also transnational problems and these 'low politics' problems include terrorism, piracy, environmental pollution, global warming, population exploration, drug trafficking, international crimes, HIV/AIDS, and so on. They have two major characteristics. One that they exist all over the globe and are related to all human beings and another, that they threaten the existence and development of all human beings.

In such a scenario, security problems can become transformed into non-traditional security problems, and non-traditional security problems can lead to traditional armed conflicts. Furthermore, traditional security threats and non-traditional security threats can become interwoven and transformed in the process. For example, weapons of mass destruction are traditional security problems. However, if terrorists get access to such weapons, it acquires the nature of a non-traditional security threat and a transnational problem. Another example is that cross-boundary attacks by terrorists are non-traditional security threats which may lead to traditional armed conflicts.

During the Cold War, the two superpowers, namely the United States and the former Soviet Union, indulged in an arms race and ignored its implications on the developing nations. Due to long-term exploitation of and ignorance exhibited towards developing nations by the developed nations, non-traditional security threats have escaped adequate attention, but are now beginning to have a greater impact. This has greatly increased the common interests of all countries in the world, and made countries cooperate more in dealing with and resolving these problems. Growing impact of non-traditional security threats on international relations and rising common interests between countries, especially major powers, has forced them to come together and to resolve disputes through consultation and coordination.

Factors Affecting Stability and Security in South Asia

There are three levels of factors which impact stability and security in South Asia:

(1) *Relations between major powers and South Asian regional powers:* During the Cold War period, the Soviet Union supported India, and the United States and China supported Pakistan against each other. However, after the end of the Cold War, the major powers including China and the United States have shared common interests in the security concerns of South Asia. They would like to see peace and stability in the region. It is not in their larger national interests to use one country against the other in South

Asia. Neither is it in their national interest to struggle against each other for a strategic position in South Asia. However, some politicians in the United States still want to use India to counterbalance China.

(2) *Relations between India and Pakistan:* India and Pakistan fought three wars against each other during the Cold War period. In May 1998, both conducted nuclear tests and continued with their apprehensive approach towards each other. From 2005 to 2008 relations between India and Pakistan had improved to some extent, which reduces the possibility of armed conflicts including nuclear exchanges, between the two countries. However, since the Mumbai terrorist attacks of 26 November 2008, India-Pakistan relations have been worsening again, because India believes that some people in Pakistan are responsible for the same.

(3) *Non-state actors:* In recent years, non-state actors have become important in international relations. Notable non-state actors include terrorist organizations, transnational companies and non-governmental organizations, multilateral organizations, and so on. Now even non-state actors have the capital and means similar to those owned by states; big transnational companies sometimes have more capital than some small states. In international domains there are many kinds of non-governmental organizations, whose roles are increasing in scope and significance. Although terrorism has been around for ages, global terrorism is a relatively new phenomenon and terrorists as non-state actors are beginning to have larger implications for international relations—9/11 being the most glaring example. Terrorism is transnational and multiethnic in its scope, with terrorists representing all walks of life, poor to rich, Third World to First World, illiterate to educated. Ironically, the same mechanisms that have fuelled economic globalization have also enabled growth of terrorism on a global scale.

In South Asia, especially India, Pakistan and Afghanistan, terrorist organizations like al Qaeda, and extremists groups such as the Taliban, pose serious threats to national governments. Other non-state actors, such as the warlords in Afghanistan, for example, also have a negative impact on the national government.

Maritime CBMs between China and India

In order to improve mutual understanding and mutual trust between China and India in the fields of defence, the two countries should make great efforts to establish the Confidence-Building Measures (CBMs) between the two navies of China and Indian.

(1) *Doctrinal exchanges:* China and India should strengthen the dialogue on strategic and security issues. At the same time, they should enhance defence exchanges and confidence-building measures so as to enhance mutual trust. China publishes its national defence white papers every two years and its military strategy guideline is positive defence. Taking advantage of this, China and India should have military doctrine exchanges every year.

(2) *Joint exercises:* In 2003, China and India had the first joint naval rescue exercise. In the future, China and India should have more joint naval exercises focused on anti-piracy and anti-terrorism mechanisms.

(3) *Disaster management at sea:* China and India should establish information exchange mechanisms on natural disasters and cooperate in disaster management in both the Pacific Ocean and the Indian Ocean. After the tsunami in the Indian Ocean in December 2004, China had to ask American aircraft carriers to deliver Chinese humanitarian assistance to Indonesia. In the future, when necessary, mechanisms have to be in place so that China can ask Indian ships to deliver Chinese humanitarian assistance to other countries. And simultaneously, if China has the capabilities India can rely upon Chinese ships to deliver Indian humanitarian assistance to other countries.

(4) *Anti-piracy measures:* Both China and India have sent warships to participate in patrol actions against piracy near the east coast of Africa. In future, the two navies should engage in more consultation and cooperation in these actions. A consensus was reached between China, EU, Combined Maritime Forces (CMF), and NATO about coordinated patrols in January 2010. In a similar vein, warships of China and India should have joint exercises on anti-piracy and joint patrol in the Gulf of Aden.

(5) *Security arrangements for the protection of important SLOCs:* China and India share common interests in protecting their trade security, especially that of energy and natural resources. On 17 February 2010, Pallam Raju, the Indian Minister of State for Defence, said that India would like to use the Indian Navy to help China to protect the sea lane of communication in the Indian Ocean. China and India should reach and sign some agreement to establish security arrangements for the protection of their SLOCs. Both countries should make greater efforts to establish multilateral

mechanisms of cooperation for navies in Asia, such as an Asia maritime partnership.

Strengthening the New Security Concept

At present there is a tension between the New Security Concept and Cold War mentality. On the one hand, new security concepts like cooperative security, coordinated security, common security and so on, have been put forward. On the other hand, Cold War-era zero-sum game theory, balance of power and geopolitics, still exist. If countries, especially major powers, can see the world through new security concepts and cooperate to deal with non-traditional security threats, such as terrorism, they can have a win-win situation. In order to effectively counter terrorism, countries should abandon the Cold War mentality and adopt some new concepts on global security like:

(1) *"Mutual security"*: The Cold War concept of zero-sum game has to give way to a concept of mutual security with changing global dynamics. Any country building its own absolute security at the disadvantage of others needs to be opposed. The concept also calls upon the nuclear powers, especially the two superpowers to speed up their process of nuclear disarmament.

(2) *Cooperation*: At present all countries facing the common problems of terrorism, environment disasters, climate change, drug trafficking, proliferation of weapons of mass destruction and so on should make common efforts and cooperate to deal with these challenges. They should pay especially more attention to nuclear non-proliferation, as it threatens the very survival of humanity.

(3) *Comprehensive security*: The emphasis should shift from military security to a comprehensive notion of security. With the growing importance of economic issues all countries should make efforts to settle their divergences and disputes through peaceful means.

The New Security Concept should become the theoretical basis for establishing Sino-Indian maritime cooperation in the 21st century. China is willing to accelerate mutual trust through dialogue and spur common security initiatives through cooperation. China understands that the only way to ensure the integrity of its sea lanes in the India Ocean and the Straits of Malacca is to cooperate with India and other countries. The final aspiration of China thus, is to build harmonious and stable Pacific and Indian Ocean zones based on mutual trust and benefit which can then be utilised for common interests of all countries in the region.

NOTES

1. He Fang, *On the Era of Peace and Development*, (*Lun heping yu fazhan shidai*), Beijing, China: Shijiezhishi Chubanshe, 2000, p. 7.
2. Yang Jiemian, *International Terrorism and Contemporary International Relations* (*Guoji kongbuzhuyi yu dangdai guoji guanxi*), Guizhou, China: Guizhou Renmin Chubanshe, 2002, pp. 22-23.
3. *Documents of the 16th National Congress of the Communist Party of China* [Zhongguo Gongchandang Dishiliuci Quanguodabiao Dahui Wenjian Huibian], Beijing, China: Foreign Language Press, 2002, p. 2.
4. *China's Document about the Position of New Security Concept*, [Zhongguo guanyu xin anquanguan lichang de wenjian], put forward by Chinese Delegation at the meeting of ASEAN Regional Forum (ARF), held in Seri Begawan, the Capital of Brunei, on 31 July 2002, Beijing, China: *People's Daily*, 2 August 2002, pp.3.
5. *People's Daily*, "Chinese Ambassador of Disarmament Hu Xiaodi's Speech at the Conference on Disarmament in Geneva", Beijing, 7 February 2002.

8

Maritime Cooperation between India and China: Drivers for Cooperation

Cdr. Kamlesh Kumar Agnihotri

In the 21st century, the Indian Ocean region is slowly emerging at the centre-stage of the global maritime map. The Ocean extends nearly 10,000 km between the Cape of Good Hope and Australia and about 13,500 km from the Persian Gulf to Antarctica.[1] A vast majority of the world's population, comprising multi-ethnic and multi-religious groups, lives in this region. Moreover, the highest tonnage of global maritime trade transits through the Indian Ocean, with about 100,000 ships plying its waters annually[2] and roughly 40 per cent of this sea-borne trade passes through the Malacca Straits. Compared to this, the Persian Gulf and adjoining region accounts for 50 per cent of the world's container cargo and 33 per cent of bulk cargo. 15.5 million barrels of oil pass through the Straits of Hormuz every day and 11 million barrels go through the Malacca and Singapore Straits.[3]

The Indian Ocean Rim comprises states with varying degrees of economic and social development, governance and political maturity. There are vibrant democracies like India and Australia, fragile states like Somalia and Yemen, isolationist regimes like Myanmar, underdeveloped nations in coastal Africa and oil-rich Arab nations. This generates complexities at various levels. Terrorism and radicalism continue to flourish in Afghanistan and Pakistan. Transnational terrorism emanating from the region has risen steeply and recent terrorist attacks in Mumbai, Jakarta and Pune are grim

The views expressed are those of the author and do not reflect the official policy or position of the Indian Navy or the National Maritime Foundation.

reminders that this threat is far from being contained. Threats to maritime order—piracy, narco-terrorism, gunrunning, smuggling and the like—plague several parts of the littoral, and can suddenly erupt into full-blown crises as coastal states face emerging economic and political challenges. The progressive deterioration of political instability and the collapse of the law and order situation in these littoral states require immediate humanitarian intervention or peacekeeping operations, as is being done in various countries of Africa.

However, as the region is so vast, it has not been possible to frame a commonly accepted and coherent vision of the security challenges in the Indian Ocean littoral. Above all, the region is exposed to natural disasters which seem to recur with alarming regularity. For instance, the Indian Ocean littoral has suffered from some of the worst natural disasters in this millennium—the 2004 Tsunami, the 2005 Pakistan earthquake, the 2006 Indonesian earthquake and the 2008 Cyclone *Nargis* in Myanmar.

The situation in the Pacific Ocean has relatively been more stable than in the Indian Ocean and the regional economy which has always been in a much better shape compared to that of the Indian Ocean region is on the upswing again as the effects of the global economic downturn are slowly, but steadily dissipating. Various mechanisms established for regional and sub-regional economic and security cooperation are progressing smoothly. Remarkable achievements have been made in the ASEAN and ASEAN plus three forums. Cooperation within the framework of the East Asia Summit (EAS) continues to make progress.[4] The Six-Party Talks on the Korean nuclear issue have somewhat softened the hard positions of North Korea and steps are again afoot to bring the country around to recommence the talks.

However, there still exist several underlying issues resulting in insecurity in the Pacific Ocean. The conflicting claims over territorial and maritime rights and interests, particularly in the East and the South China Seas remain serious and complex issues, with no scope for immediate resolution. The fragility of relations between North Korea and South Korea is evident. In November 2009, ships of both countries fired at each other across the northern limiting line (NLL), off the western coast of the peninsula, causing casualties and damage.[5] The two countries again exchanged artillery fire in January 2010, though no casualties were reported. A South Korean warship, the Cheonan was allegedly sunk by a North Korean torpedo near the maritime border on 26 March 2010 resulting in 46 fatalities and the incident was condemned by the United Nations Security Council's Presidential statement.[6] Further, the Taiwan issue remains unresolved despite the improving cross-straits relationship. The uncertainty over the occurrence of maritime and land-based natural disasters also looms large; the havoc caused by the Sichuan earthquake in May 2008 and typhoon Morakot in August 2009 that devastated parts of Taiwan are grim reminders of ever-present dangers.

Maritime Challenges

Areas of Maritime Concern for India

India has a coastline of 7,516.6 km and an exclusive economic zone (EEZ) of 2.013 million sq km.[7] The Andaman and Nicobar Island territories numbering 572 islands are located about 1,300 km from the mainland, and are in fact, much closer to some countries in Southeast Asia. The Indian peninsula juts out into one of the most important energy routes leading from the Suez Canal and Persian Gulf to the Straits of Malacca. These waters have thus, been a focus of constant attention from all actors: state as well as non-state for varied reasons. The Ocean also continues to be characterised by increasing maritime activity of extra-regional navies, mainly on account of their energy security concerns.

Indian energy and trade also largely follows the same sea route. The country's economic prosperity is thus, inseparably coupled with the ability of the Indian maritime security setup to ensure that the sea-lanes are kept free and open at all times. The Indian Navy is required to maintain unhindered connectivity between the mainland and the outlying island territories. It is also responsible for the security of Indian offshore assets, fisheries and deep sea interests within the EEZ, major and minor harbours and of the vast coastline.

The Mumbai terror attacks in November 2008 have added another huge and overriding challenge to the Indian maritime security dimension. It shows how hardened terrorists supported by smugglers, gunrunners, local criminal syndicates and the like, can use seaborne access to carry out their designs. Considerable effort is required to counter this type of threat.

Areas of Maritime Concern for China

There are various maritime challenges in the Western Pacific Ocean. Sovereignty disputes over the Paracel and Spratly islands in the South China Sea keep the security situation simmering here. Multiple parties claim territorial stakes in the Spratly and Paracel islands and the maritime areas surrounding them. The sensitive nature of the issue became evident when the Philippines and China were engaged in a two month-long standoff over the territorial sovereignty rights to Scarborough Shoal in April and May 2012. As the issues involved are quite complex, a legal settlement under the Law of the Seas becomes unfeasible. The involvement of the US which continues to maintain its strategic attention in the Western Pacific region through its military alliances and deployments is yet another matter of concern.[8]

Drivers for Joint Maritime Cooperation

Several governmental initiatives have commenced between India and China, of which the Defence and Security Consultation, the Strategic Dialogue, and the Special Representatives dialogue on the boundary question hold considerable significance. The general commonality between the maritime scenarios in both the oceans and the security challenges facing the two countries provide scope for maritime cooperation within the ambit of the Defence and Security Consultation. An identification of the drivers, which will provide the requisite focus for advancing maritime cooperative initiatives, is therefore, in order.

Collaborative Environment of Regional Stability

The predominance of a favourable maritime security environment in India's and China's immediate neighbourhoods is the most compelling driver for maritime cooperative efforts. The Indian Navy has made an effort to proactively spread this thought process through its initiatives like the *Milan* series of multilateral exercises, the last of which was held at the Andaman Islands in February 2012. The PLA Navy (PLAN) for its part has also engaged in various activities that have sought to provide a stable maritime environment in its own neighbourhood. It has been carrying out joint naval patrols with the Vietnamese Navy in the Beibu Gulf since the signing of the 26 October 2005 agreement,[9] the last being conducted in June 2011. China also signed a bilateral agreement with Japan on 18 June 2008, with the aim of resolving East China Sea territorial issues and making it a "Sea of Peace, Cooperation and Friendship".[10] Similarly, the navies of ASEAN countries are also engaged in security dialogues for enhancing maritime security in the region.

Safety of Seaborne Trade

Since the safety and freedom of each country's seaborne trade is of utmost importance, it can be ensured only through active maritime cooperation bilaterally as also multilaterally. The Indian Navy is the closest available strong naval force of a littoral state in the Indian Ocean Region. It seeks comprehensive maritime security coverage for its own as well as international commercial traffic, transiting the Indian Ocean, in collaborative partnerships with the IOR littorals. Similarly, the security of international sea lanes in the South and East China Seas may primarily rest with the countries located in the Western Pacific Rim, with due support from the countries whose merchant ships transit such sea lanes. Therefore, giving authority and legitimacy to these respective countries would benefit all.

Avenues for Maritime Cooperation

Regional stability and safe SLOCs are the desired ends, as seen from the drivers mentioned above. Since the main energy import routes of both, India and China pass through the Indian Ocean, the safety and security of these energy routes is of paramount importance to both countries, as well as to the other energy dependent nations of East Asia. This aspect therefore presents certain avenues for maritime cooperation and requires further examination.

Safeguarding International Sea Lanes (ISLs)

As the fastest growing Asian country, China has shown reliance on economic development as the bedrock of its intrinsic national strength in the last three decades. The Chinese growth model is energy-intensive and China's oil demand has been growing at more than 5 per cent and though its domestic production in 2009 was 189.4 million tonnes,[11] its dependence on imported crude oil has risen from 8 per cent in 1994 to 48 per cent in 2007,[12] and stands at about 56.5 per cent of its total demand in 2011. Uninterrupted, safe and guaranteed supply of oil and gas has therefore become a serious issue for the Chinese leadership. President Hu Jintao, during a Central Party Economic work committee meeting in 2003, reportedly raised Chinese energy security concerns by stating that more than 80 per cent of China's imported oil passed through the Malacca Strait and that China must actively adopt measures to ensure the security of its energy imports.[13]

This perception has possibly caused China to strengthen the capacity of the PLAN to operate effectively at long distances from its coastline and be in a position to safeguard China's trade and energy lifelines. Chen Mingyi, a member of the National Committee of the Chinese People's Political Consultative Conference, the top political advisory body, articulated this sentiment by stating in March 2009 that "...PLA Navy must move from coastal waters to oceans and shoulder the tasks of safeguarding territory, development of national economy and overseas interests".[14]

Meanwhile, the Indian economy is currently growing at about 7 per cent and could possibly become the third-largest economy after United States and China by mid-century if the present growth pattern is sustained. As the growth is directly related to energy consumption, India's energy demand is expected to rise at an average of 3 to 4 per cent annually over the next two decades. India holds only 0.4 per cent of the world's oil resources by current estimates, and domestic production (mainly offshore), has not been able to offset the growing demand at all. Oil currently accounts for about 36 per cent of India's primary energy supply, and 70 per cent of this demand is sourced from imports. The dependence on oil imports is expected to further increase to 95 per cent (348 out of a projected demand of 368 million tonnes) by 2025.[15] The Middle East at present remains the main source of India's energy imports, with 65 per cent of crude oil coming from this region alone.

The safe transportation of energy from the source to their destinations is the biggest concern of all the heavily energy dependent nations like United States, Japan, China and India. Most of the oil traffic from the Gulf headed towards East and Southeast Asia has to negotiate the three chokepoints in the latter region. While most of the ships go through the Malacca Straits, a few very-large and ultra-large crude carriers (VLCCs and ULCCs) have to transit through the Sunda and Lombok straits. Though incidents of piracy, robbery and maritime terrorism in Southeast Asian waters have been controlled to a large extent on account of the anti-piracy measures initiated by the littoral countries and Western navies, prospects of a rise in such incidents always remain. These littoral countries and others which stand to be severely affected in the event of a crisis cannot therefore, afford to let their guard down as the stakes involved are very high.

While piracy is generally associated with monetary gain, maritime terrorism seeks to make a political statement through premeditated violence perpetrated against non-combatants by sub-national or non-state entities. Groups like the al Qaeda are already engaged in maritime terrorism, and can generally find enough collaborators in organizations like the Jemmah Islamiyah and the Abu Sayaf group which operate in these waters. The sinking of a ship in a narrow strait or the use of a LPG/crude carrier as a bomb in a port or busy waterway are some scenarios which reveal the devastating potential of maritime terrorism.

Avenues for Collaboration—South and Southeast Asian Region

In such a maritime environment, common energy security concerns could therefore, provide the necessary incentives for strengthening cooperation and enhancing regional security networks. All maritime nations, particularly the Asian ones located in and around piracy and terrorism hotspots, should aim to collectivise their efforts by establishing a dialogue to enhance mutual understanding and forming regional institutions for achieving cooperative security. All other nations, who have an interest in the safety and security of international shipping in this region, can of course be taken along as responsible stakeholders. Some cooperative security initiatives are mentioned below.

Malacca and Singapore Straits Safety Mechanism

The 800 km-long Malacca Strait remains the most important maritime link for international trade between the Indian and Pacific Oceans. Any traffic disruption in this passage on account of collision, grounding, pollution, hijacking or terrorist strikes would have disastrous consequences for all countries. It is also known that the capabilities of the littoral states in managing such incidents are quite limited. The main issues involved in ensuring comprehensive security of the straits are thus, the installation and maintenance of modern navigational aids to regulate the ever increasing traffic density and countering piracy, terrorism and other illegal activities. As the task involved in the security and efficient management of this waterway is enormous, it should become a collective regional responsibility of nations comprising the littorals and the regional stakeholders. India and China can find many avenues for cooperation in this mechanism, along with Japan, South Korea and the ASEAN countries.

Previously, Japan, China and India have voluntarily been extending certain financial and other assistance to the littoral states under a cooperative mechanism[16] to enhance navigational safety, security and environmental protection in the Malacca and Singapore Straits. This 'Cooperative Mechanism' provides a platform for dialogue between the littoral and user states, as well as a structured framework for cooperation with the international community. India participated in the third session of the Committee on navigation aid facility fund for the Malacca and Singapore Straits as a user country in April 2009 and offered cooperation in Project 1, which deals with the removal of wrecks/submerged vessels, as well as committed $770,000 in support of Project 4, for the tide, tidal current and wind observation system. China has committed to contribute in projects 2, 4 and 6 of the above 'Cooperative Mechanism'.[17] It has promised to 'train the trainers' in the 'Hazards to Navigational Safety preparedness' as part of a capacity-building programme under Project 2. It has conducted a desktop assessment study for setting up of tidal current and wind observation stations in the Straits under Project 4 and is involved in the replacement of navigational aids damaged by the 2004 Tsunami, under Project 6. India and China could therefore, find adequate common ground within the framework of this 'Cooperative Mechanism' by virtue of being the participating stakeholders. The offer of providing active military assistance by various countries including the RMSI (Regional Maritime Security Initiative) initiative of the United States, for physical security of the strait has however, not been accepted by the Malacca Strait littoral countries. The Malaysian Deputy Prime Minister clearly stated in April 2004 "...In principle, ensuring the security of the Straits of Malacca is the responsibility of Malaysia and Indonesia and for the present we do not propose to invite the United States to join the security operations we have mounted there".[18]

Asian Maritime Partnership

An ambitious concept of '1000 Ship Navy' was mooted by two United States Admirals, in September 2005, wherein a voluntary multinational network of maritime forces would collectively undertake the task of "policing and protecting the maritime commons against a wide spectrum of threats...".[19] While this idea suffered from the expansiveness of its scale and general lack of consensus, the Asian region can actually conceptualise it at a much smaller and localised scale. The concept could be designated as the 'Asian Maritime Partnership'. It would require the regional navies to commit some naval or coast guard assets and resources to the Partnership and undertake the task of collating the integrated maritime domain awareness picture at the respective national data centres and to disseminate the information to all partners. The setting up of two regional data centres, one each for the Indian and the Western Pacific Ocean, with interconnectivity between them could also be considered. Comprehensive discussions and consultations may provide the necessary way ahead for the success of such an initiative. This includes taking due note of obstacles like the differences in legal positions and sovereignty issues.

Anti-Piracy Mission in the Gulf of Aden

The increase in piracy in the Gulf of Aden and off the Somali coast has also caused equal concern to maritime nations about the safety of their mercantile trade coming into the Indian Ocean from the Suez Canal and the Red Sea. Maritime forces of many of these countries have been deployed to stem the scourge. Though some countries are operating under existing groupings such as NATO, Combined Maritime Forces (CMF) and EU, many others are operating individually, albeit towards attainment of the same objective. However, despite the presence of so many navies in the region, piracy in the Gulf of Aden continues unabated. Out of a total of 439 piracy incidents and 45 hijackings in 2011, 237 and 28 respectively were attributed to the Somali pirates.[20]

The Indian Navy has maintained a continuous presence in the Gulf of Aden since October 2008 for anti-piracy missions and the deployed ships have fulfilled their operational roles with much success. The INS Tabar interdicted and sank a pirate mother ship on 18 November 2008. Other Indian Navy ships, their helicopters and marine commandoes have also foiled pirate attacks on 15 occasions. A total of 1,181 ships including 144 Indian flagged and 1037 from different countries, have been escorted by Indian Navy ships.[21] Additional warships are regularly deployed off Seychelles and Mauritius for EEZ patrol, in response to the pirates expanding their area of operations. As of now, Indian Navy warships are still operating on this mission, independent of other groups, and are also cooperating with other countries' ships at a tactical level when required.

The first ever 'out of area' operational mission of the PLAN commenced when an anti-piracy task force consisting of the destroyers Wuhan, Haikou and supply ship Weishanhu set sail on 26 December 2008 from China and arrived off the Somali coast on 6 January 2009. Since then, the PLAN has deployed 12 task forces consisting of two of their modern destroyers/ frigates, and a replenishment ship. A consensus in principle has been reached between China, the EU Naval Force, NATO and CMF at the fifth plenary meeting of the Contact Group on Piracy off the Coast of Somalia, at New York in January 2010.[22] Chinese warships will also reportedly collaborate with the CMF in the Internationally Recommended Transit Corridor (IRTC)[23] in the Gulf of Aden.

The distance from home ports however, is a significant factor for the sustenance of Chinese anti-piracy operations. The PLA naval units take 10 to 13 days to reach the Arabian Sea, depending on their speed of advance and from which base they get deployed. A PLA Navy Admiral therefore, proposed that China should set up a logistics base in the Indian Ocean to support the Chinese naval deployment there[24] . A 2010 article by Shen Dingli also makes a strong case for setting up Chinese military bases overseas, citing the need to enhance its capabilities for safeguarding Chinese overseas interests and prevent possible interdiction of trade routes. [25]

Both India and China are participating in patrolling operations with the same objective of securing their merchant ships against pirate attacks, and those of the other countries, on request. The very fact that the warships of the two countries are operating as part of a large, flexible, multilateral collaboration, is a step forward. It has been observed that whenever a merchant ship has faced a pirate threat and has sought the assistance of a warship, the naval ship(s) nearest to the location of the crisis has/have rendered appropriate assistance, regardless of the nationality, either of the merchant ship or that of the warship(s). It would therefore, not be wrong to presume that similar cooperation would be forthcoming from both sides, in cases related to Chinese or Indian merchant ships, should the situation so warrant.

As the multilateral anti-piracy effort progress, further opportunities for cooperation are likely to become available. An opportunity of this kind actually presented itself on 5 May 2011, when an Indian naval reconnaissance aircraft came to the assistance of a Chinese merchant ship the MV Full City which had been boarded by pirates about 450 nautical miles from the Indian coast. After a prolonged chase of more than three hours, it managed to make the pirates flee the ship, thus rescue the Chinese ship. There could not have been a better example of India-China maritime cooperation and the Chinese were appreciative of this Indian effort.[26]

Humanitarian Assistance, Disaster Relief and Other Benign Activities

Indian Maritime Capabilities and Activities[27]

With inherent attributes of mobility, sustenance, preparedness, reach and sealift capability, the Indian Navy is adequately armed to render timely Humanitarian Assistance and Disaster Relief (HADR) in the immediate aftermath of natural calamities. The Indian Navy has always been at the forefront in providing HADR in the Indian Ocean, whenever called upon to do so. For instance, post-December 2004 Tsunami, 27 Indian Navy ships were employed for a relief mission within the first 12 hours. A total of 36 ships, large numbers of aircraft, and about 5,000 naval personnel were eventually deployed, not only on India's East Coast and Island territories, but also to Sri Lanka, Maldives and Indonesia. Other instances have been the provision of large scale disaster relief to Bangladesh, post Cyclone *Sidr* in 2007 and to Myanmar post Cyclone *Nargis* in 2008.

In addition to HADR assistance, Indian naval forces have been providing other forms of assistance to Indian civil authorities during floods and other unforeseen adversities. These include maintenance of law and order, manning of essential services and diving assistance. The Indian Navy is also capable and willing to provide various forms of assistance to local and foreign government within the larger ambit of HADR/aid to civil authorities, during natural or manmade crisis situations. These include the handling of administration and logistics, medical relief, sea transportation, hydrographic survey support and search and rescue operations.

Chinese Maritime Capabilities and Activities

China similarly has had its own share of natural disasters and has managed to mount a credible, timely and appropriate response to them in the recent past. The Central Military Commission (CMC) issued a document titled

'Master Scenario for Emergency Response' in November 2006,[28] which orders all PLA units to take immediate action on occurrence of a disaster and simultaneously report to the higher authorities. China had to grapple with the colossal task of providing humanitarian assistance and handling the disaster relief in the aftermath of the May 2008 Sichuan earthquake. The Chinese defence forces played a major role in the successful conduct of the entire operation and learnt useful lessons in disaster management. More than 140,000 troops, military transport aircraft, helicopters and medical teams with over 2,160 doctors were engaged in the rescue work. The coastal areas of China and the other states in the Western Pacific have also been regularly devastated by typhoons and the various government organizations of China like the State Bureau of Surveying and Mapping, Ministries of Public Security and Health have developed certain expertise and capabilities in dealing with such disasters.

The existing sea-lift capabilities of the PLAN have been augmented by the commissioning of the *Yuzhao* class large platform dock ships,. The PLAN has also inducted a modern hospital ship the Peace Ark, which is a very important resource in providing medical relief in the post-calamity environment. The ship in fact, sailed in August 2010 on a three month-long 'Mission Harmony' to the Indian Ocean followed by an equally long trans-Pacific voyage to Latin American and Carribean nations in September 2011.[29] The Chinese Ministry of National Defense also hosted the first non-traditional security forum of the armed forces of the ASEAN, China, Japan and the ROK in June 2009[30] to build a better understanding of non-traditional threats to the Asia-Pacific Region.

Avenues for Cooperation

The possibilities of synergistically utilising the combined capacities and capabilities of the two countries for 'out of area' HADR missions, the need for which may arise without any forewarning, can be explored through mutual agreement. China could help by conducting training courses on disaster relief and non-traditional challenges for the Indian Navy and other maritime forces of the Indian Ocean Region, as was done for the Asia-Pacific Region. The PLAN's hospital ship management could also be publicised for possible emulation and each country's experiences and lessons learnt during HADR operations may be shared for imbibing best practices.

Enhancing Ongoing Naval Cooperation

Sino-Indian relations have the potential to develop manifold as all the necessary ingredients are present. Both countries are growing at a reasonable pace, have similar aspirations, a common set of social development challenges, and the same vision of comprehensive national growth. To complement this potential, the security establishments of both countries must engage more often, in order to build up confidence levels required for taking up the larger cooperative issues mentioned above. Some of these maritime domain activities that can be undertaken or enhanced include information connectivity, port calls by naval ships and interactions ashore, and joint maritime exercises.

Maritime information sharing related to non-traditional challenges will enable the two countries to combat challenges like piracy, gunrunning, human trafficking and drug smuggling. An integrated picture built on the basis of intelligence, surveillance and reconnaissance could also help in locating the source of more sinister activities like transnational terrorism and the transit of WMD—tracking their movement through the oceans, identifying and finally interdicting them at an opportune moment. This information could also be helpful if shared partially with civil agencies set up to forewarn against impending natural calamities and conducting search and rescue at sea.

The Indian Navy and the PLAN ships have been regularly calling on each other's ports and naval bases since the start of the millennium. Indian naval ships visited China in September 2000, November 2003 and April 2007 and Indian warships also participated in the International Fleet Review in April 2009 at Qingdao, Headquarters of the PLA Navy's Northern Fleet. Similarly, two PLAN ships called in at Kochi port in December 2005 and carried out various onshore interaction activities with the Indian Navy, which included the visit to Indian Naval ships, 'call on' by senior naval officers of both sides as well as sporting fixtures. A missile destroyer, the Shenzhen, docked at Kochi in August 2009, on the conclusion of its anti-piracy patrol in the Gulf of Aden. The Chinese naval training ship Zheng He also visited Kochi in May 2012 as part of its global circumnavigation voyage. Such occasions will facilitate greater navy-to-navy interactions and enable the two navies to locate and explore common grounds at the operating level.

During June 2012, a group of Indian Eastern Fleet ships visited Shanghai, while returning from their long range operational deployment to the Western Pacific. They carried out joint communication drills, station-keeping, SAR (Search and Rescue) and helicopter landing exercises with the PLAN ships. The scope of these exercises could perhaps be expanded gradually. The success of the two initiatives of joint anti-terrorism exercises between the Indian Army and the PLA ground forces should be built upon and extended into the maritime dimension also. The significance of anti-terror maritime exercises as part of the preparedness for countering seaborne terror attacks such as Mumbai 2008 also needs to be taken into account.

Conclusion

The size of their economies, recent growth profiles, strategic trade interests and the current security environments of both India and China form the common grounds for shaping their respective policy directions. Both countries must therefore, explore cooperative avenues which will enable the achievement of common goals, while economising on national security resources. While the ongoing economic engagements, people-to-people contacts and cultural interactions will bring the two countries close to a large extent, convergence of the security establishments will further supplement the process.

As India and China tentatively embark on a cooperative journey, the above-mentioned avenues for maritime cooperation will certainly provide a worthwhile route for exploration. It is pertinent to note that all cooperative ventures commence initially with benign and non-intrusive measures. The scale and scope of subsequent cooperation may be increased and expanded on the basis of experience gained and lessons learnt.

A synergistic relationship combining the will of political, economic and security establishments from both countries stands a better chance of furthering convergence between India and China. While there is adequate interaction on the political and economic realms, due attention to building security relationships will also prove to be beneficial to Sino-Indian engagement and especially so in the maritime field.

NOTES

1. Integrated Headquarters of Ministry of Defence (Navy), *Indian Maritime Doctrine 2009*, August 2009, p. 56.
2. Vice President of India, "Address of the Hon'ble Vice President of India Shri M. Hamid Ansari at the IONS Seminar 2008", Vigyan Bhavan, New Delhi, 15 February 2008, http://vicepresidentofindia.nic.in/content.asp?id=135.
3. Ibid.
4. Ministry of National Defense of People's Republic of China, "Chapter I: The Security Situation", *White Paper on China's National Defense in 2010*, http://news.xinhuanet.com/ english/2009-04/23/content_11239423.htm.
5. *CNN*, "Korean navies exchange fire", 10 November 2009, http://edition.cnn.com/ 2009/WORLD/ asiapcf/11/10/koreas.naval.clash/index.html.
6. United Nations Security Council, "Security Council condemns attack on Republic of Korea Naval Ship 'Cheonan': Stresses need to prevent further attacks, other hostilities in region", SC/9975, 9 July 2010, http://www.un.org/News/Press/ docs/2010/sc9975.doc.htm.
7. Integrated Headquarters of Ministry of Defence (Navy), *Freedom to Use the Seas: India's Maritime Military Strategy*, May 2007, Chapter 5, p. 57.

8. *White Paper on China's National Defense in 2010*, op. cit., Section I: "The Security Situation"
9. Ministry of National Defence of Peoples Republic of China, "Chinese navy ships to participate in Sino-Vietnamese joint patrol in Beibu Gulf", 2 December 2009, http://eng.mod.gov.cn/DefenseNews/ 2009-12/02/content_4108731.htm.
10. Ministry of Foreign Affairs of Japan, '"Joint Press Conference by Minister for Foreign Affairs Masahiko Koumura and Minister of Economy, Trade and Industry Akira Amari (Regarding Cooperation between Japan and China in the East China Sea)", 18 June 2008, http://www.mofa.go.jp/announce/fm_press/ 2008/6/0618.html. The original copy of the press conference is in Japanese. The English translation on the website is by an external agency.
11. *People's Daily*, "China's oil production ranks 4th in world, only meets half domestic demand", 9 February 2010, http://english.peopledaily.com.cn/90001/90778/ 90860/6891500.html.
12. Vellucci Jr., Frederic, "Extending the First Line of Defence: China's Naval Strategy and Development Prospects", in *PLA Navy Build up and ROK Navy-US Navy Cooperation*, Korean Institute for Maritime Strategy, June 2009, pp. 237-285, 267.
13. *Ibid*., p. 267.
14. *China.org.cn*, "Chinese navy urged to go from coastal waters to oceans," 7 March 2009, http://www.china.org.cn/government/NPC_CPPCC_2009/2009-03/07/ content_17397799.htm.
15. *Freedom to Use the Seas: India's Maritime Military Strategy*, op. cit., Chapter 4, p. 49.
16. International Maritime Organisation, "Milestone agreement reached on co-operation over the Straits of Malacca and Singapore", *Briefing* 29/2007, 18 September 2007, http://www.imo.org/Newsroom/mainframe.asp?topic_id=1472& doc_id =8471.
17. This information has been extracted from Yuri Gunadi, Muhammad Razif bin Ahmad, Yee Cheok Hong (Project Co-ordination Committee), "Projects 1-6: Co-Operative Mechanism", 24 November 2008; http://www.nippon-foundation.or.jp/ eng/current/malacca_sympo/8_1.ppt. This was a presentation by representatives from Malaysia, Indonesia and Singapore.
18. Mark Baker, "Malaysia rebuffs US sea force plan", *Age*, 6 April 2004, http:// www.theage.com.au/ articles/2004/04/05/1081017102019.html.
19. The proposal was made by Admirals John Morgan and Charles Martoglio at the International Sea Power Symposium at Rhode Island. See Stephen Saunders, "Executive Overview: Jane's Fighting Ships", *Jane's Fighting Ships*, 2005, http:// www.janes.com/defence/ naval_forces/news/jfs/jfs060612_1_n.shtml.
20. ICC Commercial Crime Services, "Piracy attacks in East and West Africa dominate world report', 19 January 2012, http://www.icc-ccs.org/news/711-piracy-attacks-in-east-and-west-africa-dominate-world-report
21. Indian Navy, "Anti Piracy Operations", http://indiannavy.nic.in/AntiPiracy.htm.
22. Maritime Safety Administration of PRC, "Principled consensus on escort missions reached between China, EU, NATO, CMF, 30 January 2010, http://en.msa.gov.cn/ msa/features/root/02/1243216520339/ 1265265572484.
23. The International Maritime Organisation endorsed the Internationally Recommended Transit Corridor (IRTC) for use by mariners passing the Gulf of Aden area vide IMO circular Ref. T2-OSS/2.7.1, dated 3 August 2009. International Maritime Organisation, http://www.imo.org/includes/blastDataOnly.asp/ data_id=26251/281.pdf.
24. The proposal was made by Rear Admiral Yin Zhuo, a senior researcher at the PLA Navy's Equipment Research Center. See *Reuters*, "Chinese admiral floats idea of

overseas naval bases, 30 December 2009, http://www.reuters.com/article/idUSTRE 5BT0P020091230. The Chinese transcript along with the English translation is available at http://www.accn.com/?action-viewthread-tid-214672.

25. Shen Dingli, "Don't shun the idea of setting up overseas military bases", *China.org.cn*, 28 January 2010, http://www.china.org.cn/opinion/2010-01/28/content_19324522.htm.
26. See Kamlesh K. Agnihotri, "Protection of Trade and Energy Supplies in the Indian Ocean Region," *Maritime Affairs*, Vol.8, No.1, 2012, p. 22.
27. *Indian Maritime Doctrine 2009*, op.cit., Chapter 7, pp. 120-22.
28. *White Paper on China's National Defense in 2008*, op.cit., "Section X-The Armed Forces and the People".
29. *People's Daily*, "China's 'Peace Ark' on its way home", 20 December 2011, http://english.peopledaily.com.cn/90882/7682331.html.
30. Ministry of National Defence of Peoples Republic of China, "First non-traditional security forum of armed forces of ASEAN, China, Japan and ROK held", 10 June 2009, http://eng.mod.gov.cn/ MiltaryExchanges/2009-06/10/content_4002977.htm.

9

Terrorism in South Asia and the Counter-Terrorism Cooperation between China and India

Maj. Gen. (Retd) Gong Xianfu

Counter-terrorism cooperation between China and India is a very important area for the two states to push forward their friendly relations in the new century. In recent years, global terrorist activities have been converging on South Asia, which has become the hardest-hit region—the "source" and "hotbed" of the international terrorist attacks. Governments of South Asian countries have adopted various measures to intensify their crackdown on terrorist activities and tried to maintain the social stability within their nations. Since 2009, India, Sri Lanka and Bangladesh have achieved some progress in their counter-terrorist efforts, and terrorist activities have lost some momentum in these countries. However, the Afghan government is very weak in controlling the political situation in the country, Pakistan is beset by internal and external difficulties, and the US led Af-Pak strategy has not yielded significant results. So far, the Taliban in both Pakistan and Afghanistan have continued to carry out their militant activities. The fight between terrorism and counter-terrorism is still very fierce. China and India share common interests in maintaining peace and stability in South Asia, and have great stakes in combating terrorism in the region, which demands that the two states strengthen their counter-terrorist cooperation in this regard.

Main Features of Current Terrorist Activities in South Asia

In recent years, the frequency of violent terrorist attacks has remained high in the South Asian region due to unstable domestic situations, weak government control and the impact of underlying ethnic and religious tensions. The Pakistan-Afghanistan border areas have become the main bases for terrorist organizations such as al Qaeda, the Taliban and the Islamic Movement of Uzbekistan. Terrorist activities in South Asia have presented the following characteristics.

First, South Asia has become the most important centre of terrorist activities in the world. The terrorist activities in this region have remained large in number and scale, with the tendency of localization and close collaboration through regional networks. According to the statistics of the Counter-Terrorism Research Center of the China Institute for International Strategic Studies[1], the year 2009 witnessed 404 terrorist attacks in South Asia, accounting for 46 per cent of the world's total, resulting in 2,460 deaths and 4,230 injuries. Among them, there are 17 deadly terrorist attacks causing over 100 casualties each. As of 31 March 2010, the world had seen another 145 terrorist incidents, causing 803 deaths and 1,563 injuries. 81 of these terrorist incidents had taken place in South Asia, making up 58 per cent of the world's total. At the same time, terrorist activities have become more localized. The Taliban in Afghanistan has staged a comeback, with its activities spreading again to a large part of Afghan territory. The Pakistan Taliban has bounced back dramatically, launching major terrorist attacks one after another in the heartland of the country. The terrorist organization, Lashkar-e-Taiba, in the Indian-controlled Kashmir region, has seen its capabilities to launch terrorist activities being greatly enhanced. The trend of Talibanization in both Afghanistan and Pakistan, the regionalization of the Taliban and the localization of the Indian terrorist groups are becoming more prominent.

Further, terrorists have strengthened their collaboration through regional networks. Terrorist organizations in South Asia have collaborated more closely with each other and formed regional networks across Afghanistan, Pakistan, India, Bangladesh and other countries. They have also joined hands with other international terrorist forces like al Qaeda, receiving funds from the Middle East, recruiting personnel from Central Asia, and thus forming the bases of international terrorist activities. The Lashkar-e-Taiba has set up affiliates in India, Afghanistan and Bangladesh, and has evolved from a jihad organization in India-controlled Kashmir, into a regional terrorist organization with the range of activities expanding to the surrounding areas.

Second, terrorist activities in South Asia have demonstrated the vicious effect of spillovers. Following the beginning of the Afghanistan War in 2001, al Qaeda has suffered great setbacks in its overall operational capabilities. Especially from 2009 up to now, the parties involved have stepped up mop-up operations against terrorist organizations in Afghanistan and Pakistan. Under such circumstances, terrorist activities in Afghanistan and Pakistan have shown a higher degree of the spillover effect, mainly demonstrated in the following two aspects. Firstly, the activities of the al Qaeda have become more covert and it pays more attention to exporting its action mode and terrorist ideology. The core circle of al Qaeda has speeded up working hand in glove with the local extremist forces in Afghanistan and Pakistan. The Haqqani network in Afghanistan, the Lashkar-e-Taiba in Indian-controlled Kashmir and the Pakistani Taliban are becoming increasingly interwoven and symbiotic by providing more support to each other. Some terrorist forces have aligned or affiliated themselves with al Qaeda as its branches, creating terrorist networks spanning over 70 countries around the world. For example, the Iraqi al Qaeda was founded in September 2004 and the al Qaeda in the Islamic Maghreb in Northern Africa was established in September 2006. Moreover, al Qaeda is also making better use of the Internet to spread and export terrorism and extremist ideology.

Next, terrorist organizations like the Islamic Movement of Uzbekistan (IMU) entrenched in the region have begun to withdraw from the region and are going back to Central Asia to carry out terrorist activities there. Since 2009, when the United States and Pakistan intensified their counter-terrorism operations, terrorist groups entrenched in Afghanistan and Pakistan have felt the pressure and started to move to other regions in order to avoid the crackdown and retain their strength. The IMU, which has been active in South Asia in recent years, has started to manoeuvre into the border region between Afghanistan and Tajikistan and re-infiltrate into Central Asia. Marked by the violent attack on police officers that happened in the Andizhan province of Uzbekistan on 26 May 2009, the three evil forces (terrorism, secessionism and extremism) are becoming more active in Central Asia. In 2009, there were five terrorist incidents within Uzbekistan alone. Since June 2009, Uzbekistan, Tajikistan and Kyrgyzstan have conducted several large-scale counter-terrorism operations and captured a number of members of the IMU and other terrorist organizations. The police of Kyrgyzstan have killed and rounded up more than 50 terrorists of the IMU and other terrorist organizations. In August 2009, the police of Tajikistan killed 11 terrorists and arrested another 30 of the IMU, and seized one ammunition storehouse in a military operation. The IMU is now trying to take advantage of the complicated terrain and the weak control of the border areas between Tajikistan and Afghanistan to infiltrate into the heartland of the Central Asia. It is preparing to establish bases in the east part of Tajikistan to aid its retreating members from the tribal areas along Afghanistan-Pakistan border, to use Tajikistan as the transit station and to set up underground transport networks to Kyrgyzstan, Uzbekistan and other countries. The latest turmoil in Kyrgyzstan will be deemed as a very good opportunity by terrorist organizations to expand their activities in Central Asia.

In addition, due to geographical, ethnic and economic reasons, many young people are being recruited by terrorist organizations to receive terrorist training in the border areas between Afghanistan and Pakistan. Once these young people return to Central Asia, they will form the backbone of forces used to carry out terrorist activities. According to reliable sources, the trend of foreign terrorists in South Asia is becoming more obvious.[2] Should terrorist forces support each other and coordinate their activities, a new round of integration and regrouping may take place, which will subject the regional security situation to serious challenges.

Third, fidayeen-type attacks have become the main pattern of terrorist activities and terrorist methods are getting more sophisticated. Since the 26/11 terrorist attacks in Mumbai in 2008, attacks similar to a fidayeen pattern and characterized by careful planning and multi-pronged and well-coordinated small-group attacks causing widespread devastation and destruction have become the first choice of terrorists. In 2009, most terrorist attacks with big casualties in South Asia were fidayeen-type ones. Out of the 19 massive terrorist attacks, 13 were fidayeen-type attacks, making up 70 per cent of the total, which include the 11/2 armed attack on Kabul, 3/3 attack against the Sri Lankan cricket team in Lahore, 30/3 attack on the Lahore police school, 27/5 attack on the Lahore police department, and the 10/10 attack on the Pakistani Army headquarters. In these terrorist attacks, terrorists demonstrated skill and tactics such as good coordination, successful breaking-through of defences, and multi-pronged assaults. For instance, in both cases of terrorist attacks on the Lahore police school on 30 March and on Pakistani Army headquarters on 10 October, terrorists launched a surprise assault at the entrances, created chaos and simultaneously divided themselves into several small groups to occupy strongholds and hijack hostages to confront the security forces. When surrounded and cornered they resorted to suicide by detonating explosives strapped to them. What merits more attention is that while the fidayeen-type attacks are increasingly directed against the important government and military facilities, more and more attacks are also being conducted against the living quarters of military personnel around military targets. In the deadly 10/10 terrorist attacks on the Pakistani Army headquarters and the 15/10 attacks on the police, terrorists disguised themselves as policemen and suddenly assaulted the heavily-guarded military places by employing various means. Terrorist activities in South Asia have proved that it will be very difficult to prevent fidayeen-type terrorist attacks.

Trend of Terrorist Activities in South Asia

The high occurrence of terrorist activities in South Asia has become the focus of concern for the international community. Of late, the counter-terrorism situation in South Asia has undergone some important changes in its dynamics. The United States has stepped up the implementation of the new Afghanistan strategy and will send an additional 30,000 troops. Since the start of the "joint actions" in mid-February 2010, the military forces of the United States, NATO and Afghanistan have captured Marja, an important stronghold of the Taliban, holding back the momentum of a rebounding Taliban. The coalition forces have launched the "Kandahar cooperation" offensive operations against the Taliban in the areas surrounding Kandahar since 1 September 2010, targeting the core of the Taliban, in an attempt to put the insurgency in the southern part of Afghanistan to an end. At the same time, the United States has induced and coerced Pakistan to cooperate with its counter-terrorism campaign. Although it is not allowed to deploy troops on Pakistani territory to carry out counter-terrorism activities, it has intensified its strikes against terrorists with unmanned aircraft along the border areas between Afghanistan and Pakistan. Since the beginning of last year, Pakistan has expanded the range of its counter-terrorism targets, not only hitting the Pakistan Taliban but also striking the ringleaders of the Afghan Taliban and al Qaeda within Pakistan. It has successively captured several heavyweight figures including Mullah Baradar, the No. 2 leader of the Afghan Taliban. Simultaneously, Pakistan has stepped up mopping up operations against militants of the Pakistan Taliban within the country. After cleaning up the Taliban militants in the tribal areas of Southern Waziristan at the end of 2009, it has ended its operations in the tribal areas of Bajaur in March and killed Maulana Faqir Mohammed, the ringleader of the region. Additionally, India has thwarted several plots of terrorist attacks, Bangladesh is engaging in cleaning up the religious extremist forces in the country and Sri Lanka has taken tight precautions against terrorist attacks by the remnants of the Tamil Tigers. These new developments are conducive to weakening the capabilities of terrorist groups to carry out terrorist activities.

However, on the whole, the rampant terrorist activities in South Asia cannot be held in check in a short time. On the one hand, although terrorist organizations in the region have suffered some losses, they will not stop their terrorist activities easily. As a matter of fact, they will try to seek every opportunity to take revenge by launching more terrorist attacks. Terrorist attacks happened one after another in Jaipur of India on 13 February 2010, in Kabul on 26 February 2010 and Kandahar of Afghanistan and in Lahore of Pakistan on the same day of 13 March 2010. These attacks demonstrated that terrorist organizations in South Asia will continue or even intensify their attacks.

Supporting this trend is the fact that regional counter-terrorism efforts are handicapped in various ways. First, the effectiveness of Pakistani counter-terrorism operations remains to be seen. Since April 2009, the Pakistani military has been carrying out cleanup operations against terrorists in the Swat area, containing the momentum of the Pakistan Taliban expanding to the interior of the country. So far, the Pakistani military has ousted militants of Pakistan Taliban in South Waziristan and killed some important figures. But judging from actual results of counter-terrorism operations of the Pakistani military, it killed or captured only a very limited number of terrorists. The majority of their effective strength in Pakistan has actually been preserved and transferred to other places. The supremacy of the Pakistani military does not automatically mean it can take the initiative in the fight against terrorists in the battlefield. The effectiveness of its combat against terrorists seems doubtful because it is also restrained by factors other than the military, namely those of a political, economic and social nature. After the removal of President Musharraf, the democratically-elected Pakistan coalition government has been weak and troubled by internal strife, which hinders counter-terrorism efforts in the country.

Second, the American counter-terrorism strategy in South Asia has not produced substantive results and is still facing numerous difficulties. Since the US introduced the new Af-Pak strategy in March 2009, the political reconciliation process has been proceeding very slowly. Terrorist activities there have rebounded dramatically, American military casualties have been growing and the anti-war voices of the American people are getting stronger. Under such circumstances, the Obama administration is being forced to readjust the strategy with the hope of reducing the burden of the American troops and ridding themselves of the predicament. But whether the readjusted strategy can achieve good results or not still remains to be seen.

The goal of realizing internal stability in Afghanistan is still not in sight. The efficiency of the American military operations in Afghanistan is limited by the difficult terrain there. It is no easy job to eliminate al Qaeda in such a short period of time and given that the Taliban mingle easily with the Afghan populace. Furthermore, the number and quality of the Afghan security forces cannot be greatly improved in such little time to shoulder heavy responsibilities effectively. The Obama administration has urged the international community to increase its inputs in Afghanistan to relieve the American burden. But it is obvious that the reliance on outside help to combat terrorists in Afghanistan is a one-sided wish of the US because most countries have their own considerations on the Afghan issue, and have no intention of helping the US, in order to preserve American interests. Washington's new strategy needs to gain the respect of and utilize coordination from countries in the region.

However, there are different or even opposing stances between the United States and the Afghanistan's neighbours, and so the new strategy faces an uncertain future. The United States expects the countries in Central Asia to assist in addressing the protracted Afghanistan issue, especially protecting the transport of supplies for the US and NATO forces in Afghanistan. This transportation line becomes extremely important given the frequent attacks on the important lines passing through Pakistan. The only military base in Central Asia that the US uses to station its forces and materials for the fight in Afghanistan is the Transit Center at Manas International Airport in Kyrgyzstan. Presently, Kyrgyzstan has been thrown into turmoil because of the internal struggle in that country. The change of government there has made no change over the use of the Transit Center at the Manas International Airport by the United States though, Russia has always been pressuring Kyrgyzstan to close the Manas air base and renovate its own Kant airbase, 30 kms outside the capital Bishkek. Meanwhile, Iran is becoming increasingly influential in the changing situation in Afghanistan and Central Asia. Iran shares a long frontier with Afghanistan and the Tajik people living in Afghanistan have the same origins as the Persians. These conditions make it conducive for Iran to influence Afghanistan. The Afghanistan situation has become an important bargaining chip for Iran to handle its relationship with the US.

Nevertheless, it is not easy to achieve the goal of letting the Afghans run Afghanistan effectively in a short time. The country is desperately poor and divided into many tribes. No previous Afghan central government has exercised effective control over the entire country. Karzai got less than 50 per cent votes in the first round of presidential election last year, so the run-off election was needed. Because of the withdrawal from the second round election by his rival candidate, Karzai won the presidency. Therefore, it will not be easy for him to realize national reconciliation. In a nutshell, the security situation in Afghanistan cannot be improved in the short run, and the hotbed that breeds terrorism in South Asia will, unfortunately, continue to exist for a long time.

Third, the two most important states in the South Asian sub-continent,

India and Pakistan have remained in a stalemate in their peace talks and have more often than not, blamed each other for the counter-terrorism issues in the region. In addition, they are also pursuing different strategies towards Afghanistan and have got their own supporters in that country. This has not only hindered the improvement of their bilateral relations, but also has weakened or jeopardized the concerted counter-terrorism efforts in the region.

Fourth, there are serious and complicated ethnic and religious conflicts in these countries. Terrorist activities can easily be deemed as aimed at certain ethnic and religious groups, thus aggravating or even triggering large-scale violence between different ethnic and religious groups. For example, if a Muslim terrorist in India commits a terrorist attack and that attack, by chance, is against Hindus, it will be regarded as Muslims attacking Hindus or vice versa. From the above analysis, we can surely say that terrorist activities in South Asia will remain frequent and the possibilities of intensification in some areas cannot be ruled out for a period of time to come.

Implications of Terrorist Activities in South Asia

Terrorist activities in South Asia have multi-faceted implications for the region and the world at large, which is mainly manifested in the following:

First, terrorist activities have caused great losses of lives and properties in South Asian nations. According to the statistics of the counter-terrorism research centre of the China Institute for International Strategic Studies, in 2008, more than 400 terrorist incidents occurred in South Asia, leaving more than 2,500 dead and 4,700 injured. The year 2009 saw very similar statistics as specified earlier in this essay. The series of terrorist attacks in Mumbai in November 2008 alone had left 174 people dead and 300 more injured, as well as caused tens of millions US dollars in property losses.[3] All these figures of casualties have proved the serious destructiveness of terrorist attacks in the region.

Second, because of the destructiveness and the effect on common people, terrorist activities usually create instability and even chaos in society, thus jeopardizing the political stability of the country. Moreover, there are many different ethnic and religious groups in the South Asian countries. Terrorist organizations in the region have always made use of conflicts among different ethnic and religious groups to their advantage, deliberately carrying out terrorist attacks aimed at aggravating the existing conflicts among different ethnic and religious groups, and instigating them to conduct more violent retaliations against each other. For instance, the Lal Masjid incident in July 2007 aroused great indignation among Muslims throughout Pakistan and brought about widespread violence in the country. The assassination of Benazir Bhutto in December 2007 resulted in internal political upheaval, leading to the resignation of Pakistani President, Pervez Musharraf.

Third, against the backdrop of the complicated relations between countries in the region, some terrorist activities have been aimed at sowing the seeds of discord and sabotaging relations, especially between India and Pakistan. These two countries are the largest and second largest states respectively in the South Asian subcontinent, with a total population of over 1.25 billion. The two countries have been at loggerheads with each other since their independence and have already fought three wars against each other. Terrorist groups in the region do not want to see a peaceful and stable South Asia and try to seek gains from the tensions between these two countries. Their activities have in fact, contributed to worsening relations between India and Pakistan. During the period between 2001 and 2002, India and Pakistan deployed hundreds of thousands of troops along their common border in a serious confrontation because of their disputes over terrorist attacks. However, due to joint efforts from both countries and thanks to the vigorous push by the international community, there was a remarkable improvement of their relationship by 2008. Thereafter, however, the massive terrorist attacks in Mumbai in November 2008 once again threw the two states into serious confrontation. India claimed that some terrorists launched attacks in Mumbai from Pakistani waters and acquired the necessary evidence to show that those terrorists were closely related to Pakistan. Subsequently, the process of reconciliation between the two sides stalled bringing the two nations to the verge of military conflict, which is the exact result terrorist organizations in the region want to see.

Fourth, the spillover of terrorist activities in South Asia is evident in surrounding regions and many other parts of the world as well. China, as a neighbouring country of South Asia, has suffered a lot from terrorists related to organizations like al Qaeda, Afghanistan Taliban and Pakistan Taliban. The terrorist organization East Turkistan Islamic Movement (ETIM) is supported and funded by al Qaeda and Taliban in one way or another. Some of its members were trained in Afghanistan and on the Pakistani side of the Pakistan and Afghanistan border area by al Qaeda and Taliban. This terrorist organization has sent terrorists into China and masterminded terrorist attacks mainly in Xinjiang Uygur Autonomous Region time and again. In late July 2008, just before the Beijing Olympic Games, a woman terrorist boarded a Chinese Airliner from Pakistan to Xinjiang and plotted unsuccessfully to blow up the plane with gasoline. According to a news report of the *Xinhua News Agency*, following the violent of the terrorist incident on 5 July 2009 in the Xinjiang capital of Urumqi, in which 197 people were killed, over 1,700 people were injured, more than 600 vehicles destroyed,[4] terrorist organizations outside China like the ETIM issued orders to followers in China to carry out "jihad". Similarly in Central Asia, terrorist organizations like the IMU, as stated above, have infiltrated into the region and launched many terrorist attacks in the Central Asian countries. Following the continuous heavy crackdown by the US military on its cell in Iraq in 2008, al Qaeda began to smuggle its personnel into Yemen and Lebanon and increased their terrorist activities. Al Qaeda also set up terrorist training camps in countries in the Horn of Africa like Ethiopia, Eritrea and Somalia. Muslim extremists recruited around the world were trained in these camps and then sent to Europe to launch terrorist attacks at an opportune time. Therefore, the international community is very concerned over terrorist activities in South Asia and the vicious spillover effect in other parts of the world.

Counter-terrorism Cooperation between China and India

China and India are two close neighbours and two ancient countries with a long history and great civilizations. Generally speaking, the two nations have maintained good neighbourly and friendly relations during their long history of intercourse. In the new international situation and economic globalization, as the two largest developing countries, both China and India are facing similar opportunities and challenges in developing themselves into a modern and prosperous country. It is the strategic choice of the two nations to forge a new relationship of friendly cooperation in the new century. China and India have as a result in recent years, continuously improved their relations with bilateral exchanges and cooperation greatly enhanced in the fields of politics, economy and trade, military affairs, science and technology, and culture.

In the field of counter-terrorism, China and India have many things in common. Both countries are the victims of terrorist activities in recent years and have great stakes in peace and stability of this region. The two nations have already engaged in some form of counter-terrorism cooperation, such as joint military exercises. But in the long run, China and India should make more efforts to strengthen their counter-terrorism cooperation, which is not only in the interests of the two nations, but also conducive to the peace and stability in the region and the world at large. The two states can learn from the counter-terrorism experiences of the Shanghai Cooperation Organization and think of expanding their counter-terrorism cooperation.

The Shanghai Cooperation Organization has enjoyed sound and

effective cooperation in combating terrorism in many ways. It has established a joint counter-terrorism team in Bishkek, conducted a series of joint counter-terrorism exercises, reached an agreement on the standard procedures for holding regular joint counter-terrorism exercises, set up mechanisms for consultation and intelligence sharing and so on. Possible areas of counter-terrorism cooperation between China and India are as follows:

First, the two sides could establish some kind of information-sharing mechanism on terrorist activities in the region. This could be done either through Track I official exchanges and visits at various levels or through Track II academic exchanges. On the official side, China has adopted various measures to intensify counter-terrorism efforts such as establishing a national counter-terrorism leading group headed by the minister of public security, under which the counter-terrorism office works to coordinate all counter-terrorism activities (including intelligence gathering, early warning, incident prevention and international cooperation). On the academic side, China has dozens of influential research institutions who are engaging in counter-terrorism studies. For example, the China Institute for International Strategic Studies has specifically set up a counter-terrorism research centre. Certainly, there are such centres in India. Therefore, some kind of counter-terrorism information sharing mechanism could be worked out through consultation or an agreement reached between the two governments.

Second, the two sides could exchange their experiences in combating terrorism in various fields and in protecting different facilities. Terrorist organization such as the ETIM, influenced by the three evil forces of extremism, separatism and terrorism, have carried out a number of terrorist attacks in Xinjiang and other places in China, but many of their plots to launch terrorist attacks have been foiled by Chinese security departments. Before and during the Beijing Olympic Games, various terrorist organizations outside China had conspired to sabotage the Olympic Games by launching terrorist attacks, but China succeeded in making the Olympic Games a most successful one without any terrorist incident. Through these counter-terrorism efforts, China has accumulated a lot of useful experiences. India too has its own valuable experiences in fighting terrorism. The two sides could therefore, exchange their counter-terrorism experiences and learn from each other either through official channels or by way of seminars among experts.

Third, the two sides could increase and deepen joint counter-terrorism exercises and explore ways to conduct a joint crackdown on terrorists when necessary. In recent years, the naval forces of the countries have conducted several joint training exercises in the Pacific Ocean and Indian Ocean. In 2007 and 2008, the two armies conducted two joint counter-terrorism exercises. Joint exercises held by the countries of the Shanghai Cooperation Organization are good examples of such cooperation. By learning from the experiences of joint exercises among SCO countries, China and India can work out a plan for more substantial joint counter-terrorism exercises in future. The two sides could proceed from easier ones and gradually expand and deepen joint counter-terrorism exercises. For that, some kind of road map will be desirable. This could be put into the agenda of future defence and security consultations between the two militaries.

NOTES

1. The Counter-terrorism Research Center of the China Institute for International Strategic Studies (CIISS) is one of the four research centers of the Institute. The other three are: Research Center for Arms Control and Disarmament, Research Center for Security Strategy and Research Center for Asia-Pacific Security.
2. These sources include the intelligence agencies of the Central Asian countries.
3. *Telegraph*, "Mumbai attacks: 300 feared dead as full horror of the terrorist attacks emerges", 29 November 2008, http://www.telegraph.co.uk/news/3536220/Mumbai-siege-300-feared-dead-as-full-horror-of-the-terrorist-attacks-emerges.html.
4. *Xinhua*, "Number of injured in Urumqi riot increases to 1,680", 12 July 2009, http://news.xinhuanet.com/english/2009-07/12/content_11696865.htm.

10

China and India: Countering Terrorism

Swaran Singh

In January 2011, India was elected as Chair of UN Security Council's Counter-Terrorism Committee.[1] Having deliberated on terrorism at home as also in various regional and multilateral forums for several decades, this put India in a privileged position to guide the global discourse on countering terrorism. However, at the very outset, India faced the challenge of defining terrorism which continues to be problematic. Different countries, and different groups within different countries, continue to swear by varying paradigms and often each of these carry varying connotations for each of these paradigms. As a result, anti-terrorism strategies continue to be a mosaic of different shades with limited universal appeal and limited capacity to deal with this pestering crisis with each episode of terrorist attack being responded to only on *ad hoc* basis as a knee-jerk reaction. And, this threatens to run into even greater difficulty when viewed in the context of complex equations of China and India within which these two states have been exploring possibilities of cooperation in countering terrorism.[2]

Meanwhile, at the global level, the only consensus that has evolved so far is on very broad understanding on what constitutes terrorism. Invariably, these definitions rely on their reference to specific incidents and outfits and radical Islam has lately come to be the main focus in these counter-terrorism discourses. For instance, while India sees terrorism primarily in terms of its Kashmir question and projects terrorism as a strategy, harboured (if not sponsored), by Pakistan, China's sees East Turkestan to be its major proponent and projects it as a threat to peace and stability. Both countries also increasingly underline the fact that they have been major victims of terrorism and that they have enormous experience in counter-terrorism strategies. This should make them ideal candidates to cooperate in bilateral and multilateral channels as terrorism emerges to be the major regional and international menace of 21st century. But as this chapter finds out their cooperation in countering terrorism has only been ceremonial and lukewarm, their interactions on this subject sporadic and outcomes ineffective.

The New Context

No doubt, 9/11 and the follow-up American global war on terrorism has created major triggers for China-India cooperation in countering terrorism yet, it is important to underline that their national counter-terrorism strategies as also their counter-terrorism cooperation had preceded 9/11. There are, however, few public commentaries that elaborate their institutionalised and/or implicit channels that existed and were used for exchange of information and intelligence, as also for mutual legal assistance in training and facilitating in extradition, investigations and prosecution of terrorism related cases. This is because it was normally done in far more discreet (read half-hearted) manner as China's all-weather ally, Pakistan, was invariably suspect in India for using terrorism as an instrument of its foreign policy.[3] The dynamics of the Cold War, especially Soviet intervention in Afghanistan had further circumscribed Beijing options causing it to not only ignore radical outfits gaining ground inside Pakistan but to participate (along with Pakistan, Saudi Arabia, and the United States) in the creation of mujahideen forces that worked to bleed the Soviets white in Afghanistan.[4] This process has since resulted in the rise of the Taliban and Al Qaeda as forces making this entire region a breeding ground as well as victim of international terrorism.

In the years since 9/11, terrorism has sustained itself at the centre-stage of global and regional security discourses. In particular, the realisation and conviction about the worsening situation in the Af-Pak theatre was reflected in the UN Security Council Resolution 1373 that urges nation-states to make concerted efforts, individually and collectively, to confront terrorism. This has since encouraged setting up of multiple bilateral counter-terrorism mechanisms and both China and India have set up such forums between themselves as also with other countries. The US and its NATO forces, that have been focussed in dealing with terrorism in the Af-Pak theatre are, now preoccupied with their 'exit' strategies. This has further forewarned regional powers (like China and India) to explore local solutions, thereby shifting China-India counter-terrorism cooperation beyond their bilateral innings. Afghanistan and its neighbours have begun contemplating post-

ISAF-exit strategies. These are now being debated in their multilateral forums like Shanghai Cooperation Organisation (SCO), South Asian Association for Regional Cooperation (SAARC), Russia-India-China trilateral dialogues and so on.

It is against this backdrop of growing unease of US and European countries to singularly deal with terrorism in the Af-Pak theatre and in the Gulf region that they have begun to demand burden-sharing from regional powers like Russia, Iran, China and India. Especially, in the wake of both China and India continuing to show impressive growth rates despite the global economic slowdown, Beijing and New Delhi have become attractive targets of such propositions for burden-sharing in regional security. Further, Russia may have reasons to remain reluctant to return to an Afghan quagmire, Iran may not be acceptable to Western powers and Pakistan is increasingly internally preoccupied, and so the onus of burden-sharing is likely to fall on Beijing and New Delhi. It is in this new context that this paper seeks to examine how China and India have evolved and expanded their counter-terrorism cooperation though the progress *prima facie* appears to be but seasonal, piecemeal and superficial.

Genesis of the China-India Divide

The contemporary history of terrorism-related victimhood of China and India flows from the legacies of the creation of mujahideen forces in Afghanistan from the early 1980s and has to be read against the backdrop of the Islamisation of Pakistan from the late 1970s.[5] As India at that time was close to the Soviet Union, it did not formally oppose the Soviet intervention in Afghanistan and therefore did not join any parleys or strategies to ensure the exit of Soviet forces. China, on the other hand, was part of the forces working for a Soviet exit from Afghanistan and became a close ally of United States, Saudi Arabia and Pakistan. In spite of sustained *rapprochement* between China and India since the early 1980s, some of these legacies still continue to impinge on China-India counter-terrorism initiatives.

First, while the Soviet Union withdrew from Afghanistan in 1989, India was to become its first major victim as these vast mercenary forces, created to ensure a Soviet exit, were to get active in India's Kashmir from 1989. Soon, the Soviet Union and entire Eastern bloc collapsed and this culture of violence by non-State actors continued to be the reality of Afghanistan leading later to the rise of the Taliban and al Qaeda from the late 1990s. Second, its impact on China was also substantial in terms of its rising internal unrest and incidents of terrorist violence though China has only gradually begun to publicise these, especially their external linkages. Even now China continues to fight shy of highlighting its links with Islamic radical outfits in Pakistan and while it has put on record Taliban training of Uyghurs.[6] Third, this experience has also had its impact on China-India relations. No doubt, China strongly criticised the terrorist attacks on the Indian Parliament on 13 December 2001 and in Mumbai on 26 November 2008 but given its relations with Pakistan, Beijing has been cautious in naming any terrorist outfits or states that may have provided them sanctuaries.[7] By contrast, the Chinese have officially been far too forthright in naming Dalai Lama (and indirectly indicting India) for the Lhasa riots of April 2008.[8]

It is common knowledge today that most terrorist incidents in both China and India are suspected of having links to radical groups based in the Af-Pak theatre. But while India remains overzealous to blame it on Pakistan, China faces a dilemma on how to condemn these individual actors without condemning the state of Pakistan, itself. This dilemma is unlikely to disappear even as China and India gradually evolve their counter-terrorism cooperation. However, this dilemma no longer stands in the way of China-India exploring ways to develop their training of forces, information sharing, and operational cooperation keeping in mind each other's political sensitivities. The two countries have also been working together in various regional and global multilateral forums including at the United Nations where they strongly endorse the view that all international anti-terrorism efforts should be conceived and implemented under UN auspices. Speaking at India's National Defence College on 23 March 2010, the Chinese Ambassador to India was to put this on record in the following words:

> "In fighting terrorism, the leading role of the UN and its Security Council must be given full play, and all the actions taken in this field should be in line with the purposes and principles of the UN Charter and other established norms of international law. The combat against terrorism calls for conclusive evidence and clear targets so that lives of the innocent can be spared and arbitrary enlargement of the scope of strike must be avoided. As terrorism is committed by very few extremist elements, we shall in no way confuse it with any specific nation or religion".[9]

National Counter-terrorism Strategies

China today fully supports and plays an active part in the international campaign against terrorism. Beijing had acceded to most international treaties in this regard even before 9/11. The SCO has been the main forum for China's counter-terrorism initiatives since late 1990s and SCO has been one of the first international organizations to institutionalise joint combat against separatism, extremism and terrorism. SCO had concluded the

Shanghai Convention on Combating Terrorism, Separatism and Extremism on 15 June 2001. This Convention had outlined specific directions and procedures for tackling the aforementioned threats nearly three months before the 9/11 incidents. Since 9/11, China has supported all UN anti-terrorism initiatives. It has signed the *International Convention for the Suppression of Terrorist Bombings* of May 2001 as also the *International Convention on Suppression of the Funding of Terrorism* of April 2002 and has carried out consultations and dialogues on counter-terrorism with related countries including India. What is of special significance is that recognising India's experience in combating terrorism and the convergence of their interests, New Delhi was soon invited to become an observer at the SCO from 2005 which promises to open new avenues for bilateral counter-terrorism initiatives.[10]

India has also been one of the "most terrorism battered countries in the world"[11] and had been at the forefront of the counter-terrorism debate within SAARC which had adopted its *Regional Convention on Suppression of Terrorism* way back in November 1987. In view of UNSC Resolution 1373 of 2001, SAARC agreed to add the *Additional Protocol* to the convention dealing with "collection and acquisition of funds for the purpose of committing terrorist acts and taking further measures to prevent and suppress financing of such acts".[12] While Pakistan leaders used to argue in favour of freedom fighters in Kashmir, India has been trying to push for an agreed SAARC definition of terrorism to include countries that are known for "harbouring hostile insurgent groups and criminal elements".[13] In 2005, China was included as observer at SAARC, which reinforces opportunities for China and India working together and developing chemistry for countering terrorism. Both nations today have bilateral dialogues and also counter-terrorism dialogues with other major powers like the US, Russia, UK, France, and have taken active part in the work of the Security Council Anti-Terrorism Commission.[14]

Indeed, even at the regional level, "India and China have offered closer security ties ranging from anti-drug, anti-terrorism cooperation to joint anti-piracy maritime patrol".[15] In their 10th trilateral meeting at Wuhan (China) in November 2010, the foreign ministers of Russia-India-China, for instance, had once again underlined the serious situation in the Af-Pak theatre. They devoted a full section of their joint statement on terrorism proposing SCO as the appropriate regional platform to organise counter-terrorism action.[16] The Russian Foreign Minister also reportedly, suggested that the three should have a trilateral Joint Working Group on Countering Terrorism which will be discussed further.[17]

Bilateral Parleys and a Joint Working Group

As regards their bilateral cooperation, China-India deliberations on the issue of terrorism go back to their Beijing Joint Statement of 7 September 1993 between Premier Li Peng and Prime Minister PV Narasimha Rao. This was the first time that China and India had referred to the 'threat of Islamic fundamentalism' and the two sides have gradually picked up momentum in evolving a common understanding on various aspects of terrorism.[18] This could be seen as both cause and consequence of the fact that China had been pushing Pakistan since late 1990s to rein in Taliban forces and has repeatedly made its annoyance at Pakistani inactivity obvious to Islamabad.[19] In the wake of the 1998 nuclear tests in India and Pakistan, China was also seen distancing itself from Pakistan and this was described as one of the reasons why China stood neutral and even rebuffed Islamabad during the Kargil conflict in 1999.[20]

Second, China has been one of the few countries that have kept a distance from, and occasionally even defied the US global war on terrorism while presenting an alternative paradigm in terms of how to deal with terrorism in the Asian theatre. It is in this backdrop, following 9/11 and in the wake of the India-Pakistan military stand-off following the attack on the Indian Parliament that Premier Zhu Rongji had chosen to visit India in January 2002 finalising among others, their decision on setting up a joint mechanism against terrorism.[21] China's sustained discussions within the SCO and the Russia-India-China trilateral meetings have been projecting these alternatives paradigms repeatedly and are widely appreciated in India. Again, much before 9/11, China and India had been debating terrorism in their successive annual Security Dialogues starting from March 2000. During Chinese Premier Li Peng's nine-day long visit to India in January 2001, China had frontloaded terrorism in his talks and speeches.[22] It is in this context of their continued parleys on terrorism that 9/11 have further facilitated the setting up of a Joint Working Group on Countering Terrorism.

The first meeting of the India-China Joint Working Group on Countering Terrorism was held on 23 April 2002 in New Delhi. This was the first ever formal joint mechanism meeting where China and India were directly and exclusively discussing counter-terrorism. Following the general tenor of their ongoing Security Dialogue that had been set up following India's nuclear tests of May 1998, the agenda of their Inter-Governmental Group on Countering Terrorism was also kept broad-based and the two sides exchanged views on the international terrorism situation and its repercussions in their immediate region. Besides, both sides exchanged notes on their respective national experiences in dealing with terrorism and expressed their intent in favour of strengthening cooperation in dealing with this menace within the frame of the United Nations as well as exploring possibilities for cooperation at a bilateral level. At the end, both sides described the first meeting of the dialogue mechanism as useful in enhancing mutual understanding on the subject. Later, terrorism was also the focus in Prime Minister' AB Vajpayee's visit to Beijing in June 2003 and parleys were upgraded to Strategic Dialogue at Foreign Secretary level from January 2005,[23] followed by Premier Wen Jiabao's visit to Delhi during April 2005. From here on, while their anti-terrorism cooperation began to move forward with their militaries evolving operational joint training, their political ties were to become lukewarm given India's growing interest in courting Washington that culminated in the Indo-US nuclear deal which has become a bone of contention in China-India interactions.

Military-to-Military Cooperation

Following Prime Minister Rajiv Gandhi's breakthrough visit to Beijing in December 1988, the two sides had started exchanging mid-ranking officers between the National Defence College of India and National Defence University of China. In July 1992, Sharad Pawar became the first defence minister of India to visit China and this visit resulted in an agreement to further develop academic, scientific, technical exchanges between their militaries.[24] In the backdrop of the collapse of Soviet Union, this had coincided with a new thrust for military diplomacy making military exercises an integral part of inter-State relations. The *Milan* naval exercises involving ships or representatives from countries like Singapore, Sri Lanka, Thailand, Australia, Bangladesh, Indonesia, Malaysia, Myanmar, Brunei, Philippines, Vietnam New Zealand, Japan, US, India has been one of the largest, longest and the most visible such framework since the mid-1990s.

Following this new international trend, China gradually began military exercises in the framework of the SCO since early 2000s. The recent rise of international terrorism and concerns about the US initiating a mini-NATO expansion in this region were a trigger for SCO debating and conducting anti-terrorism exercises. Indeed, this anti-terrorism agenda has resuscitated the SCO which had achieved its original agenda of defining mutual borders and trust-building by late 1990s and has since conducted several joint military exercises in the name of countering-terrorism.[25] The fact that both China and India have been participating in military exercises with several other countries has facilitated their bilateral military exercise with 9/11 and the subsequent war on terror becoming a major catalyst in accelerating these initiatives.

China-India military exercises had begun with the two navies holding their first joint 'search-and-rescue' exercise off the Shanghai coast in November 2003 following which India had proposed an 'anti-piracy' exercise near the pirate-infested Malacca Straits.[26] December 2004 and early 2005 saw both Indian and Chinese navies engaged in post-tsunami relief operations and their second naval exercise was held only in December 2005 off the coast of Kochi in the southern tip of the Indian peninsula. It included communication protocols, maneuvers and casualty evacuation. Meanwhile, their senior generals and admirals had been exchanging visits with ships making courtesy calls at each others' ports as the two have been debating and operating in the context of maritime terrorism. However, in spite of occasional news reports, exercises between their armies took some time and air forces exchanges remain in the pipeline.

To trace the beginning of army joint-exercises, the two armies had undertaken a joint mountaineering expedition to scale a 6,650meter peak in central Tibet on 28 August 2004. This was to be followed by Defence Minister Pranab Mukherjee visiting China in May 2006 and signing a MoU for Exchanges and Cooperation in the Field of Defence which provided, among other things, for joint military exercises, involving search and rescue, anti-piracy and counter-terrorism.[27] The first bilateral training exercise in counter-terrorism, called Hand-in-Hand 2007 was organised in Kunming (China) during 20-25 December2007. Based on the theme of countering-terrorism this exercise involved one armed reconnaissance company of the PLA (approximately 100 soldiers) and equivalent strength of Indian troops. It included the setting up of a joint command post, joint battle decision-making and conduct of counter-terrorism drills. Among other things, this mock counter-terrorism exercise was an anti-hijacking operation. But other than handling weapons, and counter-terrorism drills, interactions included trust-building activities like tugs-of-war to basketball matches, kung fu, yoga training and so on.[28]

The second Hand-in-Hand joint anti-terrorism exercise was held from 6 to 12 December 2008 at the Belgaum Combat School in Karnataka, in the south of India. This seven-day interaction included display of weapons and equipment, communication and tactics, joint training and comprehensive drills. The scenario for this drill was that a group of international terrorists had secretly entered two villages in the forest of north-western Belgaum and soldiers had to 'catch-or-kill' them without hurting innocent villagers. This cordon and search operation had impressive results and the Indian military attaché to China labelled the event "a new step in bilateral military cooperation".[29] Ma Xiaotian, head of the Chinese delegation, underlined its success and said that China now conducts more than 20 joint military exercises and trainings under the theme of countering terrorism with over 20 countries which are part of demonstrating China's determination "to enhance international security cooperation" but he also emphasised that these China-India joint exercises were not aimed at any third country.[30]

However, given that their bilateral relations since then have had several political hiccups, that both have been focussed on dealing with the impact of the global economic slowdown, and that India was busy transforming its relations with the United States, military exercises for 2009 were officially cancelled in September 2009.[31] Even their Annual Defence Dialogue (ADD) which was inaugurated along with the Kunming 'Hand-to-Hand' anti-terrorism exercise of 2007 and repeated in New Delhi for 2008 did not reconvene for a very long time, and the third ADD occurred only in January 2010.[32] Both sides however continue to occasionally claim that they are working to expand their interactions further and the two air forces are reported to be preparing for their first joint war games in 2012—thus realising tri-service cooperation at a bilateral level.

Regional Realities and Responsibilities

Both China and Pakistan had been US allies in ejecting Soviet forces from Afghanistan in the 1980s. Both continue to underline their serious stakes in the situation in the Af-Pak theatre though China's involvement is no longer part of US efforts directly. China is now focussed on non-military means and for long has advocated vigorous regional counter-terrorism cooperation by conducting fruitful bilateral cooperation with neighbouring countries. China also remains conscious of the external linkages to its internal security situation. Accordingly, China has primed its relevant agencies for a crackdown on terrorism, including legislative, aviation, finance, customs and other departments in order to prevent terrorist incidents on its soil.[33] China is on record having said that about 1,000 ethnic Uyghurs from Xinjiang were once trained in Afghanistan's camps, some of whom had since returned home and started a *jihad* against the Chinese government.[34]

After 9/11, the US was keen on enlisting China's full support for its global war on terrorism. This new equation has transformed China and India from being targets of US non-proliferation and deterrence strategies to being courted as 'responsible stakeholders' in the international system.[35] Both China and India have used this period to transform their relationship with the US and have also reaped certain benefits. But lately, the American focus on an 'exit' strategy in Afghanistan is making Beijing and New Delhi sit up and think seriously about evolving a regional response to deal with the fallout. According to one view, as the Americans withdraw after organising some Iraq-like patchwork and declare it a victory this "region will witness a takeover by nihilistic forces with few parallels in modern history".[36] In his address to the Chinese Academy of Social Sciences on 15 January 2008, Prime Minister Manmohan Singh had underlined India's concern when he said:

> "Perhaps the greatest danger to our development comes from extremism of all types, whether in the garb of religion or on the pretext of righting historical wrongs. Recent developments in our neighbourhood have brought home to us again the imperative need to collectively fight terrorism and extremism in all its forms".[37]

Nevertheless, bilateral counter-terrorism cooperation remains subject to very strong mutual scepticism from various constituencies with a mixed track-record of cooperation only reinforcing continued caution from both sides. Deliberations on countering terrorism, therefore, represent an overdrive in platitudes while their sporadic formal interactions and ceremonial military cooperation betrays lack of both a grip on regional realities and of preparedness to take on regional counter-terrorism responsibilities. One Indian commentator on terrorism, B. Raman, sees this counter-terrorism cooperation to be of only limited value to either New Delhi or Beijing. None of the terrorist groups that threaten India operate from China or vice versa. Thus, he says, "While there is considerable scope for the exchange of counter-terrorism-related intelligence between India and China, there is not much scope for operational cooperation between the security forces of the two countries in tackling land-based terrorism".[38] But China and India can share cooperation in anti-piracy and third country peacekeeping operations. Other sectors where the two can cooperate include tackling hostage situations, hijacking, providing post-conflict or post-disaster relief and reconstruction responsibilities.

Second, while both China and India continue to highlight their experience in counter-terrorism, their relevant agencies have had only mixed success in dealing with their internal challenges. Sustained violence by Maoists in India and the Urumqi riots in China in June 2010 are apt reminders of how both sides need to put their respective houses in order. As a first step, therefore, both must regularise the practice of brainstorming domestically before they begin working on their joint strategies and on other aspects of interoperability at the bilateral or regional levels. This remains an imperative if their military exercises have to go beyond the superficial. Both also need to be increasingly transparent and share information on a regular basis. There is a view in India that PLA exercises are more frequent with the added advantage of much better infrastructure on the Chinese side of the border. Therefore, even if mutual exposure is largely only ceremonial, it augurs well for ensuring a balanced assessment by both sides.[39]

As regards Afghanistan, while both China and India will not wish to disrupt their relations with the US, both also share the discomfiture with US counter-terrorism policies. China, for example, remains suspicious of US President Barack Obama's proposals for setting up a "new diplomatic mechanism" involving regional powers like Russia, Iran, China and India. China sees this curbing Beijing's manoeuvre room since it regards terrorism from a larger perspective involving not just attacks by terrorists but loads of other "non-traditional security threats such as drug trafficking, arms smuggling, and other cross-border crimes".[40] There is the added concern about the US and its allies using the pretext of tackling the Taliban and consolidating their military presence across Central and South Asia adding a new security dynamic to the region.

Conclusion

To conclude, while both China and India must take on an ever expanding role in burden-sharing of regional security and learn to maximise gains from their domestic experiences in dealing with terrorism around their immediate periphery, both must also see this as an important component of their overall rapprochement on which remains premised their peaceful rise in the 21st century. Terrorism cannot be tackled by any quick-fix knee-jerk reactions to specific episodes and entities but as rising Asian powers both China and India need to contemplate and evolve a shared understanding on their counter-terrorism visions and strategies. To quote again from the March 2010 speech of the Chinese ambassador,

> "To wipe out terrorism, we must address its symptoms as well as its root causes and combine short-term goals with long-term approaches... Anti-terrorism campaign is a contest between peace and violence rather than conflict between nationalities, religions or civilisations. We maintain the recognition of the diversity of the world's civilisations and the respect for differed cultural backgrounds, religious beliefs and development modes of different countries".[41]

Both China and India have a clearer understanding of terrorism at the national level, which however, gets complicated at the bilateral and multilateral levels given their diverse experiences in politics and history. This calls for putting their counter-terrorism cooperation in perspective and measuring its success as part of their larger rapprochement and in terms of their domestic dynamics. Given the rising stature and leverage of both nations, it also becomes incumbent on other major stakeholders in the international system to facilitate their co-option into multilateral efforts in dealing with terrorism and facilitating their mutual trust and understanding so as to enable China and India to play their expected vital roles in ensuring regional peace and security.

NOTES

1. The Committee was set up under UN Security Council Resolutions 1373 (of 2001) and 1624 (of 2005). The UN Security Council Counter Terrorism Committee is the highest body that works to bolster the ability of UN member-states to prevent terror acts both within their borders and across regions.
2. Jonathan Holslag, *China+India: Prospects for Peace*, New York: Columbia University Press, 2010, pp. 152-53; Zhu Chenghu, "How Tough is China's Mission to Fight Terrorism", *China Military Power*, 23 March 2010, http://www.china-defense-mashup.com/?p=5909.
3. Rushda Siddique, "The Islamic dimension of Pakistan's foreign Policy", in Hillel Frisch and Efraim Inbar (eds.), *Radical Islam and International Security: Challenges and Responses*, New York: Routledge, 2008, p. 158; Peter Brookes and Julianne Smith, "Course Correction in America's War on Terror", in Derek Chollet, Tod Lindberg and David Shorr (eds.), *Bridging the Foreign Policy Divide*, New York: Routledge, 2008, p. 58; Veena Kukreja, "Pakistan since the 1999 Coup: Prospects of Democracy", in Veena Kukreja and M.P. Singh (eds.), *Pakistan: Democracy, Development and Security Issues*, New Delhi: Sage, 2005, p. 79.
4. Ahmad Sheyeq Qassem, *Afghanistan's Political Stability: A Dream Unrealised*, Burlington: Ashgate, 2009, p. 83; Karl R. DeRouen and Uk Heo, *Civil Wars of the World: Major Conflicts since World War II (Vol. 1)*, Santa Barbara, Cal: ABC-CLIO Inc, 2007, p. 93.
5. Mohammad A. Qadeer, *Pakistan: Social and Cultural Transformations in a Muslim Nation*, New York: Routledge, 2006, p. 169; Bidanda M. Chengappa, *Pakistan, Islamisation, Army and Foreign Policy*, New Delhi: APH Publishing Corpn, 2004, p. 109.
6. Kenneth Katzman, *Afghanistan: Post-Taliban Governance, Security, and US Policy*, Washington DC: Congressional Research Service, June 2009 RL 30588, p. 52; Andrew Scobell, "Terrorism and Chinese Foreign Policy", in Yong Deng and Fei-Ling Wang (eds), *Rising China: Power and Motivation in Chinese Foreign Policy*, Lanham, Maryland: Rowman & Littlefield, 2005, p. 312.
7. B. Raman, "Counter-Terrorism: India-China-Russia Cooperation", in *South Asia Analysis Group*, 4 November 2009, http://www.southasiaanalysis.org/%5Cpapers9%5Cpaper830.html.
8. Yi Duo, "Facts exposing Dalai clique's masterminding of Lhasa violence", *Xinhua*, reproduced by China's Permanent Mission at United Nations, http://www.china-un.org/eng/zt/xzwt/t419869.htm.
9. Embassy of the People's Republic of China in India, "Speech by Ambassador Hua Junduo at the Defence College of India", 24 May 2003, http://www.chinaembassy.org.in/eng/gf/t61289.htm.
10. Amardeep Athwal, *China-India Relations: Contemporary Dynamics*, New York: Routledge, 2008, p. 115-116
11. James M. Lutz and Brenda J Lutz, *Global Terrorism*, New York: Routledge, 2004, p. 247.
12. Smruti S. Pattanaik, "Making Sense of Regional Cooperation: SAARC at Twenty", *Strategic Analysis*, Vol. 30, No. 1, January-March, 2006, p. 148.
13. *Kashmir Times*, "Pacts on Terror Tops SAARC Agenda", 30 December 2003.

14. *China.org*, "China's National Defense in 2002", http://www.china.org.cn/e-white/20021209/
15. J. Mohan Malik, "India and China", in P.R. Kumaraswamy (ed.) *Security Beyond Survival: Essays for K Subrahmanyam*, New Delhi: Sage, 2004, p. 146
16. *Xinhua*, "Joint Communique of the 10th Meeting of the Foreign Ministers of China, Russia and India", 27 November 2010, http://news.xinhuanet.com/english2010/china/2010-11/15/c_13608054.htm.
17. *Bharat Globe*, "China butts head with India on 'safe haven' language", 16 November 2010, http://www.bharatglobe.com/?p=558
18. Mao Siwei "China and the Kashmir issue", *Strategic Analysis*, Vol. XVII, No. 12, March 1995, pp.1572-1597; Swaran Singh, "Building Security and Confidence with China", in Tan Chung (ed.), *Across the Himalayan Gap: An Indian Quest for Understanding China*, New Delhi: Gyan Publishing House, 1988, p. 522.
19. Rollie Lal, "China's Relations with South Asia", Joshua Eisenman, Eric Heginboham and Derek Mitchell (eds.), *China and the Developing World: Beijing's Strategy for the twenty-first century*, Armonk, NY: M.E. Sharpe, 2007, p. 146.
20. Ajai K. Rai, *India's Nuclear Diplomacy after Pokhran II*, New Delhi: Dorling Kindersley, 2009, p. 135.
21. Jing-dong Yuan, "Sino-Indina relations: A new beginning", *Asia Times*, 19 January 2002, http://www.atimes.com/china/DA19Ad01.htm.
22. C. Raja Mohan, "China to join India in fighting terrorism", *Hindu*, 14 January 2001, p. 11.
23. Li Mingjiang, "Sino-Indian Energy Politics", in Marie Lall (ed.), *The Geopolitics of Energy in South Asia*, Singapore: Institute of South East Asians Studies, 2009, p. 155.
24. Holslag, op.cit., p. 121.
25. Clemens Stubbe Ostergaard, "The Chinese Response to 9-11 and the Anti-Terror Campaign: Sino-American Relations during Bush I", in Simon Shen (ed.), *China and Anti-terrorism*, New York: Nova Publishers, 2007, p. 85.
26. Jyotirmoy Banerjee, "Seaward Security: Modernizing the Indian Navy", in Anjali Ghosh, Tridib Chakraborti, Anindyo Jyoti Majumdar and Shibashis Chatterjee (eds.), *India's Foreign Policy*, New Delhi: Pearson, 2009, p. 82.
27. Sudha Ramachandran, "In Kunming, an exercise in uneasiness", *Asia Times*, 11 December 2007, http://www.atimes.com/atimes/South_Asia/IL11Df01.html. See also B. Raman, "Strange Bedfellows", *Foreign Policy*, 31 August 2009, http://www.foreignpolicy.com/articles/2009/08/31/strange_bedfellows.
28. Li Jianmin, "Bonhomie marks India-China joint exercises", *Hindu*, 27 December 2007, p. 1.
29. *PLA Daily*, "China, India hold joint anti-terror military training with comprehensive drill", 12 December 2008, available at *China Military Online*, http://english.chinamil.com.cn/site2/special-reports/2008-12/12/content_1582451.htm.
30. *China Daily*, "China, India conclude joint anti-terror military training", 12 December 2008, p. 9.
31. Sujan Dutta, "Hand-in-Hand drill with China loses touch", *Telegraph*, 23 September 2009, http://www.telegraphindia.com/1090923/jsp/frontpage/story_11529859.jsp.
32. Swaran Singh, "A good and timely restart for neighbors-in-arms", *China Daily*, 7 January 2010, p. 9.
33. Jia Qingguo, "Facilitating Peaceful Rise: Principles and Practices of China's Security Policy", in David A Kelly, Ramkishen S Rajan and Gillian H.L. Goh (eds.), *Managing Globalisation: Lessons from China and India*, London: World Scientific Publishing, 2006, p. 294.

34. Martin I. Wayne, *China's War on Terrorism: Counter-Insurgency, Politics, and Internal Security*, New York: Routledge, 2008, p. 10.
35. Shirley A. Kan, "US-China Counterterrorism Cooperation: Issues for US Policy", in Jannie A. Levy (ed.), *Terrorism Issues and Developments*, New York: Nova Science Publishers, 2007, p. 143; Kevin Pollpeter, *US-China Security Management: Assessing the Military-to-Military Relationship*, Santa Monica, CA: Rand, 2004, p. 30-32.
36. Amulya Ganguli, "Apocalypse next year", *New Indian Express*, 24 March 2010, http://www.expressbuzz.com/edition/story.aspx?Title=Apocalypse+ next+year&artid=cnIco2755fY=&SectionID=XVSZ2Fy6Gzo=& MainSectionID=XVSZ2Fy6Gzo=&SectionName=m3GntEw72ik=.
37. Jawed Naqvi, "India, China want to help check terrorism in Pakistan", *Dawn* (Karachi), 16 January 2008, p. 1.
38. Ramachandran, op.cit.
39. Bhartendu Kumar Singh, "The Kunming Joint Military Exercises and Sino-Indian Relations", IPCS, *Article* #2451, 28 December 2007, http://ipcs.org/article/army/the-kunming-joint-military-exercises-and-sino-indian-relations-2451.html.
40. Sun Zhuangzhi, "Afghanistan reflects US' self-obsession", *China Daily*, 24 March 2010, p. 9.
41. Embassy of the People's Republic of China, op. cit.

11

The Impact of the Media and Think-tanks on Sino-Indian Relations

Wang Fan and Zhang Yidan

The growing weight and increasing international influence of China and India has earned them the monikers of "Dragon" and "Elephant" respectively in the international arena. China-India relations were characterized by a period of "*Hindi-Chini bhai bhai*" ("Indians and Chinese are brothers") in the 1950s which however, received a grievous setback with the 1962 border war. In the 1990s, Sino-Indian relations entered a reconstruction phase though problems remained in terms of the border dispute, the Tibet issue and fierce regional competition. The development of Sino-Indian relations in the future holds a lot of significance for not only the Chinese and Indian governments, but also for the international community. More significantly, the development of Sino-Indian relations has to be seen not only in terms of hard power, such as military strength and geopolitical interests, but also in terms of soft power, such as intentions, ideas and international image. Given this latter aspect, a study of the impact of media and think-tanks on Sino-Indian relations is of great academic value and practical significance.

This paper is divided into four parts. The first part will provide a brief introduction to the prominent functions of the media and think-tanks on current international relations and a review of China's and India's media industry as well as major think-tanks. The second part analyses the impact of the media on Sino-Indian relations; it consists of two branches: the first is a study of print media by an analysis of news reports and editorials chosen from the *China Daily* (China), the *Global Times* (China) and the *Times of India* (India), the second, a research on TV programmes concentrating on several major international channels of China and India. The third part provides an analysis of the contents, attitudes and influence of Chinese and Indian think-tanks by examining their major publications. The final part brings up the conclusions of the study.

Media and Think-Tanks in China and India

In the increasingly intertwined world of the 21st century, mass media plays a remarkable role in creating a global village compressed in time and space. Quick communication of news all around the world has become the main channel for people to understand the world and further form their political judgments.[1] Transnational media empires blur the boundaries between domestic affairs and international governance. The compelling images and remarks collected from various parts of the world make common people feel associated with events and hence, make it imperative for them to participate in politics. In addition, the media provide a platform for people to express their political opinions and interact with government officials who directly affect the decision-making processes. The media also contributes to a nation-state's soft power, through which the country demonstrates its unique culture and values to the world and constructs its international images.

Compared to the media, think-tanks play a more crucial role in foreign policy formulation by offering professional advice. Successful strategic designs and sophisticated diplomacy are both highly influenced by thorough academic analysis. Nowadays, think-tanks also shoulder the responsibility of communication with other countries' intelligentsia, and conduct "track-two" diplomacy. Whether in bilateral relations or in the multilateral arena contacts between scholars, ahead of meetings of political leaders, are becoming a form of efficient and popular diplomacy.

At present, the media industry in both China and India are involved in these processes. Given the large population of these two countries, the newspaper market of China ranks the first in the world with an overall size of 98.7 million, followed by Indian newspaper market with the overall circulation of 88.9 million.[2] Meanwhile, 94 per cent of the Chinese receive TV programmes[3] while in India, half its households at least own a TV set.[4] Internet is fast becoming another battlefield for the media and also a powerful channel for political expression and international communication. According to a survey conducted by Comscore Inc., in November 2009, there are 220.8 million netizens in China over the age of 15 who access the Internet at home and work locations, making China the largest user of

Internet services in the world. India's netizen population is not as big as China and ranks 3rd in the Asia-Pacific region with 35.8 million netizens (mostly above the age of 15 and at home and work locations)[5].

However, the quality and quantity of think-tanks in China and India seem to lag behind in their overall national strength and international influence. According to the Report of the project on "The Think Tanks and Civil Societies Programme 2008: The Global 'Go-To Think Tanks'" led by James G. McGannn of the University of Pennsylvania, China has 7 think tanks among the Asian top 25 while India has only 3,[6] indicating that India may not have as many highly qualified think tanks as China.

This survey investigates 5,465 think-tanks across the world based on uniform criteria. Only 74 think-tanks from China and 121 think-tanks from India have been selected in this report according to the strict categorization, as compared to 1,777 think-tanks from the US.[7] Of these, two major think-tanks from China have been selected in the world's top 50 think-tanks (non-US), namely the Chinese Academy of Social Sciences (No.25), and Shanghai Institute of International Studies (No.34) and only one think-tank from India, Institute of Defence Studies and Analyses (No.46).[8] In addition, several other think-tanks have made it to Asia's Top 25, namely China Institute for Contemporary International Relations (CICIR) (No.9), China Institute of International Studies (CIIS) (No.13), Cathay Institute for Public Affairs (No.15), Unirule Institute of Economics (No.22) from China. From India, other than the Institute for Defence Studies and Analyses, the other think tanks in Asia's top 25 are; the Centre for Policy Research (No 10), The Institute of Peace and Conflict Studies (No 18), the Indian Council for Research on International Economic Relations (No 23) and the Liberty Institute (No.25).[9]

Though the project conducted by the University of Pennsylvania is not strictly the only guiding source of examining the quality and quantity of think-tanks in China and India, nevertheless, it still provides relevant data on think-tanks in these two countries. To sum up, both the media industry and think-tanks have grown by leaps and bounds in China and India, which is bound to have an influence on the Sino-Indian bilateral relations. The following section will look into current news reports and programmes from the media and publications from major Chinese and Indian think-tanks to illustrate how the media and think-tanks perceive and interact with each other and further analyses their impact on Sino-Indian relations.

The Media's Impact on Sino-Indian Relations—Print Media

China Daily (China), the Global Times (China), and the Times of India (India)

In order to observe the impact of the media on Sino-Indian relations, a collection of articles from newspapers like *China Daily* (China), the *Global Times* (China), and the *Times of India* (India) within the time frame of 1 January 2010 to 31 March 2010 have been studied. The selection of print media is based on the circulation, target readers, influence and social prestige.

China Daily is the most prominent official English-language newspaper in China and the *Global Times* is the leading newspaper focusing on foreign affairs in China. *China Daily* is published in an English Edition, a US Edition and in the form of online news. This study only takes into account the English edition with a circulation of 300,000 copies all around the world. The *Global Times* is published in a Chinese Edition, English Edition and in the form of online news. This study involves only the Chinese edition. The target readers of these two newspapers are usually those with white-collar jobs including public servants, company executives, and professionals. They are the main channel for foreigners to know China and for the Chinese to understand the world.

The *Times of India* is one of the most comprehensive English-language newspapers in India. It has the largest circulation among all English-language newspapers in the world with 3.14 million copies circulating in 2008 (according to the Audit Bureau of Circulations[10]). The *Times of India* has a special focus on Sino-Indian relations and China's development. Thus, it is a typical representative of Indian print media that helps to understand India's views of China.

In *China Daily*, 43 articles with the key word "India" or "Indian" in headline on the official website during the period—1 January 2010 to 31 March 2010 have been accessed.[11] For *Global Times*, 121 articles with Chinese characters of "India" or "Indian" in title in the 60 issues published during this period have been looked into.[12] Finally, for the *Times of India*, 107 articles carrying the word "China" or "Chinese" in headlines have been located through the e-paper archive.[13]

Table 1 reveals the fact that both China and India pay great attention to each other and the three main media share nearly equal coverage percentage of the number of articles concerning each other (divided by total number of international news).

Table 1: Overall Statistics of Articles in the Main Print Media of China and India

	China Daily	*Global Times*	*Times of India*
Study Period	*1 January 2010 to 31 March 2010*		
Total Issues	72	60	90
Total Number of Articles Concerning Each Other	43	121	107
Average Articles in Each Issue	0.58	2.02	1.19
Overall International News in Each Issue[14]	12.3[15]	55.7[16]	24.7[17]
The Percentage of Target News in all International News (Approximately)	4.72%	3.63%	4.82%

Created by the authors.

In order to make the study on the media's contents and attitude more effective, a comparison between the *Global Times* (*Huanqiu*) in Chinese and the *Times of India* in English is conducted. The reasons for excluding *China Daily* are that it has insufficient articles related to India, a strong official background, and lesser circulation compared to the *Global Times*.[18] In other words, a Chinese-language newspaper with large-circulation may more precisely reflect China's perceptions of India. A brief analysis on articles from *China Daily* will also be offered in the end of this section.

The contents of the *Global Times* and the *Times of India* are as follows:

Table 2: Contents of *Global Times* and *Times of India*

Content	*Global Times (Frequency/Percentage)*	*Times of India (Frequency/Percentage)*
Events	13 / 10.74%	3 / 2.80%
Political Reports	6 / 4.96%	11 / 10.28%
Economic Reports	14 / 11.57%	29 / 27.10%
Military Reports	30 / 24.79%	6 / 5.61%
Social, Legal Reports	18 / 14.88%	22 / 20.56%
Cultural Reports	2 / 1.65%	3 / 2.80%
Relations with Other Countries	16 / 13.22%	14 / 13.08%
In-Depth Reports	6 / 4.96%	4 / 3.74%
Professional Analyses	10 / 8.26%	1 / 0.93%
Others (e.g. Environment, Internet, etc.)	6 / 4.96%	14 / 13.08%
Overall	121 / 100%	107 / 100%

Created by the authors.

Table 2 reveals the content distribution of the *Global Times* and the *Times of India*. The classification is based on the subject or main theme of every article. There are also some short and descriptive news articles without a clear subject like "Rainstorms in India" or "Chopstick pierces China toddler's brain", which are included as "Event Reports".

On comparing and contrasting, the author finds the following similarities and differences in China's report contents on India and India's report on China.

Similarities

First of all, among a wide range of subjects, both China and India put great emphasis on social and legal aspects of their counterpart (China: 14.88%, India: 20.56%). The majority of these reports is heavily biased and sometimes bears negative implications. The focus is more on trivial issues, for example, the *Times of India* reports about China's 9-year-old mothers, gay parties and the lack of 24 million brides by 2030; while the *Global Times* puts much emphasis on India's gender inequality, prostitution problems, suicides and the lack of education for teenagers.

Another common theme in Chinese and Indian the media is their respective relations with a third country (China: 13.22% coverage, India: 13.08% coverage). Due to the fact that they are neighbours, Chinese and Indian media are extremely sensitive to the relations of the other side with any third country. Indian media reacts fiercely to China's economic aid to Sri Lanka as an "expansion of its influence", and China analyses Russian-Indian cooperation in order to detect potential threats. China focuses on India's relations with other great powers such as the US, Russia, Japan and Europe while India shows more concern with China's "Sphere of Influence" in South Asia.

The second similarity lies in the poor amount of cultural reports and insufficient in-depth reportage in both the *Global Times* and the *Times of India*. The only four articles found were in reference to cuisine and religion. However, without any doubts, the brilliant civilisation and cultural diversities of both the countries can help China and India to attract each other's people and publicize their ideas and values. In-depth reports, which mean a detailed report with an explicit topic of more than 500 words, are also in short supply (China: 4.96%. India: 3.73%). These kinds of reports can give readers a careful analysis of Sino-Indian relations, which would be more constructive than mere delivery of the message on the surface.

Differences

On the other hand, differences also exist between Chinese reports and Indian reports. China's first concern is India's military modernisation while India puts great emphasis on China's economic development. China's intensive coverage on India's military news is partly due to the border tension, India-Pakistan hostility and the perceived hard-line attitude of the Indian military. Besides, *Global Times* has a particular page focusing on military news around the world. For Indians, the effort is to analyse and give suggestions from China's economic development experiences. India nonetheless, holds a cautious attitude on China's achievements.

Second, *Global Times* provides more analyses by professionals than the *Times of India* (China: 8.26%, India: 0.93%)—professional analyses are usually provided by scholars in academic circles, which are helpful in expanding the readers' knowledge bases by locating Sino-Indian relations in a regional or global context. The *Times of India*, however, has a better record in describing non-traditional challenges such as environmental protection and internet security (China: 4.96%, India: 13.08%). The Indian newspaper however, exhibits a very negative tone by focussing on reporting about China's Internet espionage activities and censorship system.

In addition to content analysis, all articles in the *Global Times* and the *Times of India* also need to be considered with regards to their attitude towards each other.

Table 3: Attitude of *Global Times* and *Times of India*

Attitude	*Global Times (Frequency/Percentage)*	*Times of India (Frequency/Percentage)*
Without Clear Inclination	55 / 45.4%	36 / 33.6%
With Positive Implications	11 / 9.1%	18 / 16.8%
With Negative Implications	55 / 45.4%	53 / 49.5%
Overall	121 / 100%	107 / 100%

Created by the authors.

On the basis of Table 3, the following conclusions can be drawn. First, nearly half of the articles in both newspapers have negative implications.[19] This may have a significant priming effect on Chinese and Indian readers, considering negative reports would directly produce biased political judgments. The negative reports have a larger possibility of influencing all kinds of news analyses advocating threats or damage from the other side.

Second, the *Times of India* has more positive reports than the *Global Times*, especially in the economic domain. It shows that India recognizes China's economic achievements and at the same time wants to compete with it and surpass it in the future.

Third, the *Global Times* gives more objective reports than the *Times of India*. Exaggerated accounts and strong attitudes are notable features of the Indian media, which are also reflected in the "war of words" between the Chinese and Indian the media during the year 2009.[20] This verbal war was initiated by Indian Prime Minister Manmohan Singh's visit to "Arunachal Pradesh" and was upgraded into an unreasonable prediction of future Sino-Indian war. This finally ended with a meeting between Chinese Premier Wen Jiabao and Manmohan Singh at the ASEAN summit in an attempt to allay these fears. During this period, the Indian media frequently used aggressive gestures on issues such as the Dalai Lama's visit to "Arunachal Pradesh", China's construction of a hydropower station in Kashmir, troop deployments in disputed areas and so on, which aroused nationalistic sentiments among the Chinese public. All the above-mentioned phenomena can be seen as partly resulting from India's highly competitive media industry, and also their worries about China's development, which could have been avoided if the media had been more sensitive and promoted public interactions and mutual understanding between the two countries.

Besides the analysis of content and attitudes in the *Global Times* and the *Times of India*, articles in *China Daily* offer an alternative view on the Chinese perception of India. Except for few articles indicating certain negative implications (such as the genetic modification of food crops in India), the great majority of news reports in *China Daily* provide positive and optimistic analysis on India. *China Daily* is appreciative of India's economic development, its increasing export market, improving Indo-Pak relations, increasing presence of women in government bodies, China-India defence dialogues, environmental cooperation, and so on. In an article in the *China Daily*—"Better Media Links Help China, India"—the importance of media communication between China and India, and how to strengthen the media cooperation between the two was highlighted.[21] On the one hand, China is a diverse society with many opinions. On the other hand, Sino-Indian relations are endowed with much dynamism. Thus, *China Daily* gives the Chinese people an alternative view of India. These positive comments are not guided by the government but only reflect the constructive and beneficial perspective on Sino-Indian relations. There is further need for looking at the Sino-Indian bilateral relations through this constructive and cooperative prism.

The Media's Impact on Sino-Indian Relations—Television Media

CCTV-4 (China), NDTV 24x7 (India) and Headlines Today (India)

The television industry is flourishing in China and India with all kinds of multi-dimensional and wide-ranging TV programmes. Many large TV companies have extended popularity through their websites with live shows, reality shows and video profiles. This paper now looks at information in several major TV station's websites and attempts to give a brief analysis of the impact of TV industry on Sino-Indian relations.

A comparison between print news reports and TV programmes shows that the two differ with respect to the simplicity and objectivity of their content. Several TV programmes reflect a country's intentions and strategies through a nuanced presentation of underlying motives. With regards to China, the study looks into the programme "Focus Today" broadcast on CCTV-4 (China Central TV-International), a discussion programme hosted for two guests who are experts on international relations and specialize in the relevant topic. Sometimes, former officials from the Foreign Affairs Department or senior journalists are also invited to give comments. "Focus Today" is a daily programme reporting and analysing fiercely discussed topics in international relations and holds high prestige and authority. Correspondingly, a selection of video shows and articles from the websites of two major Indian TV Stations, *NDTV 24x7*, and *Headlines Today* are used in this paper to illustrate Indians' attitude toward China. The main contents, attitudes and impacts on people are given below.

There were about 16 programmes about India on CCTV-4 from the beginning of the year 2009 to the end of March 2010,[22] among which 11 programmes focused on the military dimension, that is India's military purchase bills, missile tests, innovations of new weapons, such as AWACS and nuclear submarines, the construction of an aircraft carrier, and joint-military exercises with the US and other countries. The remaining five programmes covered India-Pakistan relations, the Indian elections, China-India-US trilateral relations and the Sino-Indian border dispute.

Analysis of India's military modernisation is a prominent feature of "Focus Today" in observing India. It gives a careful introduction and analysis on almost every type of India's newly developed arms and munitions, such as the Brahmos missile, Prithvi-II missile, and Agni-3 ballistic missile. The programme also argues that India wants to expand its political influence and build a "half-moon encirclement" of China by exporting these advanced weapons to Southeast Asian countries. In addition, India ranks first in purchasing arms among developing countries. It signed contracts of more than US$10 billion to buy advanced arms from Russia. The fast development of India's military arouses great concern within China. It reveals India's intention to be a world power beyond South Asia. India also claims to want a strong naval force by the end of 2015 with three aircraft carriers and 145 ocean-going ships, which indicates its ambition to enter the Pacific Ocean and compete with China.[23]

Headlines Today is a popular 24-hour English language television network that carries news and current affairs in India. Several programmes with sections on "International" and "Cover Story" have been referred to for the purpose of this essay.[24] *Headlines Today* is mainly concerned about China's rise and its relation with Pakistan. It quotes a remark by SM Krishna, the Indian Minister of External Affairs of India that "India does not see China in 'antagonistic terms'," and "it believes that there is enough space for both to develop in a 'mutually supportive manner while remaining sensitive to each other's concerns and aspirations', as befits good neighbours and strategic partners".[25] This statement represents the overall attitude of Indian government and the programme.

NDTV 24x7 is another influential Indian English language television network and gives thousands of reports about China.[26] It highlights a lot of constructive aspects of Sino-Indian relations, such as the cooperation in Himalayan region over water resources, China's friendly feedback to India's on its Agni-3 missile test[27] and so on. However, some reports in NDTV also exaggerate China's threat with numerous military reports reporting negative implications. For example, it applauds India's infrastructure build-up and placement of an AN-32 transport aircraft of the Indian Air Force close to the Line of Actual Control with China,[28] which may impede Sino-Indian negotiation on resolving their border disputes. *NDTV 24x7* also actively fomented the verbal war between China and India in the year of 2009 by continuously reporting on "China's intrusion" on the "Indian territory".

To sum up, TV programmes are able to impose direct impressions on audience through compelling visual effects. Overall, the TV industry gives an objective analysis and multi-dimensional perspective on Sino-Indian relations due to competing arguments. Though extreme or biased reports also exist in Indian and Chinese TV programmes, they are far fewer compared to mainstream constructive and friendly perceptions of Sino-Indian cooperation.

Impact of Think-Tanks on Sino-Indian Relations

The number of think-tanks has grown rapidly in both China and India. Chinese think-tanks always have formal or informal linkages with the government while in India think-tanks with official connections coexist with independent ones. For the purpose of this paper, the China Institute of Contemporary International Relations (CICIR) based in China and the Institute of Peace and Conflict Studies (IPCS) in India have been taken as the main subjects of study to see the impact of think-tanks on Sino-Indian relations by examining their publications and works.

There were 26 papers published in the journal *Contemporary International Relations*, which is published by CICIR, from the beginning of 2000 to the end of 2009 that were related to India. These 26 articles covered economic, political, military and cultural aspects of India's development and gave analysis on Sino-Indian relations, Sino-Indian border dispute and the overall strategy of Indian diplomacy. However, compared to the IPCS, the analysis and comments available in *Contemporary International Relations* are not comprehensive or sophisticated enough. Though IPCS does not have a journal but it does publish short articles and issue briefs and longer special reports, research papers, and books as well as seminar reports, conference reports and book reviews. Searching with the key word—"China," the search engine produces over one thousand results from 1997 to 2010 covering almost every aspect of Sino-India relations[29] on the IPCS website. This section gives a summary and analysis of the main content and attitudes of *Contemporary International Relations* and the IPCS' published articles.

Nearly half the articles in *Contemporary International Relations* concentrate on India's rise, development trends and grand strategies. The articles argue that though India has made significant achievement in the economic and military fields, there are still many negative factors impeding its further development, such as the complex political system, fragile infrastructure and the Kashmir dispute with Pakistan.[30] The foreign policy goal of India is to be a world power and the strategy of India is to expand its influence at three levels, namely South Asia, Asia and the world.[31] Though it is unlikely that India will pursue its international status through violence, it still challenges international stability.[32] In addition, to become a world power, India manages to aggregate different thoughts, values and diverse cultures within the country by promoting the idea that all ethnic groups belong to one nation that is 'India,' it implements secular policies to eliminate religious conflicts, encourages uniform language to enhance domestic communication and carries out unified and centralized administrative system, as well as advocates democracy and the ultimate national goal of being a great power.[33]

Other papers in *Contemporary International Relations* relate to India's military modernisation, economic development and relations with other countries. India regards military modernisation as a prerequisite to becoming a world power. It intends to develop into a strong military power by the year 2015 with continuous efforts at updating military strategies, modernizing war theories, reforming the military command structure, developing information technology, and speeding up the construction of strategic nuclear forces.[34] In the economic domain, China recognizes India's achievements and potential for future development, especially in the IT industry.[35] However, except one article titled "India-Israel Strategic Cooperation and Influence," which concentrates on Indo-Israeli military and security cooperation, there are no other articles concentrating on India's relations with other countries.

The Institute of Peace and Conflict Studies in India for its part, conducts a comprehensive and thorough study of China with articles from authors from both within and outside the Institute. In the military and security domain, India is deeply concerned about East Asian security matters and is wary of China's naval ambitions. With regards to Northeast Asia, the IPCS[36] has, for example, dealt with the new contract between North Korea and China that provides China with access to the Rajin port till the year 2028. This route will not only offer China a trade route for its products from its landlocked provinces and export of Siberian gas and oil, but also presents China's naval power in the Sea of Japan an access to the Arctic Ocean.[37] In Southeast Asia, the IPCS considers China's foreign policy goals to be guided by the build-up of political, economic and military cooperation with its neighbouring countries in order to counter-balance American and Japanese influence in this region and to address the South China Sea dispute. Also, China seeks cooperation with Southeast Asian countries to implement the "string of pearls" strategy against India. Under such circumstances, India needs to seek direct linkages with ASEAN and a pan-Asia FTA, which could weaken the influence of China in this region.[38]

In addition, China's sending warships to the Somali coast and its attempts at possessing an aircraft carrier are seen by India as a display of Chinese ambition to be a naval power which arouses Indian concerns. China's ambitions result from two reasons: first of all, China seeks to protect its vital energy supply routes, and next, because it pursues the vision of being a great power. This situation results in a perception of concern among the Asian countries, which China needs to allay at multilateral forums.[39] Besides this, India pays great attention to China's aspirations for gaining a presence in the Indian Ocean by establishing a line of bases in Bangladesh, Cambodia, Myanmar, Pakistan, Thailand and the South China Sea, as well as near the Middle East and Africa. It leads India to look for cooperation with Vietnam, Indonesia, Japan and Australia to counter Chinese threats.[40]

The border dispute, mainly in "Arunachal Pradesh" and especially the "Tawang Tract", is a key issue straining the Sino-Indian diplomatic relations during the past years. Some authors published on the IPCS website argue that due to historical conflicts, India has no faith in the promises made by China.[41] "Arunachal Pradesh" is the focus of a border dispute, which is of great strategic interest for both China and India. India should upgrade the discussion to a new higher level and hasten the socioeconomic development of the state.[42] There is a feeling that besides the diplomatic efforts going on, military preparation in this area is necessary, considering the possibility that China can commence a limited or partial war against India in order to get the territory back after the death of current Dalai Lama.[43] At the same time however, there are other works holding more hopeful views of a cooperative relationship with China in dealing with disputes and disagreements.

In the economic domain, India appeals to China to address its concerns on creating a more balanced and beneficial trade relationship considering the present imbalanced trade between China and India. Of late, China has exported more value-added products to India while India's export to China mostly comprise raw materials. Thus, India is seeking appropriate economic and diplomatic measures from China to bridge the gap.[44]

Besides these aspects mentioned above, the Indian think-tank also offers incisive observations on China's relations with other countries and its domestic affairs. For example, India considers China's Xinjiang unrest in July 2009 as a learning opportunity for India, which faces similar separatist movements. It argues that to resolve such issues, dialogue may be more effective than harsh anti-terror legislations.[45] Analysing China's nationalism, the IPCS believes that managing nationalism can prove to be an effective leverage at international negotiating forums, but to keep nationalism in control requires the government to address income inequality and to deliver social justice.[46]

On the basis of the above analysis of the content and attitudes of the CICIR and IPCS, the following conclusions can be drawn. In the final analysis, both think-tanks conduct prudent and responsible studies on each other, which provide governments with reliable and comprehensive policymaking suggestions and strategies. However, certain shortcomings and deficiencies still exist in their studies. First, China assigns insufficient resources for studies on India, which does not parallel the growing importance of India in international relations and hence is far behind India's explorations on China. Not only *Contemporary International Relations* but also other publications in China focus very less on India as a region.[47] Lesser research focus obviously results in lesser attention which then proves to be an impediment to Sino-Indian relations. Second, most studies of the CICIR and IPCS are restricted to certain subjects in the economic, political, and military domains or to relations with some other country. However, as increasingly important actors in the international arena, China and India should put aside insignificant frictions to perceive their relations in a much broader way. What kind of roles China and India could play in the future and how they perceive their relations are more important aspects than short-term insignificant conflicts. Scholars should upgrade their perceptions of Sino-Indian relations to the systemic level instead of just regional or sub-regional levels and make comprehensive attempts to explore mutually beneficial solutions serving the national interests of both the countries. Third, the Cold War mentality still persists in the study of Sino-Indian relations. Due to historical reasons, China and India are used to portraying each other as potential enemies. However, this practice is dangerous and detrimental to future Sino-Indian relations. There is no chance for either China or India to become a world power if they continue with containment or confrontationist policies towards each other. The longer stereotypes exist, the worse China-India relations would become. And finally, most studies of think-tanks in China and India concentrate on hard power analysis—military modernisation and economic development being the favourite subjects. However, as a part of the soft power dimension, think-tanks should, along with the media, make contributions to the field of idea innovation and value construction. These are significant lessons that China and India can learn from Western countries.

Conclusion

The media and think-tanks in China and India wield significant and profound impact on Sino-Indian relations. On the one hand, intensive media interaction and numerous academic works promote mutual understanding between China and India while on the other, spontaneous and short-sighted public commentaries and academic efforts also result in negative impact. Especially vulnerable is the nature of nationalism in the two countries which can be exacerbated by the biased exchanges of these actors. Considering China's and India's rising status in the world system and their history of conflict, nationalism can be more devastating than useful in these two societies. Thus, how to channel the extreme patriotic sentiments into rational and constructive emotions is a challenge for Chinese and Indian governments and also a responsibility of the media and think-tanks.

Besides, given the brilliance of the two civilizations and their rich cultural histories, it does not seem appropriate and in consonance with their noble images to denigrate each other in the international arena. As rising powers, China and India should know how to construct their soft power and build positive international images to their own advantage. Thus, China and India could better leverage the media and think-tanks as strategic tools of expanding international influence and promoting world status, instead of viewing them as a battlefield for verbal wars and insignificant blame-games. More specifically, the media and think-tanks in the two countries should have a tolerant mindset and innovative spirit about each other's position in the world; they should rid themselves of the Cold War mentality and focus more on similarities instead of differences, on cultural attraction instead of social deficiencies by appropriating skills from the disciplines of journalism, communication and marketing.

Though there are some critical differences between China and India, the task for the media and think-tanks is to reduce the negative impact of tensions and prevent them from doing any further harm to Sino-Indian cooperation. After all, peaceful coexistence and cooperation are the preconditions for China's and India's pursuit of the larger goal of achieving a higher world status.

To conclude, in the long run, China and India need to carefully design their cooperative endeavours to serve their interests and aspirations for great power status. In the short term, the two countries should cooperate on subjects such as terrorism, environmental protection, poverty and development. They should act pre-emptively to cope with these challenges instead of waiting till it is too late. Similarly, the media and think-tanks in China and India should improve both their attitude and the quality of their research being done on each other. Only thus would China and India have a chance to build a favourable political environment for constructive relations in the future.

Notes

1. Lars Willnat, Joseph Graf and Paul R. Brewer, "Priming International Affairs: How the Media Influence Attitudes toward Foreign Countries", presented at the Annual Meeting of the Association for Education in Journalism and Mass Communication, George Washington University, 2000, abstract, p. 2.
2. *China Knowledge Online*, "China Media Industry", 20 March 2010, http://www.chinaknowledge.com/Business/CBGdetails.aspx?subchap=4&content=20.
3. *CRI News*, "China's TV Industry in Heated Competition", 20 March 2010, http://english.cri.cn/3166/2006/10/24/44@154376.htm.
4. Vikas Bajaj, "In India, the Golden Age of Television Is Now", *New York Times*, 11 February 2007, http://www.nytimes.com/2007/02/11/business/yourmoney/11india.html?partner=rssnyt&emc=rss.
5. Comscore, "China, India and Japan Fuel Rapid Growth in Asia Pacific Internet Audience", Inc. 16 November 2009, http://www.comscore.com/Press_Events/Press_Releases/2009/11/China_India_Japan_Fuel_Rapid_Growth_in_Asia_Pacific_Internet_Audience/(language)/eng-US.
6. James G. McGann,"The Think Tanks & Civil Societies Program—The Global Go-To-Think-Tanks", University of Pennsylvania, http://www.sas.upenn.edu/irp/documents/2008_Global_Go_To_Think_Tanks.pdf, pp. 34-35.
7. Ibid., p. 7.
8. Ibid., pp. 27, 28.
9. Ibid., pp. 34, 35.

10. ABC is a forum of the world's leading magazine and newspaper publishers, advertisers and advertising agencies. The organization provides credible, verified information essential to the media buying and selling process. ABC maintains the world's foremost electronic database of audited-circulation information and an array of verified readership, subscriber demographics and online activity data. It is a non-profit, worldwide organization founded in 1948. For more information see http://www.accessabc.com/index.html
11. Advanced search page in *China Daily*'s official website: http://search.chinadaily.com.cn/advancesearchenall.htm. Search result page with key word "India": http://search.chinadaily.com.cn/searchen.jsp?searchText=India&strTitle=&strAuthor=&strNodename=&strFromdate=2010-01-01&strTodate=2010-03-31&strSortBy=&page=4&ch=2@cndy&secondsearch=ONSearch result page with key word "Indian": http://search.chinadaily.com.cn/searchen.jsp?channelname=ICS_EN&strTodate=2010-03-31&secondsearch=ON&strFromdate=2010-01-01&searchText=Indian&ch=2@cndy&usedate=yes&f_yy=2010&f_mm=01&f_dd=01&t_yy=2010&t_mm=03&t_dd=31&strAuthor=. There is no article found with key word "Indo-". All retrieved on 5 April 2010.
12. *Global Times* is published only on weekdays.
13. Search result of "China" and "Chinese" in archive of the *Times of India* can be found at: http://epaper.timesofindia.com/Archive/skins/pastissues2/navigator.asp?login=default&AW=1268673378781. All retrieved on 5 April 2010.
14. The number of "Overall International News in Each Issue" is an average number counted from three randomly chosen issues from *China Daily*, the *Global Times* and the *Times of India* respectively during the study period.
15. Randomly counting the number of news report on 15 January, 18 February and 26 March in *China Daily* in 2010. This includes news in the the World and International pages. 2010-1-15: 12 articles, 2010-2-18: 16 articles, 2010-3-26: 9 articles; average: 12.3 articles.
16. Randomly counting the number of news report on 11 January, 25 February and 12 March in *Global Times* in 2010. This excludes news in the Taiwan Fax, Entertainment and Sports, Life, Advertisement and Picture pages. 2010-1-11: 51 articles, 2010-2-25: 54 articles, 2010-3-12: 62 articles; in average: 55.7 articles.
17. Randomly counting the number of news report on 11 January, 2 February and 3 March in the *Times of India* in 2010. This includes news in the Front, International, and Times Global pages. 2010-1-11: 26 articles, 2010-2-2: 26 articles, 2010-3-3: 22 articles; in average: 24.7 articles.
18. While the *Global Times* too is a government sanctioned newspaper, it is a self-governing institution which does not necessarily hold the same opinion as the government. Relatively speaking, it is a free forum for discussion, which always has the government's attention.
19. According to the code of ethics of the media industry, the press has the obligation of being objective. However, due to various reasons, absolute objectivity is almost unachievable. By definition, being "objective" means "expressing or dealing with facts or conditions as perceived without distortion by personal feelings, prejudices, or interpretations" (Merriam-Webster dictionary: Objective: 3-a); being "negative" means "marked by features of hostility, withdrawal, or pessimism that hinder or oppose constructive treatment or development" (Merriam-Webster Dictionary : Negative: 2-a); being "Positive" means "indication, relating to, or characterized by affirmation, addition, inclusion, or presence rather than negation, withholding, or absence" (Merriam-Webster Dictionary: Positive: 4-a). The authors classify all articles into three categories based on the above three definitions. However,

misinterpretations cannot be totally excluded. In simple term, articles containing the attitudes of approval, praise and even admiration are classified as "With Positive Implications"; articles containing hostility, pessimism, biased disapproval or criticism are tagged as "With Negative Implications"; other articles, either object or conveying unclear attitude are labeled as "Without Clear Inclination".

20. For China's side, see "US Media Worry about the out of Control of the Vituperative War of Words between China and India", *Global Times*, 24 October 2009, http://world.people.com.cn/GB/10250823.html. On the Indian side, see "How to Deal with an Aggressive China," *Headline Today*, 29 October 2009, http://indiatoday.intoday.in/site/Story/68539/Cover%20Story/How+to+deal+with+an+aggressive+China.html.
21. Hu Haiyan and Ai Yang, "Better Media Links Help China, India", *China Daily*, 31 March 2010, p. 11.
22. The official website of CCTV-4 website is http://space.tv.cctv.com/page/PAGE1221556446427735; Programmes of 2009-2010 are located at http://space.tv.cctv.com/act/platform/view/page/composePage.jsp?pageId=PAGE1234166432279693; and archive locates in http://space.tv.cctv.com/page/PAGE1252566620584105. All retrieved on 7 April 2010.
23. *CCTV-4*, "The Frequent Missile Tests and Large-scale Arms Purchases of India", Focus Today, 28 March 2010, http://space.tv.cctv.com/video/VIDE1269788259799885.
24. The home page of *Headlines Today* is http://headlinestoday.Intody.in/site/headlines_today/home.
25. *Headlines Today*, "India Concerned about China's Weapons Supply to Pakistan: Krishna", 3 January 2010, http://indiatoday.intoday.in/site/Story/77598/International/India+concerned+about+China.
26. The home page of NDTV 24x7 is http://www.ndtv.com/news/index.php. Search results of "China" retrieved on 6 April 2010, http://www.ndtv.com/news/search/result.php?cx=partner-pub-7641565019577886%3Ax0cui3-m2pp&cof=FORID%3A10&ie=ISO-8859-1&q=China&sa=Go&siteurl=www.ndtv.com%2Fnews%2 Fworld%2F&siteurl=www.ndtv.com%2Fnews%2Fworld%2F#1141.
27. *NDTV 24x7*, "Agni's not a threat, India's a friend: China", 9 February 2010, http://www.ndtv.com/news/world/india_china_does_not_pose_threat_to_each_other.php.
28. Nitin Gokhale, "Air Force Lands Plane near China Border in Ladakh", *NDTV 24x7*, 18 September 2009, http://www.ndtv.com/news/india/air_force_lands_an-32_near_china_border_in_ladakh.php.
29. The home page of IPCS is http://www.ipcs.org/, and the search result of "China" are located at in http://www.ipcs.org/search_result.php?keyword=China&search.x=13&search.y=11. All retrieved on 27 April 2010.
30. Ma Jiali, "Posture of India's Rise", *Contemporary International Relations* (6), 2006, pp. 51-55.
31. Song Dexing, "Observing India's Pursuit of Being a Great Power from the Perspective of Strategic Culture", *Contemporary International Relations* (6), 2008, pp. 27-33.
32. Zhao Gancheng, "International System and the Rise of India", *Contemporary International Relations*, (6), 2005, pp. 20-27.
33. Dao Shulin and Zhang Siqi, "The Improvement and Development of India's 'National Belief'", *Contemporary International Relations* (10), 2004, pp. 21-23.
34. Wan Wei, "India Vigorously Promotes Military Reform," *Contemporary International*

Relations, (10), 2004, pp. 13-16.
35. Zhang Minqiu, "Features and Prospects of India's Economic Development", *Contemporary International Relations*, (10), 2004, pp. 11-13.
36. The expression 'IPCS' here is used as a matter of convenience to refer to the author or authors and does not indicate an institutional point of view.
37. Gunjan Singh, "East Asian Security Perceptions", IPCS, *Article* #3076, 26 March 2010, http://www.ipcs.org/article/china/east-asian-security-perceptions-3076.html.
38. Iskander Rehman, "Sino-Indian Border Skirmishes: Towards a Limited Confrontation?", IPCS, *Issue Brief* #117, September 2009, from http://www.ipcs.org/pdf_file/issue/IB117-Iskander-IndiaChina.pdf.
39. Hayoun Ryou, "Is China Becoming Blue Water Navy?", IPCS, *Article* #2820, 27 February 2009, http://www.ipcs.org/article/military/is-china-becoming-blue-water-navy-2820.html.
40. Kriti Singh, "Chinese Naval Ambitions—Concern for India?", IPCS, *Article* #3045, 18 January 2010, http://www.ipcs.org/article/china/chinese-naval-ambitions-concern-for-india-3045.html.
41. Srikanth Kondapalli, "India's Northeast and Southeast Asia: Chinese Interests and Strategies", IPCS, *Issue Brief*, #106, June 2009, http://www.ipcs.org/pdf_file/issue/IB106-SEARP-Srikanth.pdf.
42. Mirza Zulfiqur Rahman, "The 90,000 sq kms Sino-Indian Tangle", IPCS, *Article* #2971, 18 September 2009, http://www.ipcs.org/article_details.php?articleNo=2971&submit=Jump.
43. Kondapalli, op. cit.
44. Satyajit Mohanty, "Sino-Indian Trade Ties: An Uncertain Future", IPCS, *Article* #3053, 2 February 2010, http://www.ipcs.org/article/china/sino-indian-trade-ties-an-uncertain-future-3053.html.
45. Jabin T. Jacob, "China's Xinjiang Woes: Internal and External Implications", IPCS, *Article* #2904, 14 July 2009, http://www.ipcs.org/article/china/chinas-xinjiang-woes-internal-and-external-implications-2906.html.
46. Gunjan Singh, "China at 60—Nationalism", IPCS, *Article* #2994, 30 October 2009, http://www.ipcs.org/article/china/china-at-60-nationalism-2994.html.
47. For example, another important Chinese journal, *China International Studies* published by China Institute of International Studies (CIIS), only published 13 articles about India from the beginning of 2000 to the end of 2009.

12

Bilateral Agreements and Sino-Indian Confidence-Building Measures

Jabin T. Jacob

Despite increasing political exchanges, economic interactions and people-to-people contacts, the Sino-Indian relationship remains complicated by the boundary dispute and its spillover well into the present. Chinese visa denials or issuing of stapled visas, repeated claiming of Arunachal Pradesh and their alleged incursions across the LAC form part of this spillover and have consistently managed to set back ties between India and China despite their 'strategic and cooperative partnership for peace and prosperity', announced in 2005 (*Joint Declaration by the Republic of India and the People's Republic of China*, Section III). On the Indian side, reactions to the Chinese moves often come in the form of hyperbolic statements from an aggressively market-oriented print and television media as well as from any number of strategic analysts. These too, play a role in pushing ties on a downward slope, animated as they are in general, by thinly-veiled anti-China biases. Of course, such prejudices might exist also in the Indian government and might conceivably have stymied progress in Sino-Indian relations, just as similar perceptions might have done so on the Chinese side.

That said, it is a fact that New Delhi and Beijing have concluded some major bilateral agreements—here used to refer to treaties, statements and declarations—with implications for the boundary dispute since the end of the Cold War. This is often lost sight of by analysts and the media when they discuss the state of Sino-Indian relations. Given that these agreements have been reached between two former belligerents that continue to have many reasons to be suspicious of each other, it must be surmised that they were concluded after tough negotiations and with great deliberation from both sides.

What is then important to note is that the agreements were concluded at all, and despite the many obstacles and suspicions between the two sides. While Indian foreign policy is often accused of lacking a grand strategy, these agreements suggest if not a vision for the direction of Sino-Indian relations, at least a desire to keep these stable and peaceful. Sino-Indian bilateral agreements thus put in place such measures as are required to both allay suspicions and to push things forward in a manner that enhances mutual trust and security. In other words, Sino-Indian agreements are both confidence-building measures as well as markers of the progress achieved in the relationship.

What follows is a brief examination of key agreements concluded between India and China in the post-Cold War era with implications for their boundary dispute, including the development and progression of military CBMs between the two countries.

The Agreements—Context and Content

What drove the desire for peace and stability in Sino-Indian relations despite the persistence of the boundary dispute? The answer must lie in a combination of factors.

The end of the Cold War placed both nations in a difficult position—China, because it was still recovering from the international consequences of the Tiananmen incident and would in time begin to be seen as the next big threat to the United States, and India because, it had lost a close partner and supporter in the Soviet Union. But more importantly, China in 1978, and then India in 1991, had embarked on economic reforms that required among other things, that they minimize possibilities of confrontation over their boundary dispute. As late as 1987, the two sides had seen high tension on their disputed frontier in the Sumdrung Chu incident in Arunachal Pradesh. Therefore, the *Agreement between the Government of the People's Republic of China and the Government of the Republic of India on the Maintenance of Peace and Tranquility along the Line of Actual Control in the China-India Border Areas* of 1993 is remarkable both in terms of the short distance in time travelled from 1987 before such a breakthrough was achieved, and in having been concluded so soon after the end of the Cold War, even as the world was still trying to come to grips with its consequences.

Which side had the greater motivation can be debated, but both sides clearly saw the desirability of maintaining stability on their disputed boundary. The 1993 Agreement while harking back to the Five Principles of Peaceful Coexistence or the Panchsheel principles, did not, at least from

New Delhi's point of view, fail to frame the lessons it had learned from the 1962 debacle.

For one, it calls for "effective verification measures and supervision" (Article Seven)—while acknowledging that perceptions could vary, the 1993 Agreement laid out strictures against crossing the LAC and procedures to deal with the situation when they occurred. In other words, the two sides also factored in the possibility that such incidents were inevitable. The two countries also took a big step forward in terms of confidence-building by agreeing "to reduce their military forces along the line of actual control in conformity with the requirements of the principle of mutual and equal security" (Article Two). What is notable in the present context is the fact that while the two sides might be following this stipulation on paper, the 'confidence-building' aspect of it has been given the short shrift with the buildup of troops and military infrastructure on both sides in the border areas in recent years.

A Joint Working Group was also created comprising diplomats and military personnel to help implement the Agreement and to work on the resolution of differences (Article Eight), in effect adding another layer of contact between the two sides in addition to the border patrol meetings. These contacts were probably designed to also increase the level of comfort and familiarity between the two sides but given the overall poor level of language skills on the Indian side certainly, but probably on the Chinese side as well, how far this aim has been achieved is moot.

The reliance "on the principle of good faith and mutual confidence" in the case of differences arising between the two sides (Article Eight) in fact, highlighted the fundamental weaknesses in interactions between the two sides, namely, the lack hitherto, of regular institutionalized modes of contact between the two militaries. Such institutionalization remains weak, even today. Meanwhile, in Article Six, the two sides agreed that "references to the line of actual control in this Agreement do not prejudice their respective positions on the boundary question"—underlining also that the road ahead was likely to be long and difficult.

The November 1996 *Agreement Between the Government of the People's Republic of China and the Government of the Republic of India on Confidence Building Measures in the Military Field Along the Line of Actual Control in the China-India Border Areas* was the next big step forward in terms of treaties between the two countries. Besides enjoining the two militaries not to use force against each other, Article I went on to unambiguously state the armed forces would not even, "engage in military activities that threaten the other side or undermine peace, tranquillity and stability in the China-India border areas". Given that such a formulation could be widely interpreted to cover almost any activity by either army, it would have required a rather high degree of confidence in the progression of Sino-Indian relations for the two sides to arrive at such a catch-all statement. Could this probably indicate that the boundary negotiations were making some progress and that the broad outlines of a settlement were beginning to be visible?

That said, the remainder of the treaty cannot be interpreted in so positive a light even though the two sides were able to agree on specifics such as the kind of armed units stationed on the border, and the nature and range of the weapons deployed. Suspicion or wariness is not too far from the surface as Article III.3 also states that "ceilings [on military forces and armaments] shall be determined in conformity with the requirement of the principle of mutual and equal security, with due consideration being given to parameters such as the nature of terrain, road communication and other infrastructure and time taken to induct/deinduct troops and armaments".

This is without doubt an impossible task to achieve, given that such determinations are almost entirely subjective. It is also notable that even as the two sides charged each other to "avoid holding large scale military exercises involving more than one Division (approximately 15,000 troops) in close proximity of the line of actual control" (Article IV.1), they also acknowledged that such exercises would perhaps need to be conducted. So they agreed that "the strategic direction of the main force involved shall not be towards the other side" and that "a major military exercise involving more than one Brigade Group (approximately 5,000 troops) in close proximity of the line of actual control in the China-India border areas" (Article IV.2) would require giving the other side prior notification.

Article V.2 states that "combat aircraft... shall not fly within ten kilometres of the line of actual control"—again a difficult proposition to implement given that the two sides have differing perceptions of where the LAC lies. In fact, one of the complaints on the Indian side has been the frequency of Chinese air intrusions—the very fact that 'intrusions' take place despite a 10km-wide no-fly zone indicates the distance in the respective perceptions between the two sides on the alignment of the LAC. Indeed, the 1996 treaty itself acknowledges the problem with Article X stating that the "full implementation of some of the provisions of the present Agreement will depend on the two sides arriving at a common understanding of the alignment of the line of actual control in the China-India border areas..." and therefore, the two sides would "speed up the process of clarification and confirmation of the line of actual control". This process has still not been completed and even the exchange of maps suggested in this Article has taken place so far only for the Middle Sector.

Where the 1996 Agreement relied on the China-India Joint Working Group on the Boundary Question assisted by the China-India Diplomatic and Military Expert Group, to work out the modalities of a solution, under the *Declaration on Principles for Relations and Comprehensive Cooperation between the Republic of India and the People's Republic of China* signed in 2003 each side appointed a Special Representative "to explore from the political perspective of the overall bilateral relationship the framework of a boundary settlement". In between the 1996 and 2003 agreements, the nature and direction of Sino-Indians relations had changed rather dramatically with the 1998 Indian nuclear tests in which China was more or less explicitly targeted as the cause behind India going nuclear.[1] Another event that had significant impact regionally and globally were the 9/11 attacks that brought the US back into South Asia as part of its 'war on terror'.

Together, the 1998 nuclear tests and 9/11 managed to change Chinese geopolitical perceptions of India at a time when the Chinese economy was also beginning to open up a significant gap with India and to make an impact globally. However, by 2003, India had begun to interest the Chinese even in the economic domain—it had by now begun registering significant rates of economic growth itself, and was also a prospective market for Chinese goods and companies. Thus, the political and the economic combined to set the foundation for the 2003 *Declaration* which unlike the 1993 and 1996 Agreements which placed the two militaries as the key actors in confidence-building, gave greater weight to larger political goals and their achievement as elements of confidence-building. Thus, the 2003 *Declaration* saw explicit references to the shared goals of maintaining international peace, poverty elimination, reducing the gap between developed and developing countries, strengthening the UN system, environmental protection and sustainable development—all of which have been repeated in subsequent declarations.

Once again, differences between the two countries were subtly highlighted when the treaty declared that "[e]very country has the right to choose its own political system and path to development", even as it seemed to suggest a coming together against Western reasons for military intervention in various countries. The reference to reform of the UN Security Council was a Chinese bow to India's desire to become a permanent member but has in the decade since it was put down on paper, remained a largely rhetorical commitment. Even the reference to nuclear disarmament and the elimination of nuclear weapons can be read as underscoring the differences between the two sides—China does not recognize India as a nuclear weapon state and nor is India fully satisfied that the China-Pakistan nexus in nuclear technology transfers is not being used against India.

Terrorism was another area where India and China sought to find common ground in the 2003 treaty but once again, the reference to the issue actually also brings out differences in the way both sides defined terrorism and perceived the nature of the problem within their respective territories. In other words, China remained wary of pointing fingers publicly at Pakistan either for the terrorist problem in India or for the support that Pakistani actors extended to fomenting trouble inside China.[2]

The reference to sub-regional multilateral cooperation in Asia indicated a growing interest by both countries in processes then underway. But New Delhi has until quite recently,[3] been steadfastly opposed to giving much play to such initiatives as the BCIM (Bangladesh-China-India-Myanmar) Regional Cooperation Forum, while Beijing for its part has been reluctant to acknowledge Indian claims to becoming a part of ASEAN-led economic forums such as the ASEAN+3.[4]

Another subtle hedge in the 2003 Declaration that would be thrown into sharper relief in a couple of years was the statement that "the improvement and development of India-China relations is not targeted at any third country and does not affect either country's existing friendly relations and cooperation with other countries". Clearly, China had begun to worry about the American presence in the region and the potential for closer Indo-US collaboration. The Indians for their part had begun to think of the possibility of overcoming decades of estrangement with the United States—the Strobe Talbott-Jaswant Singh talks had begun almost immediately after the 1998 nuclear tests—and probably wanted to assuage any Chinese fears on this count.

In the event, the next major agreement signed between India and China, the April 2005 *Agreement between the Government of the Republic of India and the Government of the People's Republic of China on the Political Parameters and Guiding Principles for the Settlement of the India-China Boundary Question* would be followed only a month later by the Manmohan Singh-George W Bush agreement that would set in motion the Indo-US civilian nuclear deal with all its consequences for the global nuclear regime. The deal almost completely diverted attention from the progress in Sino-Indian ties to the much more—to Indian minds, at least—comprehensible Indo-US relationship. In the end, the actual passage of the Indo-US nuclear deal through the US Congress, the Nuclear Suppliers Group and the Indian Parliament or its terms were barely comprehended by either the general Indian public or their representatives but good Indo-US ties were, nevertheless, seen as vastly more important and preferable, by large sections of the Indian government, intelligentsia and general public.

Thus, the significance of the 2005 Agreement has been missed by most

Indians bar the China specialists. Certainly, the *Protocol between the Government of the Republic of India and the Government of the People's Republic of China on Modalities for the Implementation of Confidence Building Measures in the Military Field Along the Line of Actual Control in the India-China Border Areas* signed together with the Agreement did not make any significant additions to the measures outlined in 1996 but the main Agreement itself was a landmark event.

In it, India more or less returned to a framework of accepting the status quo—in other words, it accepted a package solution to the boundary dispute with minor adjustments (Article III). China appeared to ease up a little on a major position that it had held since at least the mid-1980s that the Eastern Sector encompassing Arunachal Pradesh was the most important part of the dispute. Specifically, in Article VII which declared that "[i]n reaching a boundary settlement, the two sides shall safeguard due interests of their settled populations in the border areas", China appeared to be giving up its claim on Tawang. Birthplace of the sixth Dalai Lama and an important site of Tibetan Buddhism and of Tibetan temporal power in history, the Chinese had always insisted that Tawang had been a part of Tibet and hence a part of China. In the event, the implications that the Indians read in Article VII would soon be disputed by the Chinese government.[5] As a result, China continues to maintain that Tawang's 'return' is a minimum condition for settlement of the bilateral dispute. Nevertheless, given current realities, one must also wonder if such Chinese insistence is not simply a negotiating tactic.

And that is where in essence Sino-Indian relations and progress on confidence-building measures have stopped despite the later *Joint Declaration by the Republic of India and the People's Republic of China* signed in November 2006. In this *Declaration*, the key point related to military CBMs was the acknowledgement that the exchange of visits between defence personnel had "resulted in building of mutual trust and enhancement of mutual understanding between the defence establishments of the two countries" (Section V.19). Ironically, these exchanges of visits have been affected in the last few years with Indian military officials being denied visas on grounds ranging from service in the 'disputed' region of Jammu and Kashmir to being domiciled in Arunachal Pradesh.

In order to further develop defence cooperation, the *Joint Declaration* used as its institutional framework the *Memorandum of Understanding between the Ministry of Defence of the Republic of India and the Ministry of National Defence of the People's Republic of China for Exchanges and Cooperation in the Field of Defence*, signed earlier in May 2006. In this *Memorandum* is the suggestion for an Annual Defence Dialogue which commenced in 2007.

Meanwhile, it needs to be asked if, in the explicit reference to "the relevant purposes and principles of the Charter of the United Nations" and to the "endeavour...to hold joint military exercises and/or training programmes in the fields of search and rescue, anti-piracy, counter-terrorism and other areas of mutual interest" (Article 1(c)) there was a desire to get the two militaries to work together in traditional and non-traditional security missions. In the event, promising as it is, such cooperation has yet to take off. The *Memorandum* also talks about establishing "study tours for each other's senior and middle level military officers and relevant civilian officials" (Article 1(d))—these have started but have not reached any substantial numbers in terms of either officers visiting or those studying at each other's institutions.

Despite the Special Representatives entering into discussions of a possible 'political' solution to the dispute, the Joint Working Group on the India-China Boundary Question continues to be tasked with expediting its work, "including on the clarification and confirmation of the line of actual control and the implementation of confidence building measures" (*Joint Declaration*, Section VI.22). The same section goes on to reiterate that the two sides had to complete "the process of exchanging maps indicating their respective perceptions of the entire alignment of the LAC on the basis of already agreed parameters as soon as possible". It is important to note at this point that one of the factors that have vitiated relations between China and India and called into question the efficacy of confidence-building measures between the two sides in recent years, is the reported 'incursions' by the Chinese across the LAC. Indian media coverage on the issue has been especially high and the tone of such reports particularly strident, suggesting that Chinese activity in this regard, has been increasing and become more aggressive. However, sources within the Indian government, including the Indian Army, themselves discount any such increase either in frequency or in terms of aggressive behaviour. According to them, there has been no major change in the patterns of Chinese 'incursions' across the LAC—the Chinese continue to do as they have always done over the years and Indian troops too, continue their usual pattern of activity.

At the same time, the 2008 *A Shared Vision for the 21st Century of the People's Republic of China and the Republic of India* suggests that the two countries realized that there was a need to remedy impressions gaining ground that each was engaged in aligning or hedging against the other. The document reflects this sentiment when it declares "the right of each country to choose its own path of social, economic and political development". While in 2003, a similar statement could have been seen as expressing concern about American actions in Iraq, Afghanistan and elsewhere, in 2008, with Indo-US relations getting warmer as the civilian nuclear deal progressed, it suggested that the United States was however, no cause for differences between India and China.

Meanwhile, in the bilateral military context, the huge attention that LAC incursions have generated over the last few years is probably what has compelled the two sides to conclude the latest *Agreement between the Government of the Republic of India and the Government of the People's Republic of China on the Establishment of a Working Mechanism for Consultation and Coordination on India-China Border Affairs* of January 2012.

This agreement in fact goes one step below the Special Representatives to establish a hotline between the Joint Secretary (East Asia) in the Indian Ministry of External Affairs and his counterpart at the level of a Director General level official in the Chinese Ministry of Foreign Affairs (Article II). Article IV notes that "[t]he Working Mechanism will explore the possibility of cooperation in the border areas that are agreed upon by the two sides" but unlike 1996 *Agreement* where very specific details were available, there are none whatsoever in the 2012 *Agreement* indicating perhaps that the two sides found it difficult to reach agreement on how to achieve such cooperation.

And, in the very categorical statement of Article V that the Working Mechanism "will not discuss resolution of the Boundary Question or affect the Special Representatives Mechanism" it would appear somewhat counter-intuitively that even if the latter mechanism is seen as the primary forum, it might take a break, while the former "will address issues and situations that may arise in the border areas that affect the maintenance of peace and tranquillity and will work actively towards maintaining the friendly atmosphere between the two countries" (Article VI). A reason for such a break may be justified in that Dai Bingguo the Chinese Special Representative since the beginning of the process, is due to retire in March 2013, and his replacement might take a while to get around to dealing with India. While there might be the issue of taking time to develop some understanding and expertise of India, it might also well be that the situation in China's neighbourhood in the east, whether the Korean peninsula or the South China Sea, could require the newcomer's primary attention.

What of the Future?

The establishment of the Working Mechanism and its low declared frequency of contact (Article VIII) could also indicate that it is a stopgap arrangement during a difficult passage in Sino-Indian negotiations. On the Chinese side, there is a leadership transition underway in 2012-2013, and in the case of India, the present government appears too short of political capital and clout domestically, to expend any on foreign policy issues. These conditions suggest that any forward movement on the boundary dispute is unlikely for the immediate term. In other words, there will be increasing dependence on the CBMs already enshrined in various treaties to maintain peace and stability on the Sino-Indian border areas. At the same time, given the vastly changed domestic, regional and international contexts from the time the first CBM treaties were signed following the end of the Cold War, the efficacy of these CBMs will also come under closer scrutiny.

This in turn begs the question, if confidence can really be achieved in a state of asymmetry of military capabilities. When the first military CBM treaties were signed between India and China, the capabilities gap in favour of China was not as serious an issue as it is perceived today. Despite the presence of nuclear weapons on both sides, their respective nuclear postures and self-image as (responsible) global powers, create a situation where an 'edge' (for China) or 'parity' (for India) (howsoever defined) in conventional weapons capabilities, appears necessary before real 'confidence' is created on the LAC. Of course, a middle ground between the two positions is possible if China were to accept 'parity' or India were to be comfortable with 'near parity'—but this seems far from being the case, at least for the moment.

In short, how their bilateral CBMs will stand the test of political and military uncertainty and flux in India and China, and outside their borders, will play an important role in determining the future path of Sino-Indian relations.

NOTES

1. *New York Times*, "Nuclear Anxiety; Indian's Letter to Clinton on the Nuclear Testing", 13 May 1998, http://www.nytimes.com/1998/05/13/world/nuclear-anxiety-indian-s-letter-to-clintonon-the-nuclear-testing.html?pagewanted=1?pagewanted=1.
2. For China's dilemmas when it comes to dealing with Pakistani-origin terrorism, see Jabin T. Jacob, "China's Pakistan Quandary," IPCS, *Article* #2714, 24 October 2008, http://www.ipcs.org/article/terrorism/chinas-pakistan-quandary-2714.html.
3. On the BCIM specifically, after years of somewhat desultory attention to its activities, the Indian Foreign Secretary Ranjan Mathai in his keynote speech at the forum's 10th edition in Kolkatta in February 2012, signaled a significantly greater government interest in and support for its role in pushing India's engagement with the countries of the sub-region and larger region. Ranjan Mathai, "Speech by Foreign Secretary on India's Look East Policy at the 10th Meeting of the BCIM (Bangladesh, China, India, Myanmar) Cooperation Forum," *Speeches/Statements*, Ministry of External Affairs, Government of India, 18 February 2012, http://meaindia.nic.in/mystart.php?id=530119048.
4. For an explanation of China's reluctance see Li Mingjiang, "China and Asian

Regionalism: Pragmatism Hinders Leadership," RSIS, *Working Papers*, No. 179, http://www.rsis.edu.sg/publications/WorkingPapers/WP179.pdf.

5. Chinese Foreign minister Yang Jiechi told his Indian counterpart Pranab Mukherjee in Hamburg early June 2007 that the 'mere presence' of settled populations did not affect China's claims. Pranab Dhal Samanta, "At ADB, Beijing blocks India's $60-m project for Arunachal", *Indian Express*, 14 April 2009, http://www.indianexpress.com/news/at-adb-beijing-blocks-indias-60m-project-for-arunachal/446709/0.

APPENDICES

Major Bilateral Agreements Since the End of the Cold War

Appendix 1

Agreement between the Government of the People's Republic of China and the Government of the Republic of India on the Maintenance of Peace and Tranquility along the Line of Actual Control in the China-India Border Areas

7 September 1993

The Government of the People's Republic of China and the Government of the Republic of India, (hereinafter referred to as the two sides), have entered into the present Agreement in accordance with the Five Principles of mutual respect for sovereignty and territorial integrity, mutual non-aggression, non-interference in each other's internal affairs, equality and mutual benefit and peaceful coexistence and with a view to maintaining peace and tranquility in areas along the line of actual control in the China-India border areas.

Article One

The two sides are of the view that the China-India boundary question shall be resolved through peaceful and friendly consultations. Neither side shall use or threaten to use force against the other by any means. Pending an ultimate solution to the boundary question between the countries, the two sides shall strictly respect and observe the line of actual control between the two sides. No activities of either side shall overstep the line of actual control. In case personnel of one side cross the line of actual control, upon being cautioned by the other side, they shall immediately pull back to their own side of the line of actual control. When necessary, the two sides shall jointly check and determine the segments of the line of actual control where they have different views as to its alignment.

Article Two

Each side will keep its military forces in the areas along the line of actual control to a minimum level compatible with the friendly and good neighbourly relations between the two countries. The two sides agree to reduce their military forces along the line of actual control in conformity with the requirements of the principle of mutual and equal security to ceilings to mutually agreed. The extent, depth, timing and nature of reduction of military forces along the line of actual control shall be determined through mutual consultations between the two countries. The reduction of military forces shall be carried out by stages in mutually agreed geographical locations sectorwise within the areas along the line of actual control.

Article Three

Both sides shall work out through consultations effective confidence building measures in the areas along the line of actual control. Neither side will undertake specified levels of military exercises in mutually identified zones. Each side shall give the other prior notification of military exercises of specified levels near the line of actual control permitted under this Agreement.

Article Four

In case of contingencies or other problems arising in the areas along the line of actual control, the two sides shall deal with them through meetings and friendly consultations between border personnel of the two countries. The form of such meetings and channels of communications between the border personnel shall be mutually agreed upon by the two sides.

Article Five

The two sides agree to take adequate measures to ensure that air intrusions across the line of actual control do not take place and shall undertake mutual consultations should intrusions occur. Both sides shall also consult on possible restrictions on air exercises in areas to mutually agreed near the line of actual control.

Article Six

The two sides are agreed that references to the line of actual control in this Agreement do not prejudice their respective positions on the boundary question.

Article Seven

The two sides shall agree through consultations on the form, method, scale and content of effective verification measures and supervision required for the reduction of military forces and the maintenance of peace and tranquillity in the areas along the line of actual control under this Agreement.

Article Eight
Each side of the China-India Joint Working Group on the boundary question shall appoint diplomatic and military experts to formulate, through mutual consultations, the implementation measures for the present Agreement. The experts shall advise the Joint Working Group on the resolution of differences between the two sides on the alignment of the line of actual control and address issues relating to redeployment with a view to reduction of military forces in the areas along the line of actual control. The experts shall also assist the Joint Working Group in supervision of the implementation of the Agreement, and settlement of differences that may arise in that process, based on the principle of good faith and mutual confidence.

Article Nine
The present Agreement shall come into effect as of the date of signature and is subject to amendment and addition by agreement of the two sides.

Signed in duplicated at Beijing on September 7, 1993 in the Chinese, Hindi and English languages, all three texts having equal validity.

APPENDIX 2

Agreement Between the Government of the People's Republic of China and the Government of the Republic of India on Confidence Building Measures in the Military Field Along the Line of Actual Control in the China-India Border Areas

29 November 1996

The Government of the People's Republic of China and the Government of Republic of India (hereinafter referred to as the two sides),

Believing that it serves the fundamental interests of the peoples of China and India to foster a long-term good-neighbourly relationship in accordance with the Five Principles of mutual respect for sovereignty and territorial integrity, mutual non-aggression, non-interference in each other's internal affairs, equality and mutual benefit and peaceful co-existence,

Convinced that the maintenance of peace and tranquillity along the line of actual control in the China-India border areas accords with the fundamental interests of the two peoples and will also contribute to the ultimate resolution of the boundary question,

Reaffirming that neither side shall use or threaten to use force against the other by any means or seek unilateral military superiority,

Pursuant to the Agreement between the Government of the People's Republic of China and the Government of Republic of India on the Maintenance of Peace and Tranquillity Along the Line of Actual Control in the China-India Border Areas, signed on 7 September 1993,

Recognizing the need for effective confidence building measures in the military field along the line of actual control in the border areas between the two sides,

Noting the utility of confidence building measures already in place along the line of actual control in the China-India border areas,

Committed to enhancing mutual confidence and transparency in the military field,

Have agreed as follows:

Article I

Neither side shall use its military capability against the other side. No armed forces deployed by either side in the border areas along the line of actual control as part of their respective military strength shall be used to attack the other side, or engage in military activities that threaten the other side or undermine peace, tranquillity and stability in the China-India border areas.

Article II

The two sides reiterate their determination to seek a fair, reasonable and mutually acceptable settlement of the boundary question. Pending an ultimate resolution of the boundary question, the two sides reaffirm their commitment to strictly respect and observe the line of actual control in the China-India border areas. No activities of either side shall overstep the line of actual control.

Article III

The two sides agree to take the following measures to reduce or limit their respective military forces within mutually agreed geographical zones along the line of actual control in the China-India border areas:

1. The two sides reaffirm that they shall reduce or limit their respective military forces within mutually agreed geographical zones along the line of actual control in the China-India border areas to minimum levels compatible with friendly and good-neighbourly relations between the two countries and consistent with the principle of mutual and equal security.
2. The two sides shall reduce or limit the number of field army, border defence forces, para-military forces and any other mutually agreed category of armed force deployed in mutually agreed geographical zones along the line of actual control to ceilings to be mutually agreed upon. The major categories of armaments to be reduced or limited are as follows: combat tanks, infantry combat vehicles, guns (including howitzers) with 75 mm or bigger calibre, mortars with 120 mm or bigger calibre, surface-to-surface missiles, surface-to-air missiles and any other weapon system mutually agreed upon.
3. The two sides shall exchange data on the military forces and armaments to be reduced or limited and decide on ceilings on military forces and armaments to be kept by each side within mutually agreed geographical zones along the line of actual control in the China-India border areas. The ceilings shall be determined in conformity with the requirement of the principle of mutual and equal security, with due consideration being given to parameters

such as the nature of terrain, road communication and other infrastructure and time taken to induct/deinduct troops and armaments.

Article IV

In order to maintain peace and tranquillity along the line of actual control in the China-India border areas and to prevent any tension in the border areas due to misreading by either side of the other side's intentions:

1. Both sides shall avoid holding large scale military exercises involving more than one Division (approximately 15,000 troops) in close proximity of the line of actual control in the China-India border areas. However, if such exercises are to be conducted, the strategic direction of the main force involved shall not be towards the other side.
2. If either side conducts a major military exercise involving more than one Brigade Group (approximately 5,000 troops) in close proximity of the line of actual control in the China-India border areas, it shall give the other side prior notification with regard to type, level, planned duration and area of exercise as well as the number and type of units or formations participating in the exercise.
3. The date of completion of the exercise and deinduction of troops from the area of exercise shall be intimated to the other side within five days of completion or deinduction.
4. Each side shall be entitled to obtain timely clarification from the side undertaking the exercise in respect of data specified in Pargragh 2 of the present Article.

Article V

With a view to preventing air intrusions across the line of actual control in the China-India border areas and facilitating overflights and landings by military aircraft:

1. Both sides shall take adequate measures to ensure that air intrusions across the line of actual control do not take place. However, if an intrusion does take place, it should cease as soon as detected and the incident shall be promptly investigated by the side operating the aircraft. The results of the investigation shall be immediately communicated, through diplomatic channels or at border personnel meetings, to the other side.
2. Subject to Paragraphs 3 and 5 of this Article, combat aircraft (to include fighter, bomber, reconnaissance, military trainer, armed helicopter and other armed aircraft) shall not fly within ten

kilometres of the line of actual control.

3. If either side is required to undertake flights of combat aircraft within ten kilometres from the line of actual control, it shall give the following information in advance to the other side, through diplomatic channels:
   (a) Type and number of combat aircraft;
   (b) Height of the proposed flight (in meters);
   (c) Proposed duration of flights (normally not to exceed ten days);
   (d) Proposed timing of flights; and
   (e) Area of operations, defined in latitude and longitude.
4. Unarmed transport aircraft, survey aircraft and helicopters shall be permitted to fly up to the line of actual control.
5. No military aircraft of either side shall fly across the line of actual control, except by prior permission. Military aircraft of either side may fly across the line of actual control or overfly the other side's airspace or land on the other side only after obtaining the latter's prior permission after providing the latter with detailed information on the flight in accordance with the international practice in this regard.
   Notwithstanding the above stipulation, each side has the sovereign right to specify additional conditions, including at short notice, for flights or landings of military aircraft of the other side on its side of the line of actual control or through its airspace.
6. In order to ensure flight safety in emergency situations, the authorities designated by the two sides may contact each other by the quickest means of communications available.

Article VI

With a view to preventing dangerous military activities along the line of actual control in the China-India border areas, the two sides agree as follows:

1. Neither side shall open fire, cause bio-degradation, use hazardous chemicals, conduct blast operations or hunt with guns or explosives within two kilometres from the line of actual control. This prohibition shall not apply to routine firing activities in small arms firing ranges.
2. If there is a need to conduct blast operations within two kilometres of the line of actual control as part of developmental activities, the other side shall be informed through diplomatic channels or by convening a border personnel meeting, preferably five days in advance.
3. While conducting exercises with live ammunition in areas close to

the line of actual control, precaution shall be taken to ensure that a bullet or a missile does not accidentally fall on the other side across the line of actual control and causes harm to the personnel or property of the other side.

4. If the border personnel of the two sides come in a face-to-face situation due to differences on the alignment of the line of actual control or any other reason, they shall exercise self-restraint and take all necessary steps to avoid an escalation of the situation. Both sides shall also enter into immediate consultations through diplomatic and/or other available channels to review the situation and prevent any escalation of tension.

Article VII

In order to strengthen exchanges and cooperation between their military personnel and establishments in the border areas along the line of actual control, the two sides agree:

1. To maintain and expand the regime of scheduled and flag meetings between their border representatives at designated places along the line of actual control;
2. To maintain and expand telecommunication links between their border meeting points at designated places along the line of actual control;
3. To establish step-by-step medium and high-level contacts between the border authorities of the two sides.

Article VIII

1. Should the personnel of one side cross the line of actual control and enter the other side because of unavoidable circumstances like natural disasters, the other side shall extend all possible assistance to them and inform their side, as soon as possible, regarding the forced or inadvertent entry across the line of actual control. The modalities of return of the concerned personnel to their own side shall be settled through mutual consultations.
2. The two sides shall provide each other, at the earliest possible, with information pertaining to natural disasters and epidemic diseases in contiguous border areas which might affect the other side. The exchange of information shall take place either through diplomatic channels or at border personnel meetings.

Article IX

In case a doubtful situation develops in the border region, or in case one of the sides has some questions or doubts regarding the manner in which the other side is observing this Agreement, either side has the right to seek a clarification from the other side. The clarifications sought and replies to them shall be conveyed through diplomatic channels.

Article X

1. Recognizing that the full implementation of some of the provisions of the present Agreement will depend on the two sides arriving at a common understanding of the alignment of the line of actual control in the China-India border areas, the two sides agree to speed up the process of clarification and confirmation of the line of actual control. As an initial step in this process, they are clarifying the alignment of the line of actual control in those segments where they have different perceptions. They also agree to exchange maps indicating their respective perceptions of the entire alignment of the line of actual control as soon as possible.
2. Pending the completion of the process of clarification and confirmation of the line of actual control, the two sides shall work out modalities for implementing confidence building measures envisaged under this Agreement on an interim basis, without prejudice to their respective positions on the alignment of the line of actual control as well as on the boundary question,

Article XI

Detailed implementation measures required under Article I to Article X of this Agreement shall be decided through mutual consultations in the China-India Joint Working Group on the Boundary Question. The China-India Diplomatic and Military Expert Group shall assist the China-India Joint Working Group in devising implementation measures under the Agreement.

Article XII

This Agreement is subject to ratification and shall enter into force on the date of exchange of instruments of ratification. It shall remain in effect until either side decides to terminate it after giving six months notice in writing. It shall become invalid six months after the notification.

This Agreement is subject to amendment and addition by mutual agreement in writing between the two sides.

Signed in duplicate in New Delhi on 29 November 1996 in the Chinese, Hindi and English languages, all three texts being equally authentic. In case of divergence, the English text shall prevail.

Appendix 3

Declaration on Principles for Relations and Comprehensive Cooperation between the Republic of India and the People's Republic of China

23 June 2003

At the invitation of Premier of the State Council of the People's Republic of China H.E. Wen Jiabao, Prime Minister of the Republic of India H.E. Atal Bihari Vajpayee paid an official visit to the People's Republic of China from 22 to 27 June 2003.

During this visit, Premier Wen Jiabao held talks with Prime Minister Vajpayee. Their Excellencies President Hu Jintao of the People's Republic of China, Chairman Jiang Zemin of the Central Military Commission, Chairman Wu Bangguo of the Standing Committee of the National People's Congress and Vice President Zeng Qinghong of the People's Republic of China held separate meetings with Prime Minister Vajpayee. The talks and meetings were held in a sincere and friendly atmosphere.

Leaders from both countries noted with satisfaction the progress made over recent years in bilateral relations. This is conducive not only to their respective development, but also to regional stability and prosperity. The two sides recalled the historical depth of their friendly contacts. India and China are the two largest developing countries of the world with centuries-old civilization, unique history and similar objectives. Both noted that the sustained economic and social development in the two countries, representing one third of humanity is vital for ensuring peace, stability and prosperity not only in Asia but also in the whole world.

The two sides agreed that India and China have a mutual desire for good neighborly relations and have broad common interests. They agreed to fully utilize the substantial potential and opportunities for deepening mutually beneficial cooperation.

Friendship and cooperation between the two countries meets the need to:

- promote the socio-economic development and prosperity of both India and China;

- maintain peace and stability regionally and globally;
- strengthen multipolarity at the international level; and
- enhance the positive factors of globalization.

Both sides affirmed that they would abide by the following principles, promote a long-term constructive and cooperative partnership and, on this basis, build a qualitatively new relationship:

- Both sides are committed to developing their long-term constructive and cooperative partnership on the basis of the principles of Panchsheel, mutual respect and sensitivity for each other's concerns and equality;
- As two major developing countries, India and China have a broad mutual interest in the maintenance of peace, stability and prosperity in Asia and the world, and a mutual desire in developing wider and closer cooperation and understanding in regional and international affairs;
- The common interests of the two sides outweigh their differences. The two countries are not a threat to each other. Neither side shall use or threaten to use force against the other; and
- Both sides agree to qualitatively enhancing the bilateral relationship at all levels and in all areas while addressing differences through peaceful means in a fair, reasonable and mutually acceptable manner. The differences should not be allowed to affect the overall development of bilateral relations.

Both sides agreed to hold regular high-level exchanges between the two countries. This will greatly enhance mutual understanding and expand bilateral relations. With a view to deepening their coordination and dialogues on bilateral, regional and international issues, both sides agreed on the need for annual meetings between Foreign Ministers of the two countries. They also agreed that personnel exchanges and friendly contacts between ministries, parliaments and political parties of the two countries should be further enhanced.

The two sides welcomed the positive momentum of bilateral trade and economic cooperation in recent years and shared the belief that continued expansion and intensification of India-China economic cooperation is essential for strengthening bilateral relations.

Both sides shared the view that existing complementarities between their two economies provide an important foundation and offer broad prospects for further enhancing their economic relations. In order to promote trade and economic cooperation, both sides will take necessary measures consistent with their national laws and rules and international obligations to remove impediments to bilateral trade and investment. They reaffirmed the importance of the ministerial meeting of the Joint Economic Group (JEG) and agreed to hold the next (seventh) JEG meeting within the year.

The two sides will set up a compact Joint Study Group (JSG) composed of officials and economists to examine the potential complementarities between the two countries in expanded trade and economic cooperation. The JSG would also draw up a programme for the development of India-China trade and economic cooperation for the next five years, aimed at encouraging greater cooperation between the business communities of both sides. The Group should present a study report and recommendations to the two Governments on measures for comprehensive trade and economic cooperation by the end of June 2004.

The two countries will launch a financial dialogue and cooperation mechanism to strengthen their dialogue and coordination in this sector.

The two sides agreed to enhance cooperation at the World Trade Organization, which is not only to mutual benefit but also in the broader interest of developing countries. The two sides will hold dialogues on a regular basis in this regard.

Historical and cultural links between India and China will be strengthened, inter-alia, through the promotion of exchanges in culture, education, science and technology, media, youth and people-to-people relations. They agreed to set up Cultural Centers in each other's capitals and facilitate their establishment.

Both sides will work towards the enhancement of direct air and shipping links, tourism, exchange hydrological data in flood season on common rivers as agreed, cooperation in agriculture, dairy, food processing, health and other sectors.

They agreed on the need to broaden and deepen defence exchanges between the two countries, which will help enhance and deepen the mutual understanding and trust between the two armed forces. They confirmed that the exchange of visits by their Defence Ministers and of military officials at various levels should be strengthened.

The two sides exchanged views on the India-China boundary question and expounded their respective positions. They reiterated their readiness to seek a fair, reasonable and mutually acceptable solution through consultations on an equal footing. The two sides agreed that pending an ultimate solution, they should work together to maintain peace and tranquility in the border areas, and reiterated their commitment to continue implementation of the agreements signed for this purpose, including the clarification of the Line of Actual Control.

The two sides agreed to each appoint a Special Representative to explore from the political perspective of the overall bilateral relationship the framework of a boundary settlement.

The Indian side recognizes that the Tibet Autonomous Region is part of the territory of the People's Republic of China and reiterates that it does not allow Tibetans to engage in anti-China political activities in India. The Chinese side expresses its appreciation for the Indian position and reiterates that it is firmly opposed to any attempt and action aimed at splitting China and bringing about "independence of Tibet".

The Indian side recalled that India was among the first countries to recognize that there is one China and its one China policy remains unaltered. The Chinese side expressed its appreciation of the Indian position.

India and China recognized the primacy of maintaining international peace. This is a prerequisite for the socio-economic development of all developing countries, including India and China. The world is marked by diversity. Every country has the right to choose its own political system and path to development. As two major developing countries, India and China acknowledged the importance of their respective roles in the shaping of a new international political and economic order. The international community must help the developing countries to eliminate poverty and narrow the gap between the North and the South through dialogue and cooperation so as to achieve common prosperity.

The two sides acknowledged the vital importance of the role of the United Nations in world peace, stability and development. They are determined to continue their efforts in strengthening the UN system. They reaffirmed their readiness to work together to promote reform of the UN. In reform of the UN Security Council, priority should be given to enhancing representation of the developing countries.

Both sides stood for continued multilateral arms control and disarmament process, undiminished and equal security for all at progressively lower levels of armament and for multilateral negotiations aimed at nuclear disarmament and elimination of nuclear weapons. They are firmly opposed to introduction of weapons in outer space, use or threat of force against space-based objects and support cooperation in development of space technology for peaceful purposes.

The two sides recognised the threat posed by terrorism to them and to global peace and security. They resolutely condemned terrorism in any form. The struggle between the international community and global terrorism is a comprehensive and sustained one, with the ultimate objective of eradication of terrorism in all regions. This requires strengthening the global legal framework against terrorism. Both sides shall also promote cooperation on counter-terrorism through their bilateral dialogue mechanism.

India and China face special and similar challenges in their efforts to protect the environment while simultaneously forging ahead with rapid social and economic development of their countries. In this context, the two sides agreed to work together in a practical manner to cooperate on preserving the environment and ensuring sustainable development and to coordinate positions on climate change, biodiversity and other issues in relevant multilateral fora.

The two sides supported multilateral cooperation in Asia, believing that such cooperation promotes mutually beneficial exchanges, economic growth as well as greater cohesion among Asian countries. The two sides viewed positively each other's participation in regional and sub-regional multilateral cooperation processes in Asia.

The two sides stated that the improvement and development of India-China relations is not targeted at any third country and does not affect either country's existing friendly relations and cooperation with other countries.

The two sides agreed that the official visit of the Prime Minister of India to the People's Republic of China has been a success, has contributed to enhancing mutual understanding and trust between the Governments, leaders and peoples of the two countries, and marks a new step forward in strengthening the all-round cooperation between India and China in the new century.

Prime Minister Vajpayee invited Premier Wen Jiabao to visit India at a mutually convenient time and conveyed to President Hu Jintao an invitation from President Abdul Kalam to visit India. The Chinese side accepted the invitations with appreciation. The dates of the visits will be settled through diplomatic channels. On behalf of the Government and the people of India, H.E Prime Minister Atal Bihari Vajpayee thanked the Government and the people of China for the warm welcome received by him and his delegation.

Signed in Beijing on 23 June 2003 in the Hindi, Chinese and English languages.

(Atal Bihari Vajpayee)	(Wen Jiabao)
Prime Minister	Premier of the State Council
The Republic of India	The People's Republic of China

Appendix 4

Joint Statement of the Republic of India and the People's Republic of China

11 April 2005

I. H.E. Mr. Wen Jiabao, Premier of the State Council of the People's Republic of China, is currently paying a state visit to the Republic of India from 9 to 12 April 2005 at the invitation of H.E. Dr. Manmohan Singh, Prime Minister of the Republic of India.

During the visit, Premier Wen Jiabao held talks with Prime Minister Dr. Manmohan Singh, called on President Dr. A.P.J. Abdul Kalam and Vice President Shri Bhairon Singh Shekhawat, and met with Chairperson, United Progressive Alliance Smt. Sonia Gandhi. External Affairs Minister Shri K. Natwar Singh and Leader of Opposition, Lok Sabha Shri L.K. Advani will call on him. Premier Wen paid a visit to Bangalore and will deliver a speech at the Indian Institute of Technology in New Delhi.

Leaders of the two countries had an in-depth exchange of views in a sincere, friendly and constructive atmosphere and reached broad consensus on bilateral relations and international and regional issues of common concern.

II. The two sides reviewed the friendly contacts and progress in their bilateral relations in recent years and agreed that India-China relations have entered a new stage of comprehensive development. Both sides noted with satisfaction that with the frequent exchange of visits between leaders of the two countries, the process of building trust and understanding has gained momentum. Rapid growth of trade and economic cooperation has been coupled with the expansion of exchanges and cooperation in other fields. The two sides have made incremental progress in addressing outstanding issues. The two sides have also maintained good communication and collaboration in international and regional affairs. Both sides agreed that India and China have made satisfying progress in developing their long-term constructive and cooperative partnership.

The two sides recalled the Declaration on Principles for Relations and Comprehensive Cooperation between the two Prime Ministers on 23 June 2003 and reiterated that the Declaration provided a shared vision of bilateral relations and an agreed framework for cooperation.

III. In the light of the development of their bilateral relations, in order to promote good neighbourliness, friendship and mutually beneficial cooperation and taking into account the profound changes in the regional and international situation, the two sides agreed that India-China relations have now acquired a global and strategic character. The leaders of the two countries have, therefore, agreed to establish an India-China Strategic and Cooperative Partnership for Peace and Prosperity.

Such a partnership is based on the principles of Panchsheel, mutual respect and sensitivity for each other's concerns and aspirations, and equality; provides a sound framework for an all-round and comprehensive development of bilateral relations based on mutual and equal security, development and prosperity of the two peoples; and contributes to jointly addressing global challenges and threats. It reflects the readiness of the two sides to resolve outstanding differences in a proactive manner without letting them come in the way of the continued development of bilateral relations.

IV. The two sides agreed that high-level exchanges between the governments, parliaments and political parties of the two countries play an important role in expanding overall bilateral cooperation. They conveyed their determination to maintain and strengthen the momentum of such exchanges in future and agreed to hold regular meetings between the leaders of the two countries. In this context, the two sides also reiterated their intention to promote regular ministerial-level exchanges and make full use of the India-China strategic dialogue and other bilateral dialogue mechanisms.

V. The year of 2005 marks the 55th anniversary of the establishment of diplomatic relations between India and China. To mark the occasion, the two countries will organize a series of commemorative activities. It was noted that "Cultural Festival of China" was currently underway in India and that a corresponding "Cultural Festival of India" would be organized in China later in the year. The two sides would also organize other cultural activities to further promote mutual awareness and deepen the friendship between the two peoples. The two sides declared 2006 as the "year of India-China friendship".

Both sides expressed satisfaction with strengthened exchanges in the area of culture, and affirmed that mutual understanding and cultural exchanges would facilitate development of cooperation in other areas as well. In order to reinforce traditional cultural links, an agreement was concluded for the construction of an Indian-style Buddhist temple at Luoyang in Henan Province of China.

VI. The two sides stressed that an all-round expansion of India-China economic cooperation, including trade and investment, constitutes an important dimension of a stronger India-China relationship. The two countries agreed to make joint efforts to increase the bilateral trade volume to US$ 20 billion or higher by 2008. The two sides welcomed the report of the Joint Study Group (JSG) that was set up to examine the potential complementarities between the two countries in expanded trade and economic cooperation. The JSG in its Report has identified a series of measures related to trade in goods, trade in services, investments and other areas of economic cooperation, and recommended their expeditious implementation to remove impediments and facilitate enhanced economic engagement between India and China. The two Prime Ministers tasked the Ministerial-level India-China Joint Economic Group (JEG) to consider these recommendations and coordinate their implementation. For this purpose, the two sides will make their best endeavour to hold the next meeting of the JEG within the next six months. The JSG has also recommended an India-China Regional Trading Arrangement, comprising of trade in goods and services, investments, identified understandings for trade and investment promotion and facilitation, and measures for promotion of economic cooperation in identified sectors. The Prime Ministers agreed to appoint a Joint Task Force to study in detail the feasibility of, and the benefits that may derive from, the India-China Regional Trading Arrangement and give recommendations regarding its content.

Both sides noted that the Agreement on the Establishment of a Financial Dialogue Mechanism would further facilitate the dynamic and diversifying economic cooperation between the two sides. They will continue consultations on concluding the Bilateral Investment Promotion and Protection Agreement.

The two sides noted with satisfaction that the two countries have signed the SPS Protocols for the export of grapes and bitter gourd from India to China. The two sides also agreed to constitute a Joint Working Group to implement expeditiously the MOU on Application of SPS between the Chinese General Administration of Quality Supervision, Inspection and Quarantine and the Indian Ministry of Agriculture.

China positively evaluates market access for Indian rice to the Chinese market and will launch as early as possible the risk analysis procedure of the Indian rice in accordance with relevant Chinese laws and regulations.

VII. The two sides agreed to further promote the cooperation in the spheres of education, science and technology, healthcare, information, tourism, youth exchange, agriculture, dairy development, sports and other fields on the basis of mutual benefit and reciprocity. The two sides decided to establish an India-China Steering Committee on Scientific and Technological Cooperation chaired by their Ministers for Science and Technology, and start consultations on an agreement on mutual recognition of academic certificates and degrees between India and China. The two sides announced the launching of regular youth exchange activities. China will invite 100 Indian youth to China within the year of 2005 and hold an exhibition this year on advanced and applicable technologies in India.

VIII. The two sides recognized the importance of strengthening mutual connectivity and agreed to jointly work towards further enhancement of direct air and shipping links, tourism and people-to-people contacts. It was noted with satisfaction that an MOU on major liberalisation of civil aviation links between India and China was concluded during the visit.

IX. The two sides will continue to cooperate in exchanging flood-season hydrological data of the trans-border rivers as agreed between them.

In response to concerns expressed by the Indian side, the Chinese side agreed to take measures for controlled release of accumulated water of the landslide dam on the river Parechu, as soon as conditions permit. It was noted with satisfaction that an agreement concerning the provision of hydrological data on Sutlej/Langqen Zangbo was concluded during the visit and that the two sides had also agreed to continue bilateral discussions to finalize at an early date similar arrangements for the Parlung Zangbo and Lohit/Zayu Qu Rivers.

The two sides agreed to cooperate in the field of energy security and conservation, including, among others, encouraging relevant departments and units of the two countries to engage in the survey and exploration of petroleum and natural gas resources in third countries.

X. The two sides noted the useful exchanges and interaction in the military field and decided to further promote such exchanges and interaction. They agreed that broadening and deepening of defense exchanges between the two countries was of vital importance in enhancing mutual trust and understanding between the two armed forces, and to ensuring a peaceful environment in which they could pursue their respective national development objectives. The two sides decided to further strengthen effective contacts and exchanges in this field.

XI. During the visit, the two sides exchanged views on the India-China boundary question and reiterated their readiness to seek a fair, reasonable and mutually acceptable solution, through equal and friendly consultations and proceeding from the overall interests of bilateral relations. They expressed satisfaction over the progress made in the discussions between the Special Representatives of the two countries and welcomed the conclusion of the Agreement on the Political Parameters and Guiding Principles for the Settlement of the Boundary Question. Both sides are convinced that an early settlement of the boundary question will advance the basic interests of the two countries and should therefore be pursued as a strategic objective. They expressed their commitment to the mechanism of Special Representatives for seeking a political settlement of the boundary question in the context of their long-term interests and the overall bilateral relationship.

Pending a final resolution, the two sides will continue to make joint efforts to maintain peace and tranquility in the border areas in accordance with the Agreements of 1993 and 1996. Both sides agreed that while continuing the discussions between the Special Representatives, it is also important that the Joint Working Group (JWG) continues its work to seek an early clarification and confirmation of the Line of Actual Control (LAC). Progress made so far on the clarification of the LAC in the India-China border areas was noted. It was agreed to complete the process of exchanging maps indicating their respective perceptions of the entire alignment of the LAC on the basis of already agreed parameters, with the objective of arriving at a common understanding of the alignment, as soon as possible.

The two sides expressed satisfaction at the progress achieved in the implementation of the Agreements of 1993 and 1996 and agreed to fully implement them expeditiously. Towards that end, they concluded a Protocol on Modalities for the Implementation of Confidence Building Measures in the Military Field along the Line of Actual Control in the India-China Border Areas.

XII. The Indian side reiterated that it recognized the Tibet Autonomous Region as part of the territory of the People's Republic of China and that it did not allow Tibetans to engage in anti-China political activities in India.

The Indian side recalled that India was among the first countries to recognize that there is one China and its one China policy remains unaltered. The Indian side stated it would continue to abide by its one China policy.

The Chinese side expressed its appreciation for the Indian positions.

XIII. Both sides reviewed with satisfaction the implementation of the memorandum on the border trade through the Nathula Pass between the Tibet Autonomous Region of the People's Republic of China and the Sikkim State of the Republic of India.

XIV. The two sides noted with satisfaction that through friendly consultations an agreement in principle had been reached between the two countries to solve the long-pending issue of property originally belonging to Indian Consulate General in Shanghai with the Chinese side agreeing to provide a plot of land in lieu of the premises of the original Consulate General of India.

XV. As two large developing countries, both India and China were aware of each other's important role in the process of promoting the establishment of a new international political and economic order. Both sides share common interests in the maintenance of peace, stability and prosperity in Asia and the world at large, and share the desire to develop closer and more extensive understanding and cooperation in regional and international affairs.

The two sides are supportive of democratization of international relations and multilateralism, stand for the establishment of a new international political and economic order that is fair, rational, equal and mutually beneficial, and promote North-South Dialogue and South-South Cooperation. The two sides believe that the international community should eliminate poverty, narrow the gap between North and South, and achieve common prosperity through dialogue and cooperation.

XVI. The two sides reiterated the importance of the United Nations in global peace, stability and common development and expressed their determination to continue their efforts, together with the international community, in strengthening the UN system to develop a sound multilateral basis to address global issues. Both India and China agree that reform of the United Nations should be comprehensive and multi-faceted and should put emphasis on an increase in the representation of developing countries. The Indian side reiterated its aspirations for permanent membership of the UN Security Council. The Chinese side also reiterated that India is an important developing country and is having an increasingly important influence in the international arena. China attaches great importance to the status of India in international affairs. It understands and supports India's aspirations to play an active role in the UN and international affairs. The two sides reaffirmed their readiness to conduct close consultations and cooperation in the process of UN reforms.

XVII. The two sides, aware of the threats posed by terrorism to the peace and security of the two countries and the whole world, resolutely condemn terrorism in any form. The struggle between the international community and global terrorism is a comprehensive and sustained one, with the ultimate objective of eradication of terrorism in all regions. This requires strengthening the global legal framework against terrorism. Both sides noted the positive outcome of the meetings held so far of their bilateral dialogue mechanism on counter-terrorism and agreed to further strengthen and consolidate their discussions and cooperation. It was agreed to hold the next meeting of the dialogue mechanism on counter-terrorism later this year.

XVIII. Both sides agreed to conduct regular exchange of views on major international and regional issues, strengthen cooperation in the WTO and other international multilateral organizations, and to continue the consultations on other issues of common concern. They agreed to work together to preserve stability and growth in the global economy and reduce disparities between developed and developing countries. They supported an open, fair, equitable and transparent rule-based multilateral trade system and resolved to safeguard the legitimate rights and interests of the developing countries.

XIX. Aware of their linked destinies as neighbours and the two largest countries of Asia, both sides agreed that they would, together, contribute to the establishment of an atmosphere of mutual understanding, trust and cooperation in Asia and the world at large, and facilitate efforts to strengthen multilateral coordination mechanisms on security and cooperation.

XX. During the visit, the two sides signed and/or released the following documents.

i. Agreement on Political Parameters and Guiding Principles for the Settlement of the India-China Boundary Question

ii. Report of India-China Joint Study Group on Comprehensive Trade and Economic Cooperation
iii. Protocol on Modalities for the Implementation of CBMs in the Military Field Along the Line of Actual Control in the India-China Border Areas
iv. Agreement on Mutual Administrative Assistance and Cooperation in Customs Matters
v. MOU on the Launch of the India-China Financial Dialogue
vi. MOU on Civil Aviation
vii. Protocol of Phytosanitary Requirement for Exporting Grapes from India to China
viii. Protocol of Phytosanitary Requirement for Exporting Bitter Gourds from India to China
ix. MOU on Provision of Hydrological Information of the Sutlej / Langqen Zangbo River in Flood Season by China to India.
x. Protocol on India-China Film Cooperation Commission
xi. MOU on Cooperation between the Indian Council of World Affairs and the Chinese People's Institute of Foreign Affairs
xii. Memorandum on the Construction of an Indian-style Buddhist Temple on the Western side of the White Horse Temple in Luoyang, China

XXI. The two sides believed that Premier Wen Jiabao's highly successful State visit to the Republic of India marked a new level of India-China relationship and opened a new chapter in the friendly relations and cooperation between the two countries.

Premier Wen Jiabao, on behalf of the Chinese Government and people, expressed his appreciation to the Government and the people of India for their warm hospitality, and invited Prime Minister Manmohan Singh to visit China at a mutually convenient time. Prime Minister Manmohan Singh appreciated the invitation and accepted it with pleasure. The Indian side also reiterated the invitation to President Hu Jintao to visit India. The exact time of the visit will be decided through diplomatic channels.

Prime Minister of the Republic of India

Premier of the State Council of the People's Republic of China

New Delhi
April 11, 2005

APPENDIX 5

Agreement between the Government of the Republic of India and the Government of the People's Republic of China on the Political Parameters and Guiding Principles for the Settlement of the India-China Boundary Question

11 April 2005

The Government of the Republic of India and the Government of the People's Republic of China (hereinafter referred to as the two sides),

Believing that it serves the fundamental interests of the peoples of India and China to foster a long-term constructive and cooperative partnership on the basis of the Five Principles of Peaceful Co-existence, mutual respect and sensitivity for each other's concerns and aspirations, and equality,

Desirous of qualitatively upgrading the bilateral relationship at all levels and in all areas while addressing differences through peaceful means in a fair, reasonable and mutually acceptable manner,

Reiterating their commitment to abide by and implement the Agreement on the Maintenance of Peace and Tranquillity along the Line of Actual Control in the India-China Border Areas, signed on 7 September 1993, and the Agreement on Confidence Building Measures in the Military Field along the Line of Actual Control in the India-China Border Areas, signed on 29 November 1996,

Reaffirming the Declaration on Principles for Relations and Comprehensive Cooperation between India and China, signed on 23 June 2003,

Recalling that the two sides have appointed Special Representatives to explore the framework of settlement of the India-China boundary question and the two Special Representatives have been engaged in consultations in a friendly, cooperative and constructive atmosphere,

Noting that the two sides are seeking a political settlement of the boundary question in the context of their overall and long-term interests,

Convinced that an early settlement of the boundary question will advance the basic interests of the two countries and should therefore be pursued as a strategic objective,

Have agreed on the following political parameters and guiding principles for a boundary settlement:

Article I

The differences on the boundary question should not be allowed to affect the overall development of bilateral relations. The two sides will resolve the boundary question through peaceful and friendly consultations. Neither side shall use or threaten to use force against the other by any means. The final solution of the boundary question will significantly promote good neighbourly and friendly relations between India and China.

Article II

The two sides should, in accordance with the Five Principles of Peaceful Coexistence, seek a fair, reasonable and mutually acceptable solution to the boundary question through consultations on an equal footing, proceeding from the political perspective of overall bilateral relations.

Article III

Both sides should, in the spirit of mutual respect and mutual understanding, make meaningful and mutually acceptable adjustments to their respective positions on the boundary question, so as to arrive at a package settlement to the boundary question. The boundary settlement must be final, covering all sectors of the India-China boundary.

Article IV

The two sides will give due consideration to each other's strategic and reasonable interests, and the principle of mutual and equal security.

Article V

The two sides will take into account, inter alia, historical evidence, national sentiments, practical difficulties and reasonable concerns and sensitivities of both sides, and the actual state of border areas.

Article VI

The boundary should be along well-defined and easily identifiable natural geographical features to be mutually agreed upon between the two sides.

Article VII

In reaching a boundary settlement, the two sides shall safeguard due interests of their settled populations in the border areas.

Article VIII

Within the agreed framework of the final boundary settlement, the delineation of the boundary will be carried out utilising means such as modern cartographic and surveying practices and joint surveys.

Article IX

Pending an ultimate settlement of the boundary question, the two sides should strictly respect and observe the line of actual control and work together to maintain peace and tranquillity in the border areas. The India-China Joint Working Group and the India-China Diplomatic and Military Expert Group shall continue their work under the Agreements of 7 September 1993 and 29 November 1996, including the clarification of the line of actual control and the implementation of confidence building measures.

Article X

The Special Representatives on the boundary question shall continue their consultations in an earnest manner with the objective of arriving at an agreed framework for a boundary settlement, which will provide the basis for the delineation and demarcation of the India-China boundary to be subsequently undertaken by civil and military officials and surveyors of the two sides.

Article XI

This Agreement shall come into force as of the date of signature and is subject to amendment and addition by mutual agreement in writing between the two sides.

Signed in duplicate in New Delhi on 11 April, 2005, in the Hindi, Chinese and English languages, all three texts being equally authentic. In case of divergence, the English text shall prevail.

For the Government of the Republic of India

For the Government of the People's Republic of China

New Delhi
11 April 2005

APPENDIX 6

Protocol between the Government of the Republic of India and the Government of the People's Republic of China on Modalities for the Implementation of Confidence Building Measures in the Military Field Along the Line of Actual Control in the India-China Border Areas

11 April 2005

The Government of the Republic of India and the Government of the People's Republic of China (hereinafter referred to as the two sides),

Recalling that both sides are committed to developing their long-term constructive and cooperative partnership on the basis of the Five Principles of Peaceful Co-existence, mutual respect and sensitivity for each other's concerns and aspirations, and equality, Reaffirming that the two sides seek a fair, reasonable and mutually acceptable settlement of the boundary question,

Reaffirming their commitment that, pending an ultimate solution to the boundary question, both sides shall strictly respect and observe the Line of Actual Control in the India-China border areas,

Noting the utility of confidence building measures already in place along the Line of Actual Control in the India-China border areas,

Recognising that the maintenance of peace and tranquillity along the Line of Actual Control in the India-China border areas accords with the fundamental interests of the two sides, and will facilitate the process of early clarification and confirmation of the alignment of the Line of Actual Control,

Convinced of the need for agreed modalities for the implementation of confidence building measures between the two sides in the military field along the Line of Actual Control in the India-China border areas, and

Recalling further the relevant provisions of the Agreement on the Maintenance of Peace and Tranquillity along the Line of Actual Control in the India-China Border Areas signed in September 1993 and Agreement on Confidence Building Measures in the Military Field along the Line of

Actual Control in the India-China Border Areas signed between the two sides in November 1996,

Have agreed on the modalities as follows:

Article I

In accordance with Article II of the Agreement on Confidence Building Measures in the Military Field along the Line of Actual Control in the India-China Border Areas signed between the two sides in November 1996, the two sides should strictly respect and observe the Line of Actual Control and work together to maintain peace and tranquillity in the border areas.

Article II

In accordance with Article IV of the Agreement on Confidence Building Measures in the Military Field along the Line of Actual Control in the India-China Border Areas signed between the two sides in November 1996,

(a) Both sides shall avoid holding large-scale military exercises involving more than one Division (approximately 15,000 troops) in close proximity to the Line of Actual Control. However, if such exercises are to be conducted, the strategic direction of the main force involved shall not be towards the other side.

(b) If either side conducts a military exercise involving more than one Brigade Group (approximately 5,000 troops) in close proximity to the Line of Actual Control, it shall not be targeted against the other side. The side undertaking the exercise shall give, through Flag Meetings, the other side prior intimation 15 days in advance of the exercise with regard to type, level, planned duration and area of exercise as well as the number and type of units or formations participating in the exercise.

(c) Each side shall be entitled to obtain timely clarification within 15 days from the side undertaking the exercise in respect of data specified in paragraph (b) above of the present article, through Flag Meetings.

(d) Each side shall give prior intimation of changes in the timing of any scheduled exercise 15 days in advance, through Flag Meetings.

Article III

In accordance with Article V of the Agreement on Confidence Building Measures in the Military Field along the Line of Actual Control in the India-China Border Areas signed between the two sides in November 1996,

(a) In the event of an alleged air intrusion of its controlled airspace by the military aircraft of the other side, either side may seek a Flag Meeting within 48 hours of the alleged air intrusion in order to seek a clarification. The investigation shall be completed by the other side and its results communicated through a Flag Meeting within a period of four weeks.

(b) If a military aircraft of either side is required to fly across the Line of Actual Control or to overfly the airspace of the other side, prior permission shall be sought from the other side according to procedures and formats to be mutually agreed upon.

(c) If a military or civilian aircraft of either side is required to fly across the Line of Actual Control or to land on the other side of the Line of Actual Control in an emergency situation, the two sides will ensure flight safety in such situations by adhering to procedures to be mutually agreed upon.

Article IV

In accordance with Article VI of the Agreement on Confidence Building Measures in the Military Field along the Line of Actual Control in the India-China Border Areas signed between the two sides in November 1996, if the border personnel of the two sides come to a face-to-face situation due to differences on the alignment of the Line of Actual Control or any other reason, they shall exercise self-restraint and take all necessary steps to avoid an escalation of the situation. To this end, they shall follow the procedures as given below:

(a) Both sides shall cease their activities in the area, not advance any further, and simultaneously return to their bases.

(b) Both sides shall then inform their respective Headquarters and, if necessary, enter into immediate consultations through border meetings or diplomatic channels so as to prevent an escalation of the situation.

(c) Throughout the face-to-face situation, neither side shall use force or threaten to use force against the other.

(d) Both sides shall treat each other with courtesy and refrain from any provocative actions. Neither side shall put up marks or signs on the spots.

Article V

In accordance with Article VII of the Agreement on Confidence Building Measures in the Military Field along the Line of Actual Control in India-China Border Areas signed between the two sides in November 1996,

(a) Both sides shall hold two additional border meetings each year at Spanggur Gap in the Western Sector, Nathu La Pass in the Sikkim Sector and Bum La in the Eastern Sector respectively in celebration of the National Day or Army Day of either side. Specific arrangements shall be decided through consultation between the border forces of the two sides.

(b) Both sides agree in principle to expand the mechanism of border meeting points to include Kibithu-Damai in the Eastern Sector and Lipulekh Pass/Qiang La in the Middle Sector. The precise locations of these border meeting points will be decided through mutual consultations.

(c) Both sides shall conduct exchanges between the relevant Military Regions of China and Army Commands of India. Specific arrangements shall be decided upon through mutual consultations between the relevant agencies under the Ministries of Defence of the two sides.

(d) Both sides shall strengthen exchanges between institutions of training of the two armed forces, and conduct exchanges between institutions of sports and culture of the two armed forces. Specific arrangements shall be decided upon through mutual consultations between the relevant agencies under the Ministries of Defence of the two sides.

Article VI

In accordance with Article VIII of the Agreement on Confidence Building Measures in the Military Field along the Line of Actual Control in the India-China Border Areas signed between the two sides in November 1996,

(a) In case the personnel of one side in the border areas cross over to the other side due to force majeure such as natural disasters:

i. The side having discovered it should promptly contact and notify the other side;

ii. The personnel crossing over to the other side should, in the light of the prevailing circumstances, take measures to return to their own side or proceed to places designated by the other side en route to return to their own side;

iii. The receiving side will provide all possible assistance to the personnel from the other side and ensure their earliest possible return; and

iv. At the request of the side affected by the natural disaster, the other side may consider all possible measures to help alleviate the situation.

(b) In order to prevent infectious diseases in specific areas on either side in the border areas from spreading to the other side:

i. Both sides should share relevant information promptly through border meetings or diplomatic channels;

ii. Each side should take measures to prevent the spread of

diseases from spilling onto the other side; and

iii. At the request of the side suffering from spread of infectious diseases, the other side may consider all possible measures to help alleviate the situation.

Article VII

The Protocol shall enter into force on the date of signature of this Protocol and will automatically be rendered invalid if the Agreement on Confidence Building Measures in the Military Field along the Line of Actual Control in the India-China Border Areas signed between the two sides in November 1996 ceases to be in force. Subject to agreement after mutual consultations between the two sides, the Protocol may be amended and supplemented at any time.

Done in duplicate in New Delhi on April 11, 2005 in the Hindi, Chinese and English languages, all three texts being equally authentic. In case of any divergence, the English text shall prevail.

For the Government of the Republic of India

For the Government of the People's Republic of China

New Delhi
11 April 2005

Appendix 7

Memorandum of Understanding between the Ministry of Defence of the Republic of India and the Ministry of National Defence of the People's Republic of China for Exchanges and Cooperation in the field of Defence

29 May 2006

Pursuant to the Declaration on Principles for Relations and Comprehensive Cooperation between India and China signed in June 2003 and the Joint Statement signed in April 2005 by the Prime Minster of the Republic of India and the Premier of the State Council of the People's Republic of China, the Ministry of Defence of the Republic of India and the Ministry of National Defence of the People's Republic of China (hereinafter referred to as "the two sides") are committed, in accordance with the relevant purposes and principles of the Charter of the United Nations, to developing the strategic and cooperative partnership for peace and prosperity between India and China. Such a partnership is based on the principles of the Five Principles of Peaceful Co-existence, mutual respect and sensitivity for each other's concerns and aspirations and equality.

The two sides note the utility of confidence building measures between them, including their armed forces.

The two sides reiterate that strengthening effective contacts in the field of defence is of vital importance to enhancing mutual trust and understanding between their two armed forces, ensuring a peaceful environment in which they can pursue their respective national development objectives, and maintaining peace and stability in the region and the world at large. In order to broaden and deepen defence exchanges between the two countries, the two sides have, through friendly consultations, reached the following understanding:

Article 1

(a) Maintain frequent exchanges between the leaders and high-level functionaries of the Defence Ministries and the armed forces of India and China. An annual programme of exchange of visits will be worked out through consultations for timely implementations;

(b) Convene an Annual Defence Dialogue at a mutually agreed level, to be hosted alternately by the two sides. The dialogue will review progress in defence exchanges and make suggestions for future exchanges. It will also exchange views on international, security and strategic issues;

(c) Endeavour to hold joint military exercises and/or training programmes in the fields of search and rescue, anti-piracy, counter-terrorism and other areas of mutual interest. Each side will invite senior military officers of the other side to witness designated military exercises;

(d) Establish a mechanism of study tours for each other's senior and middle level military officers and relevant civilian officials, in order to facilitate better understanding of foreign, defence and national development policies of the host side, and participation in seminars and discussions on themes to be agreed upon. Specific arrangements will be decided through consultations;

(e) Establish a mechanism for military officers to study in the military academies of the other side to be identified by the host side. Carry out exchanges between counterpart military academies. The number of officers and academies involved in the above-mentioned exchanges can be increased if necessary; and

(f) Have exchanges in other mutually agreed fields to be decided through consultations.

Article 2

For the high level delegations as undertaken under clause (a) of Article 1 and other delegations designated by the two sides, on the basis of balance and reciprocity, the host will bear the local expenses for boarding, lodging and transportation. Other delegations will be self-financed. The delegations may comprise both military and civilian officials. The host will facilitate the visits and assist with visa and other travel arrangements, as necessary.

Article 3

This Memorandum of Understanding shall come into effect on signature by the two sides. It shall remain in force for five years unless terminated in advance by either side giving written notice for termination at least three months in advance. At the end of the five-year period, the Memorandum of Understanding shall be automatically extended by another five-years, unless either side gives written notice for its non-extension at least three months before the expiry date.

Done at Beijing on May 29, 2006 in two originals, each in the Hindi, Chinese and English languages, all texts being equally authentic. In case of any divergence in interpretation, the English text shall prevail.

Sd/-	Sd/-
Defence Minister of the Republic of India	Defence Minister of the People's Republic of China

Appendix 8

Joint Declaration by the Republic of India and the People's Republic of China

21 November 2006

1. H.E. Mr. Hu Jintao, President of the People's Republic of China, is currently paying a State visit to the Republic of India from 20 to 23 November 2006 at the invitation of H.E. Dr. A.P.J. Abdul Kalam, President of the Republic of India.
2. President Hu Jintao held talks with Prime Minister Dr. Manmohan Singh, earlier today. He will call on President Dr. A. P. J. Abdul Kalam later in the day. Vice President Shri Bhairon Singh Shekhawat, Speaker, Lok Sabha Shri Somnath Chatterjee, and Leader of the Opposition in Lok Sabha Shri L.K. Advani will pay courtesy calls on President Hu Jintao. Smt. Sonia Gandhi, Chairperson, United Progressive Alliance, will meet him. Earlier today, Minister of External Affairs Shri Pranab Mukherjee called on the visiting Chinese President. President Hu Jintao will deliver a policy address at the Vigyan Bhawan and attend the India-China Friendship Year commemorative function. He will also visit Agra and address a business summit in Mumbai, among other engagements.
3. The leaders of the two countries have noted with satisfaction the all-round progress made over recent years in India-China relations and their regional and multilateral cooperation. They reiterate the shared vision and fundamental principles for the future development of India-China relations, as embodied in the Declaration on Principles for Relations and Comprehensive Cooperation of 23 June 2003 and the Joint Statement of 11 April 2005 signed between the Prime Ministers of the two countries.
4. Both sides agree that the relationship between India and China, the two biggest developing countries in the world, is of global and strategic significance. Both countries are seeking to avail themselves of historic opportunities for development. Each side welcomes and takes a positive view of the development of the other, and considers the development of either side as a positive contribution to peace, stability and prosperity of Asia and the world. Both sides hold the view that

there exist bright prospects for their common development, that they are not rivals or competitors but are partners for mutual benefit. They agree that there is enough space for them to grow together, achieve a higher scale of development, and play their respective roles in the region and beyond, while remaining sensitive to each other's concerns and aspirations. Strategic partnership between the two countries with a similar worldview is consistent with their roles as two major developing countries. With the growing participation and role of the two countries in all key issues in today's globalising world, their partnership is vital for international efforts to deal with global challenges and threats. As two major countries in the emerging multi-polar global order, the simultaneous development of India and China will have a positive influence on the future international system.

5. In order to promote the sustainable socio-economic development of India and China, to fully realise the substantial potential for their cooperation in a wide range of areas, to upgrade India-China relations to a qualitatively new level, and to further substantiate and reinforce their Strategic and Cooperative Partnership, the leaders of the two countries have committed themselves to pursuing the following "ten-pronged strategy":

I. Ensuring Comprehensive Development of Bilateral Relations:

6. Both sides are committed to making the positive development and diversification of India-China relations in recent years an irreversible trend.
7. The two sides agree to hold regular Summit-level meetings, in each other's country and in multilateral forums. They agree that high-level exchanges between Governments, Parliaments and political parties play an important role in expanding overall bilateral cooperation.
8. In order to sustain, facilitate and promote greater engagement between the two countries, an additional Consulate General shall be opened in each other's country. The Indian side shall open a new Consulate General in Guangzhou, while the Chinese side shall open a new Consulate General in Kolkata. In this context, the mutually satisfactory resolution of the long-pending issue of the property of the Consulate General of India in Shanghai is a positive development.

II. Strengthening Institutional Linkages and Dialogue Mechanisms:

9. The two sides shall strengthen institutional linkages between their Governments in different areas and levels with a view to foster synergy and cooperation and promote greater understanding of each other's policies and positions on important national, regional and international

issues. The concerned ministries and organisations of the two countries shall intensify exchanges under the existing dialogue mechanisms and revitalise those that have not been regularly used. The signing of the Protocol of Cooperation between the Ministry of External Affairs of India and the Ministry of Foreign Affairs of China during the visit is an important step in this direction.

III. Consolidating Commercial and Economic Exchanges:

10. Both sides believe that comprehensive economic and commercial engagement between India and China is a core component of their Strategic and Cooperative Partnership. They will endeavour to raise the volume of their bilateral trade to US$ 40 billion by 2010. They shall make joint efforts to diversify their trade basket, remove existing impediments, and optimally utilise the present and potential complementarities in their economies, in order to sustain and further strengthen bilateral commercial and economic cooperation. Towards this end, both sides will attach utmost priority to an early implementation of the decisions taken in March 2006 by the Ministerial-level Joint Economic Group, including the recommendations of the Joint Study Group, through mechanisms already created for this purpose. The Joint Task Force set up to study the feasibility and benefits of an India-China Regional Trading Arrangement shall complete its work by October 2007.
11. The conclusion of the Bilateral Investment Promotion and Protection Agreement during the visit is a welcome development that will provide the institutional and legal basis to encourage and promote greater investment flows between the two countries.
12. The Chinese side has invited India to participate in the World Exposition Shanghai 2010. The Indian side expressed its appreciation and stated that it will actively support and participate in the event.

IV. Expanding All-Round Mutually Beneficial Cooperation:

13. The two sides agree to further strengthen positive trends in the all-round development of relations and fully realize the substantial potential of cooperation, including in trade, industry, finance, agriculture, water resources, energy, environment, transportation, infrastructure, information technology, health, education, media, culture, tourism, youth affairs and other fields.
14. Both sides agree to fully implement the provisions of the Memorandum on Cooperation in the field of Oil and Natural Gas signed in January 2006 and encourage collaboration between their enterprises, including

through joint exploration and development of hydrocarbon resources in third countries.

15. Given the complementarities that India and China enjoy in the area of information and communication technology, the two sides agreed to strengthen mutually beneficial cooperation in this sector, through closer policy dialogue and enhanced collaboration among their enterprises, including in third countries.
16. The two sides shall fully implement the Memorandum of Understanding on Agricultural Cooperation, step up the exchange of experience in the field of agriculture and rural development, including food security, and hold discussions and consultations on the standards for agricultural goods at an early date in order to facilitate trade in such goods.
17. The two sides will set up an expert-level mechanism to discuss interaction and cooperation on the provision of flood season hydrological data, emergency management and other issues regarding trans-border rivers as agreed between them. The on-going provision of hydrological data for the Brahmaputra/Yarlung Zangbo and the Sutlej/Langqen Zangbo Rivers by the Chinese side to the Indian side has proved valuable in flood forecasting and mitigation. The two sides agree to continue bilateral discussions to finalise at an early date similar arrangements for the Parlung Zangbo and Lohit/Zayu Qu Rivers.
18. Both sides shall intensify their consultations, bilaterally and in multilateral fora, on sustainable development, bio-diversity, climate change and other related environmental issues of common concern. The cooperation in wildlife conservation, particularly in tiger conservation, shall be stepped up.

V. Instilling Mutual Trust and Confidence through Defence Cooperation:

19. The exchange of visits in the field of defence has resulted in building of mutual trust and enhancement of mutual understanding between the defence establishments of the two countries. Both sides shall fully implement the provisions of the Memorandum of Understanding for Exchanges and Cooperation in the field of Defence signed on 29 May 2006, which provides a sound foundation and institutional framework for further development of defence cooperation.

VI. Seeking Early Settlement of Outstanding Issues:

20. Both sides are committed to resolving outstanding differences, including on the boundary question, through peaceful means and in a fair, reasonable, mutually acceptable and proactive manner, while ensuring that such differences are not allowed to affect the positive development of bilateral relations.

21. The Special Representatives of India and China on the boundary question have taken steps and shall continue to strive to arrive at a boundary settlement on the basis of the Agreement on Political Parameters and Guiding Principles for the Settlement of India-China Boundary Question signed on 11 April 2005. An early settlement of the boundary question will advance the basic interests of the two countries and shall, therefore, be pursued as a strategic objective. The Special Representatives shall complete at an early date the task of finalising an appropriate framework for a final package settlement covering all sectors of the India-China boundary. Pending the resolution of the boundary question, both sides shall maintain peace and tranquillity in the border areas in accordance with the agreements of 1993, 1996 and 2005.
22. Along with the talks between the Special Representatives, the Joint Working Group on the India-China Boundary Question shall expedite their work, including on the clarification and confirmation of the line of actual control and the implementation of confidence building measures. It was agreed to complete the process of exchanging maps indicating their respective perceptions of the entire alignment of the LAC on the basis of already agreed parameters as soon as possible.

VII. Promoting Trans-border Connectivity and Cooperation:

23. Both sides shall promote greater trans-border cooperation at mutually agreed sites in India-China border areas with the objective of transforming their border from being a dividing line into a bridge that unites them in cooperative pursuits. In this context, border trade between India and China, including the recent resumption of border trade through the Nathula La Pass, is of significant importance. The two sides shall strengthen border trade through the existing locations, while continuing to explore the possibility of opening additional trading routes in India-China border areas.
24. The two sides welcome the organisation of a car rally, recommended by the BCIM Forum, between Kolkata and Kunming via Bangladesh and Myanmar.
25. The Chinese side shall provide greater facilitation to Indian pilgrims for the Kailash Mansarovar Yatra. Both sides shall explore the possibility of opening an additional route for the Yatra.

VIII. Boosting Cooperation in Science and Technology:

26. Bearing in mind the priority attached by India and China to scientific and technological development and innovation as a cornerstone of their efforts towards sustainable socio-economic development, the two sides shall establish an India-China Partnership in Science and Technology.

The two sides welcome the establishment of the Ministerial-level Committee on Science and Technology Cooperation as a positive step in guiding, coordinating and facilitating cooperative activities. They agree to launch joint projects in the areas of (i) earthquake engineering, (ii) climate change and weather forecasting, (iii) nano-technology with focus on advanced materials, and (iv) biotechnology and medicines with focus on bio-nano. The cooperation framework shall include entrepreneurs on both sides, besides the two Governments and their respective institutions.

27. Considering that for both India and China, expansion of civilian nuclear energy programme is an essential and important component of their national energy plans to ensure energy security, the two sides agree to promote cooperation in the field of nuclear energy, consistent with their respective international commitments. As two countries with advanced scientific capabilities, they stress the importance of further deepening cooperation bilaterally as well as through multilateral projects such as ITER, and enhance exchanges in the related academic fields.

28. As countries, which have made advances in space technologies, both sides reiterate their commitment to the use of outer space for peaceful purposes. They agree to strengthen their cooperation in the use of space-based technologies for peaceful and developmental applications, including through satellite remote sensing, satellite communications, satellite meteorology and satellite launch services. Cooperation in practical applications of space technology, such as those related to disaster management and distance education, shall also be actively explored. Towards this end, both sides shall fully implement the provisions of the Memoranda of Understanding on the peaceful use of outer space signed between India and China in December 1991 and January 2002.

IX. Revitalising Cultural Ties and Nurturing People-to-People Exchanges:

29. The centuries-old cultural contacts between the two peoples provide a strong foundation for enduring friendship between India and China. The initiatives to rediscover these historical linkages and revitalise them in the present day context, including through an early completion of the Xuanzang Memorial in Nalanda and the Indian-style Buddhist Shrine in Luoyang, will further strengthen these bonds. The two sides agree to strengthen cooperation in the area of spiritual and civilizational heritage, discuss collaboration in the digitisation of Buddhist manuscripts available in China as well as the re-development of Nalanda as a major centre of learning with the establishment of an international university on the basis of regional cooperation. In order

to promote greater awareness of each other's culture, the two sides shall organise a "Festival of India" in China and a "Festival of China" in India, with a joint logo. Detailed modalities in this regard will be decided by the concerned authorities through mutual consultations.

30. In order to promote greater academic exchanges between India and China, the two sides agree to work towards the establishment of an "India-China Exchange Foundation". Detailed modalities of the Foundation will be worked out through mutual consultations.
31. India-China relations in the field of education will be further strengthened through a new Educational Exchange Programme concluded during the visit.
32. The two sides also agree to launch a five-year programme for mutual exchange of youth delegations. In this context, the Chinese side invites five hundred youth from India over the next five years.
33. With a view to vigorously promoting tourism between India and China, the two sides shall organise the "India-China Year of Friendship Through Tourism" in 2007 with a joint logo and take other initiatives, such as opening of the office of the China National Tourism Administration in India and an Indian Tourism Office in China, improved air connectivity, and continued liberalisation of the visa regime.
34. The two sides welcome cooperation linkages between the Indian States and the Chinese provinces in order to promote greater people-to-people exchanges.

X. Expanding Cooperation on Regional and International Stage:

35. The two sides shall hold regular exchange of views on the emerging security environment in the Asia-Pacific and in the world, and undertake proactive consultations on issues of immediate and emerging concern, so as to coordinate their positions and to make positive contribution towards peaceful resolution of such issues. They shall also have regular consultations on issues pertaining to regional peace, security and stability, such as regional maritime security, proliferation of weapons of mass destruction and related materials and their means of delivery, pandemics, natural disasters, illegal trafficking in arms, narcotics and people, and environmental degradation.
36. The two sides positively assess the trilateral dialogue mechanism among India, China and Russia and agree that exchanges and cooperation under it should be further substantiated.
37. Recognising that terrorism constitutes a crime against humanity that cannot be justified on any ground and condemning it in all forms and manifestations, the two sides agree to revitalise and broaden the India-

China Dialogue Mechanism on Counter-Terrorism. They shall strengthen their efforts, bilaterally as also in the international fora, to fight against terrorism, separatism and extremism, and the linkages between terrorism and organized crime and illicit arms and drugs trafficking.

38. Recognising the central role of the United Nations in promoting international peace, security and development, both sides reiterate their determination to strengthen the UN system. The reform of the UN should be comprehensive, ensure balanced representation of developing and developed countries in the UN Security Council, and add to the efficiency and efficacy of the UN and its Security Council. The two sides shall conduct consultations on the question of UN reform, including the reform of the UN Security Council. The Indian side reiterates its aspirations for permanent membership of the UN Security Council. China attaches great importance to the status of India in international affairs. It understands and supports India's aspirations to play a greater role in the United Nations.
39. Energy security constitutes a vital and strategic issue for producing and consuming countries alike. It is consistent with the common interest of the two sides to establish an international energy order, which is fair, equitable, secure and stable, and to the benefit of the entire international community. Both sides shall also make joint efforts, bilaterally as well as in multilateral fora, to diversify the global energy mix and to increase the share in it of renewable energy sources. Global energy systems should take into account and meet the energy needs of both countries, as part and parcel of a stable, predictable, secure and clean energy future. In this context, international civilian nuclear cooperation should be advanced through innovative and forward-looking approaches, while safeguarding the effectiveness of international non-proliferation principles.
40. Both countries are committed to non-proliferation objectives and agree to expand their dialogue on the related issues, in bilateral and international fora.
41. As two large developing countries with relatively successful developmental experiences, India and China share unique responsibilities to protect and promote the interests of the developing world in the emerging international order and to help them benefit from the positive forces of globalisation. In this context, the two sides shall hold a two-part international seminar in Beijing and New Delhi, co-hosted by their Ministries of Finance, to share their developmental experience with other developing countries and the international community at large.

42. The two sides agree to strengthen their cooperation in the World Trade Organisation. They support the establishment of an open, fair, equitable, transparent and rule-based multilateral trading system, early resumption of Doha negotiations, and are determined to safeguard the legitimate rights and interests of the developing countries. As founder Members of the G-20 and the G-33, they are determined to strengthen their cooperation and to coordinate with other members of the WTO, especially the developing countries, in order to secure an early resumption of the negotiations on the Doha Work Programme, placing the development dimension at its heart.
43. Recognising that regional integration is an important feature of the emerging international economic order, the two sides agree to expand their coordination within regional organisations and explore a new architecture for closer regional cooperation in Asia. They positively view each other's participation in Asian inter-regional, regional and sub-regional cooperation process, including in the progress towards the East Asian Community. In this context, the two sides agree to cooperate closely in the East Asia Summit. The Indian side welcomes China's attainment of observer status in the South Asian Association for Regional Cooperation. The Chinese side welcomes India's membership of the Asia-Europe Meeting. The two sides agree to expand their cooperation on issues on common interest under the Shanghai Cooperation Organisation.
44. The Indian side recalls that India was among the first countries to recognize that there is one China and that its one China policy has remained unaltered. The Indian side states that it would continue to abide by its one China policy. The Chinese side expresses its appreciation for the Indian position.
45. The Indian side reiterates that it has recognized the Tibet Autonomous Region as part of the territory of the People's Republic of China, and that it does not allow Tibetans to engage in anti-China political activities in India. The Chinese side expresses its appreciation for the Indian position.
46. The following agreements were signed during the visit:
    i) Protocol on the Establishment of Consulates-General at Guangzhou and Kolkata;
    ii) Protocol on Cooperation between the Ministry of External Affairs of India and the Ministry of Foreign Affairs of China;
    iii) Agreement on the Issue of Property of the Consulate General of India in Shanghai;
    iv) Agreement on Bilateral Investment Protection and Promotion;

v) Memorandum of Understanding on Inspection of Export Cargo (Iron Ore);

vi) Protocol on Phytosanitary Requirements for Exporting Rice from India to China;

vii) Memorandum of Understanding between Forward Markets Commission of India and China Securities Regulatory Commission regarding Commodity Futures Regulatory Cooperation;

viii) Memorandum of Understanding on Cooperation between the Indian Institute of Public Administration and the Central Party School of the Communist Party of China;

ix) Agreement on Forestry Cooperation;

x) Memorandum of Understanding between the Indian Council of Agricultural Research and the Chinese Academy of Agricultural Sciences;

xi) Exchange Programme on Cooperation in the Field of Education;

xii) Memorandum of Understanding on Cooperation in the Conservation of Cultural Heritage; and

xiii) Agreement on Preventing Theft, Clandestine Excavation and Illicit Import and Export of Cultural Property.

47. The two sides believe that the highly successful visit of President Hu Jintao to India marks the high point of the India-China Friendship Year in 2006, promotes mutual understanding and trust, helps in substantiating the Strategic and Cooperative Partnership between the two countries and leads to a qualitative and quantum improvement in bilateral relations. They also agree that this Joint Statement provides a valuable blueprint for enduring development and diversification of the relations between India and China and sustained enrichment of their strategic partnership.

48. President Hu Jintao extended invitations to President Dr. A.P.J. Abdul Kalam and Prime Minister Dr. Manmohan Singh to visit China. The invitations were accepted with appreciation. The timing of the visits will be decided through diplomatic channels.

New Delhi
21 November 2006

Appendix 9

A Shared Vision for the 21st Century of the People's Republic of China and the Republic of India

14 January 2008

H.E. Dr. Manmohan Singh, Prime Minister of the Republic of India and H.E. Mr. Wen Jiabao, Premier of the State Council of the People's Republic of China, meeting in Beijing on 14 January 2008, resolve to promote the building of a harmonious world of durable peace and common prosperity through developing the Strategic and Cooperative Partnership for Peace and Prosperity between the two countries.

India and China (hereinafter referred to as the "two sides") are the two largest developing nations on earth representing more than one-third of humanity. The two sides recognize that both India and China bear a significant historical responsibility to ensure comprehensive, balanced and sustainable economic and social development of the two countries and to promote peace and development in Asia and the world as a whole.

The two sides are convinced that it is time to look to the future in building a relationship of friendship and trust, based on equality, in which each is sensitive to the concerns and aspirations of the other. The two sides reiterate that India-China friendship and common development will have a positive influence on the future of the international system. India-China relations are not targeted at any country, nor will it affect their friendship with other countries.

The two sides believe that in the new century, *Panchsheel*, the Five Principles of Peaceful Co-existence, should continue to constitute the basic guiding principles for good relations between all countries and for creating the conditions for realizing peace and progress of humankind. An international system founded on these principles will be fair, rational, equal and mutually beneficial, will promote durable peace and common prosperity, create equal opportunities and eliminate poverty and discrimination.

The two sides hold that the right of each country to choose its own path of social, economic and political development in which fundamental human rights and the rule of law are given their due place, should be respected. An international system founded in tolerance and respect for diversity will promote the cause of peace and reduce the use, or threat of use, of force. The two sides favour an open and inclusive international system and believe that drawing lines on the ground of ideologies and values, or on geographical criteria, is not conducive to peaceful and harmonious coexistence.

The two sides believe that the continuous democratization of international relations and multilateralism are an important objective in the new century. The central role of the United Nations in promoting international peace, security and development should be recognized and promoted. The two sides support comprehensive reform of the United Nations, including giving priority to increasing the representation of developing countries in the Security Council. The Indian side reiterates its aspirations for permanent membership of the UN Security Council. The Chinese side attaches great importance to India's position as a major developing country in international affairs. The Chinese side understands and supports India's aspirations to play a greater role in the United Nations, including in the Security Council.

The two sides support and encourage the processes of regional integration that provide mutually beneficial opportunities for growth, as an important feature of the emerging international economic system. The two sides positively view each others' participation in regional processes and agree to strengthen their coordination and consultation within regional cooperation mechanisms including the East Asia Summit, to explore together and with other countries a new architecture for closer regional cooperation in Asia, and to make joint efforts for further regional integration of Asia. The two sides will strengthen their coordination under the framework of Asia-Europe Meeting, and are committed to strengthening and deepening Asia-Europe comprehensive partnership.

The two sides take a positive view on each other's participation in sub-regional multilateral cooperation processes between like-minded countries, including South Asian Association for Regional Cooperation, Bay of Bengal Initiative for Multi-Sectoral Technical and Economic Cooperation and Shanghai Cooperation Organization. The two sides hold that this does not affect either country's existing friendly relations or cooperation with other countries.

The two sides welcome the positive facets of economic globalization, and are ready to face and meet its challenges, and will work with other countries towards balanced and mutually beneficial economic globalization. The two sides believe that the establishment of an open, fair, equitable, transparent and rule-based multilateral trading system is the common aspiration of all countries. The two sides favour the early conclusion of the Doha Development Round, placing the issues that affect the poorest of the poor at its core. The two sides are determined to strengthen their coordination with other developing countries in order to secure their shared objectives.

The two sides are convinced that it is in the common interest of the international community to establish an international energy order that is fair, equitable, secure and stable, and to the benefit of the entire international community. The two sides are committed to making joint efforts to diversify the global energy mix and enhance the share of clean and renewable energy, so as to meet the energy requirements of all countries.

The two sides welcome the opportunity for their outstanding scientists to work together in the International Thermonuclear Experimental Reactor (ITER) project, which is of great potential significance in meeting the global energy challenge in an environmentally sustainable manner. As two countries with advanced scientific capabilities, the two sides pledge to promote bilateral cooperation in civil nuclear energy, consistent with their respective international commitments, which will contribute to energy security and to dealing with risks associated with climate change.

The two sides recognize the challenge that humankind faces from climate change. The two sides take the issue of climate change seriously and reiterate their readiness to join the international community in the efforts to address climate change. The two sides also stand ready to enhance technological cooperation between the two countries. The two sides welcome the outcome of the United Nations Framework Convention on Climate Change (UNFCCC) meeting in Bali in December 2007 and agree to work closely during the negotiation process laid out in the Bali Road Map for long term cooperative action under the Convention. The two sides emphasise the importance of addressing climate change in accordance with principles and provisions of the UNFCCC and its Kyoto Protocol, in particular the principle of common but differentiated responsibilities.

The two sides appeal to the international community to move forward the processes of multilateral arms control, disarmament and non-proliferation. Outer space is the common heritage of humankind. It is the responsibility of all space-faring nations to commit to the peaceful uses of outer space. The two sides express their categorical opposition to the weaponisation and arms race in outer space.

The two sides strongly condemn the scourge of terrorism in all its forms and manifestations, and in all regions of the world. The two sides pledge to work together and with the international community to strengthen the global framework against terrorism in a long-term, sustained and comprehensive manner.

The two sides believe that cultural and religious tolerance and dialogue between civilizations and peoples will contribute to overall peace and stability of our world. The two sides endorse all efforts to promote inter-civilizational and inter-faith dialogues.

The two sides believe that their bilateral relationship in this century will be of significant regional and global influence. The two sides will therefore continue to build their Strategic and Cooperative Partnership in a positive way. As major economies in their region, the two sides believe that the strong growth in their trade and economic relations is mutually beneficial, and welcome the conclusion of a Feasibility Study on a Regional Trading Arrangement (RTA) between the two countries. According to the report of the Feasibility Study, a India-China RTA will be mutually advantageous. Against the backdrop of accelerating regional economic integration in Asia, the two sides agree to explore the possibility of commencing discussions on a mutually beneficial and high-quality RTA that meets the common aspirations of both countries, and will also benefit the region.

The two sides will continuously promote confidence building measures through steadily enhanced contacts in the field of defence. The two sides therefore welcome the commencement of the India-China Defence Dialogue and express their satisfaction at the successful conclusion of the first joint anti-terrorism training between their armed forces in December 2007. The two sides also welcome their efforts to set an example on trans-border rivers by commencing cooperation since 2002. The Indian side highly appreciates the assistance extended by China on the provision of flood season hydrological data which has assisted India in ensuring the safety and security of its population in the regions along these rivers. The two sides agree that this has contributed positively to building mutual understanding and trust.

The two sides remain firmly committed to resolving outstanding differences, including on the boundary question, through peaceful negotiations, while ensuring that such differences are not allowed to affect the positive development of bilateral relations. The two sides reiterate their determination to seek a fair, reasonable and mutually acceptable solution to the boundary question and to build a boundary of peace and friendship on the basis of the Agreement on Political Parameters and Guiding Principles for the Settlement of the India-China Boundary Question concluded in April 2005. The Special Representatives shall complete at an early date the task of arriving at an agreed framework of settlement on the basis of this Agreement.

The Indian side recalls that India was among the first countries to recognize that there is one China and that its one China policy has remained unaltered. The Indian side states that it would continue to abide by its one China policy, and oppose any activity that is against the one China principle. The Chinese side expresses its appreciation for the Indian position.

The two sides recognize the responsibilities and obligations of the two countries to the international community. The two sides are determined to enhance mutual understanding and friendship between the peoples of India and China, for the betterment of both countries and to bring about a brighter future for humanity.

Dr. Manmohan Singh
Prime Minister of the
Republic of India

Wen Jiabao
Premier of the State Council of
the People's Republic of China

Beijing
14 January 2008

Appendix 10

Agreement between the Government of the Republic of India and the Government of the People's Republic of China on the Establishment of a Working Mechanism for Consultation and Coordination on India-China Border Affairs

17 January 2012

The Government of the Republic of India and the Government of the People's Republic of China (hereinafter referred to as the "two sides");

Firmly believing that respecting and abiding by the Line of Actual Control pending a resolution of the Boundary Question between the two countries as well as maintaining and strengthening peace and tranquility in the India-China border areas is very significant for enhancing mutual trust and security between the two countries, for resolving the Boundary Question at an early date and for building the India-China Strategic and Cooperative Partnership for Peace and Prosperity;

Desiring to materialize the spirit of the Agreement between the Government of the Republic of India and the Government of the People's Republic of China on the Maintenance of Peace and Tranquility Along the Line of Actual Control in the India-China Border Areas signed on 7th September 1993, the Agreement between the Government of the Republic of India and the Government of the People's Republic of China on Confidence Building Measures in the Military Field Along the Line of Actual Control in the India-China Border Areas signed on 29th November 1996 and the Protocol between the Government of the Republic of India and the Government of the People's Republic of China on Modalities for the Implementation of Confidence Building Measures in the Military Field Along the Line of Actual Control in the India-China Border Areas signed on 11th April 2005;

Aiming for timely communication of information on the border situation, for appropriately handling border incidents, for earnestly undertaking other cooperation activities in the India-China border areas, have agreed as follows:

Article I

The two sides agree to establish a Working Mechanism for Consultation and Coordination on India-China Border Affairs (hereinafter referred to as "the Working Mechanism") to deal with important border affairs related to maintaining peace and tranquility in the India-China border areas.

Article II

The Working Mechanism will be headed by a Joint Secretary level official from the Ministry of External Affairs of the Republic of India and a Director General level official from the Ministry of Foreign Affairs of the People's Republic of China and will be composed of diplomatic and military officials of the two sides.

Article III

The Working Mechanism will study ways and means to conduct and strengthen exchanges and cooperation between military personnel and establishments of the two sides in the border areas.

Article IV

The Working Mechanism will explore the possibility of cooperation in the border areas that are agreed upon by the two sides.

Article V

The Working Mechanism will undertake other tasks that are mutually agreed upon by the two sides but will not discuss resolution of the Boundary Question or affect the Special Representatives Mechanism.

Article VI

The Working Mechanism will address issues and situations that may arise in the border areas that affect the maintenance of peace and tranquillity and will work actively towards maintaining the friendly atmosphere between the two countries.

Article VII

The Working Mechanism will hold consultations once or twice every year alternately in India and China. Emergency consultations, if required, may be convened after mutual agreement.

Article VIII

This Agreement shall come into force on the date of its signature. It may be revised, amended, or terminated with the consent of the two sides. Any revision or amendment, mutually agreed by the two sides, shall form an integral part of this Agreement.

Signed in duplicate in Hindi, Chinese and English languages at New Delhi, on 17th January 2012, all three versions being equally authentic. In case of divergence the English text shall prevail.

For the Government of the Republic of India

For the Government of the People's Republic of China

Index